Praise for Katherine Ramsland's books

TRUE STORIES OF C.S.I.

"*C.S.I.* fans . . . will enjoy this professional—and professionally morbid—treatment of their favorite T.V. crime dramas."

—*Publishers Weekly*

BEATING THE DEVIL'S GAME

"A great forensic thriller, and once again Katherine Ramsland has brilliantly captured the insights and drama of some fascinating cases." —Dr. Henry C. Lee

THE C.S.I. EFFECT

"Ramsland expands upon the scientific and investigation procedures that viewers see on the [C.S.I.] show. Using real examples such as the BTK murders and the O. J. Simpson case as well as episodes from the three C.S.I. shows, Ramsland analyzes the ways technology such as the Internet and DNA testing are revolutionizing the way law enforcement apprehends killers and obtains convictions. Ramsland also looks at how a case can get derailed when eyewitness testimony contradicts the physical evidence or when the handling of the evidence is called into question. A fascinating must-read for C.S.I. fans and anyone interested in criminal justice." —*Booklist*

continued . . .

THE FORENSIC SCIENCE OF C.S.I.

"With the mind of a true investigator, Katherine Ramsland demystifies the world of forensics with authentic and vivid detail."
—John Douglas, former FBI profiler and coauthor of
Mindhunter: Inside the FBI's Elite Serial Crime Unit

"Fascinating . . . this book is a must for anyone who wonders how the real crime-solvers do it."
—Michael Palmer, *New York Times* bestselling author of
The Second Opinion

THE HUMAN PREDATOR

"Extraordinary, well-researched, written in a flowing, easy-to-understand style. Unique in the field—for anyone interested in either forensic science and psychology or serial murder, this book is a must-have."
—Court TV Crime Library

THE UNKNOWN DARKNESS
Coauthored with Gregg O. McCrary

"One of the most intensely readable and gripping accounts of serial murder I have ever read."
—Colin Wilson, author of
Serial Killer: A Study in the Psychology of Violence

Also by Katherine Ramsland

*The Devil's Dozen: How Cutting-Edge Forensics
Took Down 12 Notorious Serial Killers*

True Stories of C.S.I.

*Into the Devil's Den: How an FBI Informant Went into the
Aryan Nations and an FBI Agent Got Him Out Alive*
(with Dave Hall and Tym Burkey)

Inside the Minds of Healthcare Serial Killers

*Beating the Devil's Game: A History of Forensic Science
and Criminal Investigation*

*The Human Predator: A Historical Chronicle of Serial Murder
and Forensic Investigation*

Inside the Minds of Serial Killers: Why They Kill

Inside the Minds of Mass Murderers: Why They Kill

The C.S.I. Effect

A Voice for the Dead
(with James E. Starrs)

The Science of Cold Case Files

The Unknown Darkness: Profiling the Predators Among Us
(with Gregg McCrary)

The Science of Vampires

The Criminal Mind: A Writer's Guide to Forensic Psychology

The Forensic Science of C.S.I

The Forensic Psychology of
CRIMINAL MINDS

KATHERINE RAMSLAND

BERKLEY BOULEVARD, NEW YORK

THE BERKLEY PUBLISHING GROUP
Published by the Penguin Group
Penguin Group (USA) Inc.
375 Hudson Street, New York, New York 10014, USA
Penguin Group (Canada), 90 Eglinton Avenue East, Suite 700, Toronto, Ontario M4P 2Y3, Canada
(a division of Pearson Penguin Canada Inc.)
Penguin Books Ltd., 80 Strand, London WC2R 0RL, England
Penguin Group Ireland, 25 St. Stephen's Green, Dublin 2, Ireland (a division of Penguin Books Ltd.)
Penguin Group (Australia), 250 Camberwell Road, Camberwell, Victoria 3124, Australia
(a division of Pearson Australia Group Pty. Ltd.)
Penguin Books India Pvt. Ltd., 11 Community Centre, Panchsheel Park, New Delhi—110 017, India
Penguin Group (NZ), 67 Apollo Drive, Rosedale, North Shore, 0632, New Zealand
(a division of Pearson New Zealand Ltd.)
Penguin Books (South Africa) (Pty.) Ltd., 24 Sturdee Avenue, Rosebank, Johannesburg 2196,
South Africa

Penguin Books Ltd., Registered Offices: 80 Strand, London WC2R 0RL, England

This book was not authorized, prepared, approved, licensed, or endorsed by any entity involved in creating or producing the *Criminal Minds* television series.

The publisher does not have any control over and does not assume any responsibility for author or third-party websites or their content.

PRINTING HISTORY
Berkley Boulevard trade paperback edition / February 2010

Library of Congress Cataloging-in-Publication Data

Ramsland, Katherine M., 1953-
    The forensic psychology of criminal minds / Katherine Ramsland.
        p. cm.
    Includes bibliographical references and index.
    ISBN 978-0-425-23226-2
 1. Criminal psychology. I. Title.
    HV6080.R26 2009
    614'.15—dc22   2009015693

PRINTED IN THE UNITED STATES OF AMERICA

10 9 8 7 6 5 4 3 2 1

For Robert Ressler and Gregg McCrary,
former members of the FBI BSU/BAU,
who were most instrumental in helping me
to understand the process of profiling.

CONTENTS

ACKNOWLEDGMENTS

Having gotten my start by working on *The Cases That Haunt Us* with John Douglas leads me to thank him first. Then both Robert Ressler and Roy Hazelwood agreed to interviews about their work, and through that I learned quite a bit more about special areas of criminal profiling. Ressler also went into detail about some of his investigations. Around the same time, I worked with Gregg McCrary on turning his cases into a book, *The Unknown Darkness: Profiling the Predators Among Us.* To them I owe a lot as well as to more recent personnel: Mark Hilts, Mary Ellen O'Toole, and Mark Safarik, who've all spoken to me about their experiences. In addition, I listened to *Criminal Minds (CM)* producer Andrew Wilder describe how he worked with FBI consultants to write episodes of *CM*, and I've long known and learned from Robert Hare, the world's acknowledged expert on psychopathy. At the same time, I've learned much from my colleagues in the forensic sciences or investigation, notably Henry C. Lee, Cyril Wecht, M. Fredric Rieders, Traci Ardinger, James E. Starrs, Lee Lofland, and Michael Baden.

I also want to thank Kristin Sell for her assistance with proofreading the manuscript, and Marie Gallagher, Pelli Wheaton, and Ruth Osborne for believing in me.

My agent, John Silbersack, was quick to see the potential in this book, and I thank him for his friendship—twenty years now!—and enthusiastic support. The same goes for my editor, Ginjer Buchanan. My gratitude to both, and to Kim Lionetti for getting me started with this series of books.

The Forensic Psychology of
CRIMINAL MINDS

INTRODUCTION

–Forensic Psychology and the Profiler–

Most crime scenes tell a story. The ability of the investigator to perceive the details of this story depends on his or her ability to analyze the crime scene.

—JOHN DOUGLAS

Pop culture has merged with criminal investigation to the point at which the shows most in demand generally involve murder. While the "good guys" still outwit the "bad guys," experiments that subvert such expectations have also proven popular. Notable is a series about Dexter Morgan, a serial killer who holds a job with the Miami police as a blood pattern analyst and whose personal code dictates that he slice and dice other killers. Because he's both a good *and* a bad guy, with a certain amount of flair, he's a potential role model.

At least Canadian filmmaker Mark Twitchell thought so. He became so enamored of Dexter that during the fall of 2008 he decided to start killing, too. Earlier, Twitchell had filmed a movie in which a killer lured men to a brutal death by offering an Internet encounter with a nonexistent woman. It seems that Twitchell then crossed the line. After baiting actual victims with the same Internet ruse, he'd lure them to his garage and meet them wearing a hockey mask and wielding a chain saw. The first man fled, but John Brian Altinger was not so lucky. He turned up missing.

When he'd quit his job by e-mail and claimed to have taken off with a woman, a friend grew suspicious of this uncharacteristic behavior and contacted the police. The friend provided the address where he knew Altinger had gone, and in Twitchell's garage investigators discovered evidence that someone had been strapped to a chair and murdered.

In Twitchell's script, the killer worked for the police, just like Dexter, and on the status line of his Facebook page Twitchell had written, "Mark has way too much in common with Dexter Morgan." It was just a matter of time before some unstable person like Twitchell merged himself with this character.

Ironically, a case like this—life imitating fiction—is perfect for fiction that imitates life. In fact, the majority of episodes on CBS's *Criminal Minds* (*CM*) are based on actual cases (including copycats), and it's not difficult to identify them. Several of the first-generation members of the FBI's Behavioral Science Unit, or BSU (now the Behavioral Analysis Unit, or BAU) have written books about their most interesting or high-profile cases. In addition, because the "profilers" have been elevated in our culture to elite status, books devoted to profiling have proliferated, from a biography of the BAU to collections of scholarly articles to pop overviews.

While the show focuses on profilers, in fact there is no such job designation at the FBI. Members of the BAU are special agents trained in criminal investigative analysis, which includes the activity of behavioral profiling. Just to be clear:

From the FBI's website:

BAU assistance to law enforcement agencies is provided through the process of "criminal investigative analysis." Criminal investigative analysis is a process of reviewing crimes from both a behavioral and investigative perspective. It involves reviewing and assessing the facts of a criminal act, interpreting offender behavior, and interaction with the victim, as exhibited during the commission of the crime, or as displayed in the crime scene. BAU staff conduct detailed analyses of crimes for the purpose of providing one or more of the following services: crime analysis, investigative suggestions, profiles of unknown offenders, threat analysis, critical incident analysis, interview strategies, major case management, search warrant assistance, prosecutive and trial strategies, and expert testimony.

Yet because the show refers to BAU members as profilers, we'll adopt this terminology at times.

Criminal Minds first aired in September 2005, and it features an elite team of FBI agents who travel around the country to assist with investigations involving the most disturbing crimes. They determine the type of crime committed, perform a victim assessment, profile the unknown perpetrator(s), describe the specific psychological aberration involved, and assist in the capture and interrogation. They also interview convicted offenders. At times, they even get involved in legal proceedings.

A prominent agent since the third season began is David Rossi. He's a founding BSU member who'd retired to write books but who has returned to replace a burned-out Jason Gideon. Both characters reflect actual members of the earliest days of the BSU. Each BAU profiler has an area of specialization, and one—Dr. Spencer Reid—is a socially awkward genius with an encyclopedic knowledge about serial killers. Unit Chief Aaron Hotchner—"Hotch"—is a former prosecutor, Supervisory Special Agent (SSA) Derek Morgan is an expert in self-defense and handling explosives, and SSA Emily Prentiss offers help with translation. Each plays off the others' strengths to work against the clock to prevent further crimes and bring killers, arsonists, and rapists to justice. (The public relations liaison, "J J" Jareau, explains that as requests for help come in they engage in a murder triage—assessing which case presents the most imminent danger.) Unlike other series that feature a number of forensic methods, this unit focuses strictly on the criminal mind.

In the pilot episode, "Extreme Aggressor," the agents describe what had happened in famous past cases: the Mad Bomber, the Lipstick Killer, and even the Footpath Killer (a combination of the real-life Trailside Killer and Footpad Murderer). Featuring the Seattle Strangler, the plot is reminiscent of a case involving the first generation of profilers, Seattle's Green River Killer. In fact, Gideon is recovering from a leave of absence due to extreme stress, similar to SSA John Douglas, who grew dangerously ill while on the Green River case. (Gideon's post-traumatic stress disorder, or PTSD, was the result of an order he once gave that caused the deaths of six agents.)

The producers of *Criminal Minds* claim to have based the series on concepts actually used by the FBI, but this fictional team's activity has little in common with BAU procedures. First, the *CM* profilers are often in danger and they usually catch the perpetrator themselves, slighting the local jurisdiction. Second, the entire team (usually five or six) travels together on a corporate jet to a jurisdiction in need. Third, they rely on a computer wiz who's both squeamish and often professionally inappropriate. In addition, they constantly reference the behavior of some past killer to ponder a case they currently face, and we won't even talk about how the female agents dress for sex appeal. In reality, there's no jet, the agents merely consult (one or two at a time), and they rely on statistically analyzed databases, not isolated examples of lone perpetrators, to devise their profiles. In short, aside from the cases and buzzwords, little in this show mirrors the BSU or BAU, despite the writers' access to FBI consultants. Still, expert consultants are better suited to documentaries than sizzle TV, so for the sake of entertainment the changes were made.

Since the premise of criminal behavioral analysis relies on the long history of research and clinical practice in the fields of criminology and forensic psychology and psychiatry, let's summarize what's involved. First, the basics.

THE PSYCHOLOGY OF CRIME—

Forensic psychology focuses on psychological issues and situations in the law, by the law, and of the law. Professionals in this field use their expertise with human behavior, motivation, and psychopathology to provide assessment services for the courts and may also consult in criminal investigations. Each episode of *Criminal Minds* shows an angle on this, whether it's psychosis, perversion, or protocol. "The Big Game," for example, illustrates crimes arising from multiple personality disorder and "North Mammon" features the effects of psychological terrorism during captivity.

Experts in forensic psychology may appraise behaviors such as malingering (faking symptoms of an illness), confessing to a crime, or acting suicidal. Although most such practitioners are clinicians with a specialization in forensic issues, this applied discipline also involves investigators who study psychology (Reid on *CM*) and researchers who examine issues relevant to legal situations. These subjects include assessing threats, determining the fitness of a parent for guardianship, crystallizing the influences on false confessions, and testing eyewitness accuracy. Forensic psychologists may also assist a forensic artist with behavioral quirks that affect appearance, help attorneys select jury members, or assist coroners to resolve ambiguous death determinations.

Some forensic psychologists work for police departments to

screen for fitness for duty or the need for trauma counseling. Many work in prisons or psychiatric hospitals, and quite a few develop a private practice that's affiliated with the courts. To be effective, they must be familiar with the way the criminal justice system works. Whether it's to evaluate an offender's knowledge of right and wrong at the time of a crime, assess trauma to a child, or profile a crime scene, psychologists and other mental health professionals are an integral part of the pursuit of justice.

As part of the field of forensic psychology, profiling is itself a complex arena with many different facets. Each chapter that follows focuses on an area in which professionals with specialized training in criminal psychology and psychological logic apply their skills.

Culturally, one of the earliest mass-market fictional renderings of the FBI's form of profiling came from author Thomas Harris. He received unprecedented access to the BSU, attending meetings and learning about the agents and their cases. He then devised the novels *Red Dragon* (1981) and *The Silence of the Lambs* (1988). The latter was made into a movie in 1991, winning five Academy Awards, including Best Picture, which brought considerable fame to the unit. The news magazine show *60 Minutes* then featured the agents who were members of the BSU at the time. Yet Harris didn't exactly get it right.

In *The Silence of the Lambs*, agent-in-training Clarice Starling is sent to the prison cell of brutal serial killer and cannibal, Dr. Hannibal Lecter, to get him to describe the mind and methods of "Buffalo Bill," a murderer who is holding a woman hostage. (This killer was based on a combination of real-life killers Ted Bundy, Gary Heidnik, and Ed Gein.) In reality, candidates for the BAU have a minimum of three years of field experience (usually much more), and in any event, no one would send a young female recruit alone on what they all view as a dangerous and important assignment. While members of the BSU who read the script suggested changes, reportedly there was little regard for their opinions.

Around this time, several of the first-generation members of the BSU, now retired, were publishing books. The former profilers were soon touted in the media as super-sleuths, each one a contemporary Sherlock Holmes. While Robert Ressler was the first to publish, it was former BSU chief John Douglas who achieved the greatest visibility. He penned an international bestseller, *Mind Hunter*, and, right or wrong, came to be linked with Jack Crawford, head of the BSU, in *The Silence of the Lambs*. As a result, he became a popular spokesperson, and in *Mind Hunter* he states, "I use a formula, How plus Why equals Who. If we can answer the hows and whys in a crime, we generally can come up with the solution." In other words, based on the idea that people tend to be slaves to their psychology and will inevitably leave clues, a profile is an educated attempt to provide parameters from behavioral evidence at a crime scene that reveal the type of person who committed it.

This idea spawned a television series, *Profiler*, in which a female FBI agent possessed extra-sensory powers. The public came to regard profiling—just one tool among many others in a criminal investigation—as the ultimate tool. Having a profiler on the case seemed to guarantee a serial killer's capture, and the professionals who could achieve this were thought to possess larger-than-life abilities. Fictional media enhanced this notion and redesigned serial killers to be clever and worthy adversaries. The two-part *CM* episodes, "The Evilution of Frank" and "Masterpiece" are examples.

Soon, the media began to misrepresent the activity of profiling. Journalists talked about "the profile of a serial killer" as if it were a set generic blueprint for a type of offender rather than the unique analysis of behavior specific to a crime scene. While responsible investigators resisted journalists' demands to reinforce this notion, there were always pseudo-profilers willing to step up and supply the sound-bites. Thanks to fiction and film, the phrases were readily available, and some people even used them to design weekend seminars that fraudulently certified eager young novices as profilers. The FBI was not amused. However, there was little the agents could do except continue to use profiling as it was meant to be used to assist local jurisdictions.

Yet, forensic behavioral analysis is not solely the province of the FBI. Psychologists with a specialty in criminal behavior, as well as some criminologists, have developed their own ideas on the subject, and even their own methods. The FBI gets credit for making the subject media worthy, but they weren't the first profilers or even necessarily the best.

Whether people enter this discipline via law enforcement or psychological consulting, they must still learn the ropes. They need to know the process of investigation and the methods used to determine if a death is a suicide, an accident, or a homicide. They must understand the typical signals of a staged crime as well as the way a psychopath operates. They also need to know about evidence collection, courtroom protocol, and how to interview different types of people—from victims' families and friends to rapists, pedophiles, and murderers.

Academic psychologists can also provide research support, and the FBI has hired them to become part of the National Center for the Analysis of Violent Crime (NCAVC). Even outside the FBI, researchers who hope to bring a more scientific basis to behavioral profiling have designed studies with statistical analysis. For example, in 1990 and 2000, experiments pitted trained profilers against students and police officers to see who fared best on predicting an offender's characteristics from the facts in sample cases. It turns out that experienced profilers do have an edge, although there was significant variability among them. In other words, some were outstanding while others were no better than an average person.

The FBI, too, hopes to inject more science into its practices. Geographical profiling uses computerized maps, for example. An analysis of behavior in eighty-three arson cases offered enough data to characterize six distinct styles. In England, crime scene data from a hundred serial homicides helped identify the most distinguishing perp behaviors, whereas some FBI agents have used the Psychopathy Checklist (PCL-R) to try to understand apparently motiveless serial crimes. The agency continues to analyze interviews with convicted criminals and to build up comparative records in the computerized database, Violent Criminal Apprehension Program (ViCAP). There's even pattern-recognition software that strives for accuracy in providing profiles of serial crime by computer. But more about this later.

In *Criminal Minds*, we see not only the activity of crime scene analysis and reconstruction but also how to assess a variety of criminal psyches, how to deal with hostage situations, and what can happen to professionals who focus so intensely on extreme offenders. The subject of torture is obviously high on the list, but we also see child abuse, stalking, terrorism, organized crime, and kidnapping. Across the course of several seasons, one agent has abandoned the unit, another was temporarily suspended, a third became a drug addict, and a fourth took justice into her own hands, ending her career. The other agents often face personal issues mirrored in their cases, from child abuse to rape to divorce. So, as the *CM* profilers say when they're ready to go, "Wheels up." Let's see how behavioral profiling evolved through a series of infamous crimes.

ONE

—Criminal Profiling—

ITS HISTORY AND PURPOSE

The blood-dimmed tide is loosed and everywhere
The ceremony of innocence is drowned.

—W. B. YEATS, "THE SECOND COMING"

A female pawnbroker and her stepsister are murdered in their shop. The pawnbroker has been bludgeoned, while the second victim sustained injuries from an ax blade. No weapon turns up at the scene, and although money is missing, other items of value remain. The detective first performs a victimology: He interviews everyone who knows or has had business with either victim. He also learns about the victims' habits. Then he devises a profile, based on the crime scene and his experience, to decide on a range of characteristics for the unknown perpetrator. He now has an idea about the type of person he's looking for.

This was the task that Inspector Porfiry faced in one of the earliest examples in fiction of working up a criminal profile, Fyodor Dostoevsky's 1866 novel, *Crime and Punishment*. As Porfiry makes a list of clients, he examines their lives and discovers that a student named Raskolnikov has not paid his rent. Thus, he could be in need of money. More interesting, this same young man has just published a passionate article on the idea that extraordinary men can commit crimes without moral accountability. In addition, Raskolnikov has recently fallen ill—perhaps from the stress of guilt. Since no other customers prove to have motives, Raskolnikov emerges as a solid suspect. Porfiry meets and pressures him, and eventually the guilt-ridden young man confesses to the double homicide.

In real life, identifying a suspect and provoking a confession are not this easy, yet thanks largely to fiction and to entertainment shows that pass as news, the general public has come to believe that profiling borders on the supernatural. While it is true that psychological analysis of behavioral evidence at a crime scene can assist—sometimes significantly—it does not necessarily enhance the chance of making an arrest.

As we make our way through the evolution of forensic psychological analysis, we'll see how it began as a rudimentary interpretation of serious crime but grew into a specialized and detailed tool that involves increasingly more research and scientific calculation.

WHO IS JACK?—

A surgeon drew up one of the earliest documented profiles in 1888, two decades after Dostoevsky penned his tale. Dr. Thomas Bond, who read the autopsy reports of the murder victims attributed to Jack the Ripper and assisted in one of the autopsies, offered his own ideas. In fact, the episode "Jones" refers to this infamous spree when the *Criminal Minds* team encounters an apparent copycat killer in post-Katrina New Orleans.

The official story of the Ripper focuses on the murders of five prostitutes in different areas of London's East End slums in the fall of 1888. Some criminologists (and Ripperologists) believe there were more than five victims, but to avoid getting involved in the arguments, we'll concentrate on the five on which most experts agree.

The first was forty-five-year-old Mary Ann "Polly" Nichols. On the night of August 31, an hour after a friend spotted her, she was killed, blitz-style, where she stood. Her skirt was pulled up to her waist, her legs were parted, and there were severe cuts into her abdomen and throat. About a week later, Annie Chapman ended up on the wrong side of a similar knife. Her throat was cut, her stomach was ripped open, and her intestines pulled out. Her bladder and uterus were missing.

A note arrived on September 29 that appeared to be a lead. Signed, "Yours Truly, Jack the Ripper," the author claimed that he was "down on whores" and would continue to kill them. The next night, September 30, saw the murders of two women, not far apart, Elizabeth Stride and Catherine Eddowes. Stride's throat was cut, but Eddowes's intestines were removed and placed over her right shoulder, her uterus and kidney were gone, and her face was oddly mutilated.

Then came a letter "from Hell" to the head of the Whitechapel vigilante organization, enclosed with half of a pickled kidney that seemed to be afflicted with Bright's disease—a disorder from which Eddowes had reportedly suffered. The note's author indicated that he'd fried and eaten the other half. He offered to send "the bloody knife" in due time, and taunted, "Catch me when you can." The police were unable to learn who had sent the gruesome package, but the handwriting was different from that in the Jack the Ripper letter.

It was the last victim, Mary Kelly, twenty-four, who took the brunt of the offender's frenzy. On November 8, she apparently invited a man into a rented room, and after he killed her, he spent about two hours skinning and disemboweling her.

Bond's assessment of the type of person who would commit

such crimes was dated November 10, 1888. Excerpts from Bond's profile:

> All five murders were no doubt committed by the same hand. In the first four, the throats appear to have been cut from left to right. . . . All circumstances surrounding the murders lead me to form the opinion that the women must have been lying down when murdered and in every case the throat was first cut. . . .
>
> In each case the mutilation was inflicted by a person who had no scientific nor anatomical knowledge. In my opinion, he does not even possess the technical knowledge of a butcher or horse slaughterer or any person accustomed to cut up dead animals. . . .
>
> The murderer must have been a man of physical strength, and great coolness and daring. There is no evidence that he had an accomplice. He must, in my opinion, be a man subject to periodic attacks of homicidal and erotic mania. The character of the mutilations indicates that the man may be in a condition sexually, that may be called Satyriasis. It is of course possible that the homicidal impulse may have developed from a revengeful or brooding condition of mind, or that religious mania may have been the original disease, but I do not think that either hypothesis is likely. The murderer in external appearance is quite likely to be a quiet inoffensive looking man, probably middle-aged, and neatly and respectably dressed. I think he might be in the habit of wearing a cloak or overcoat, or he could hardly have escaped notice in the streets if the blood on his hands or clothes were visible. . . .
>
> [H]e would probably be solitary and eccentric in his habits, also he is most likely to be a man without regular occupation, but with some small income or pension. He is possibly living

among respectable persons who have some knowledge of his character and habits, and who may have grounds for suspicion that he is not quite right in his mind at times.

Bond believed the offer of a reward would garner clues from people who knew the man but who were otherwise hesitant to come forward. He was also certain the same man was responsible for the 1889 murder of a sixth woman, Alice McKenzie, whose autopsy he performed as well.

Many scholars agree with the idea that the Ripper was a sexually depraved individual, but another idea emerged after a Ripperologist measured the distance from each crime scene to the others. Since the distances were evenly balanced (he claimed), he believed that the murder sites themselves were significant, not the specific victims. They had merely been in the wrong place at the wrong time. In addition, while many theorists believe the murders stopped with Mary Kelly, others think the Ripper merely moved on to another place and continued elsewhere, or remained inactive for a while and emerged later. A similar murder occurred in 1889 in Scotland, and upon his arrest, that man hinted he was the Ripper. In San Francisco, two young women were killed in the spring of 1895, one of them attacked in a Ripper-like manner. Thus Bond's profile might have been based on too few crimes, too many, or perhaps not all the facts. The precise series of crimes and the motive for them would affect any assessment of the perpetrator. Because no one knows exactly which victims can be attributed to the London maniac, no profile at this time can be affirmed as accurate.

In any event, "Jack" was never caught, and within a few decades, criminal profiling had moved onto the couch of criminal psychiatrists. Freud and his followers had a few things to say about what precipitated crime, but mental health experts who focused on specific figures seemed to best appreciate the psychological modus operandi at a crime scene. Richard von Krafft-Ebing was the first to do this, publishing *Psychopathia Sexualis* in 1887, and forensic pathologist Alexandre Lacassagne (who had an interest in the criminal mind) initiated the first "prison autobiographies," inspired by cases in which he had testified. For example, in 1897 a tramp from France named Joseph Vacher was accused of sexual crimes against fourteen people, including eleven murders. Vacher, twenty-nine, claimed he suffered from an irresistible impulse that drove him. Having been bitten by a rabid dog when he was a child, he insisted that his blood had been poisoned, so as his victims died he'd drunk their blood to refresh his own.

Lacassagne decided that Vacher was faking a mental illness. In court, the famed pathologist demonstrated how he believed the defendant had carried out the crimes and Vacher reportedly said, "He's very good." Indeed, Lacassagne's reputation and commanding stance helped convict Vacher, who was executed two months later by guillotine. Lacassagne did more interviews with offenders, encouraging several to write about themselves. Each week he checked their notebooks, correcting and guiding these men and women toward some insight about their behavior. He found that their family histories were full of violence, tension, and disease, and he inspired many psychiatrists who followed his work to analyze the psychosexual development of serial killers.

BLOOD CRIMES—

Ernst August Ferdinand Gennat was director of the Berlin Criminal Police, starting shortly after a separate homicide division was created in 1902. He organized a homicide squad, the Zentrale Mordinspektion, which he led to an impressive record of success. By 1931, they were solving nearly 95 percent of the crimes they investigated, and some have credited Gennat with developing the basis for psychological profiling and even with suggesting the phrase *serial killer.* He used *serienmörder* in reference to the case of Peter Kürten. Yet it's Dr. Karl Berg, who questioned Kürten extensively in prison in 1930, who is most closely linked with the infamous offender. After Kürten was charged with numerous counts of assault and murder, Berg set out to study him. While this was not the activity of a profiler, since the killer's identity was known, it was among the early attempts to thoroughly understand the abnormal mind of a repeat offender. As such, it would assist the emerging BSU decades later. Kürten's confessions became the basis for Berg's book *The Sadist,* and for those aspects of the murders in which Kürten took great pleasure, his memory was detailed and accurate. He even reeled off details about crimes he'd perpetrated for which he had not even been accused, culminating in seventy-nine different criminal incidents (including thirteen murders). He displayed no remorse to his interviewers and in fact took delight whenever he provoked a reaction. Although Kürten claimed he had slaughtered his victims to inflict harm on society, Berg believed the crimes were sexually motivated.

Kürten started killing, he said, after a neighbor taught him how to rape and torture animals. At the age of nine, he'd set up an "accident" in which two other boys died. He'd enjoyed that, so he'd become a predator.

In 1913, he entered the second-floor room of an inn at Koln-Mulheim in the Rhine River Valley, where he sliced the throat of a ten-year-old girl and drank her blood as it spurted from the artery. He admitted that this act had resulted in an orgasm.

Kürten went to prison on unrelated crimes, but upon emerging years later, he stabbed an eight-year-old girl thirteen times, set fire to her corpse, and stuffed it under a hedge. That same week, Kürten stabbed a forty-five-year-old mechanic in the skull. Six months went by before he killed two girls at the fairgrounds, strangling the five-year-old and beheading the fourteen-year-old.

He attacked but did not kill a few others, but then used a hammer to slaughter a teenager after he raped her. Then Kürten sent a letter to police to lead them to the body of a five-year-old child, stabbed thirty-six times. The letter also described the location of the corpse of another young woman who'd been missing for months. Finally, Kürten let a rape victim go who then turned him in. Under arrest, he admitted to drinking blood from his victims because it excited him. After his conviction for nine murders, Kürten was executed in 1931.

One of the important facets of Kürten's modus operandi was his claim that he had no conscience. "Never have I felt any misgivings in my soul," he told the judge. "Never did I think to myself that what I did was bad." He blamed the "torture" he'd received in prison and believed that any Higher Being would approve of his behavior. He also added, "I derived the sort of pleasure from these visions [of harm to others] that other people would get from thinking about a naked woman."

Thus Kurten stands as an example of a depraved sadistic psychopath with no particular victim preference who would have continued to kill had he not been stopped. He is also one of the few serial killers who knowingly made an error in releasing a victim, and one of the rare such perpetrators who used a variety of murder weapons and activities. He tortured animals and other children as a child, but he was married and, once caught, went to great lengths to ensure that his wife would live out her days a rich widow. In other words, Kürten presented an odd collection of traits and behaviors, some of them contradictory, which defy the serial killer stereotypes we have today.

THE CONFUSION BEGINS—

The word, *profile* is used in three different ways, so before we move on, let's clarify. The one on which this book focuses is about the activity of developing a collection of traits and behaviors from a crime scene or series of crime scenes. We'll refer to this as criminal profiling or crime-scene profiling. It's a retrospective activity, after the fact and based on specific incidents.

Prospective profiling, which the media tend to use, is akin to racial profiling, a form of risk assessment. It reinforces the erroneous notion that there is a blueprint for what we understand about the type of person who commits serial murder, and various offenders can be compared to this blueprint to see how closely they match. While prospective profiling has its place, its use for an active serial crime investigation is limited.

The third, and most awkward notion of profiling, which *CM* occasionally promotes, is that profiling is an ability to psychoanalyze or "read" people from their behavior and habits. Reid even states this on "52 Pickup," as they proceed to read the behavior of a specific man whom they believe is teaching serial killers how to stalk women. In addition, the agents on *CM* sometimes deflect a colleague's analysis of them or comment on the fact that a profiler can't profile—read—the people right in front of him. Hotchner does it to some effect in "Tabula Rasa," when a defense attorney tries to discredit him in the courtroom. Then and there, he reads the man, accurately describing his traits from his behaviors. Yet interpreting the behavior of a known person is not the same skill as criminal profiling of an unknown subject (unsub). All three of these activities are related in that they seek to draw up a portrait through psychological analysis. However, offering hypotheses about a known person versus an unknown one are quite different activities, calling on different skill sets. It's unfortunate that we have conflated the three concepts into a single word, because confusion abounds.

For example, many histories of profiling include the analysis done on Hitler during World War II in 1942, as if this were the same procedure as Bond's attempt to understand the unsub responsible for the Ripper crimes. Dr. Walter C. Langer, a psychoanalyst based in New York, offered a 135-page long-range evaluation of what Hitler was probably like and what he might do if he believed he were going to lose the war. In other words, Langer offered a risk assessment, not a criminal profile, because the Office of Strategic Services wanted a psychological basis for making plans, given likely options.

To devise a predictive portrait, Langer used speeches, a lengthy biography, Hitler's book *Mein Kampf,* and interviews with people who had known Hitler. He noted that Hitler was meticulous, conventional, and prudish about his body. He was in good health, so it was unlikely he would die from natural causes, but his actions and orders indicated that he was deteriorating mentally. Yet he would not try to escape to some neutral country to save himself. He showed strong streaks of narcissism and sadism, and he tended to speak in long monologues rather than engaging in conversations. Because he appeared to be delusional, it was possible that in the face of imminent defeat his psychological structures would collapse. The most likely scenario, Langer predicted, was that Hitler would end his own life, via one of his henchmen.

It should be clear from Langer's analysis that looking at information about a known person, especially one for whom there are abundant resources, has little in common with analyzing evidence at crime scenes to try to devise a behavioral and personality portrait. The latter is a much more difficult activity, riskier, and more prone to error. Even so, a skilled observer of people will do a better job of reading such evidence than someone with only a passive grasp of his or her environment. Let's return to the history of criminal profiling.

PSYCHOLOGICAL IMPRESSIONS—

It was the work of psychiatrist James A. Brussel that offered significant inspiration to what was to become the FBI's Behavioral Science Unit. In fact, the case for which Brussel provided a psychiatric analysis is the basis for the *CM* episode, "Empty Planet." Almost every book on the subject of profiling documents this case, in part because it was surprising, but also in part because it grounded a historic turning point for the FBI.

Three investigators went to the Manhattan offices of Dr. Brussel one afternoon in 1956. They showed him a collection of letters and photos from the unsolved sixteen-year spree of the infamous "Mad Bomber" of New York City. More than three dozen explosions had occurred in Manhattan between 1940 and 1956, in public places such as Radio City Music Hall and Grand Central Station, and the perpetrator had sent a barrage of angry letters to area newspapers, politicians, and Consolidated Edison. While no bomb had yet been lethal, the attacks had grown more dangerous. At the time, the idea of using a psychiatric consultant for crime scene analysis was unprecedented, but the detectives had tried everything else. They were at an impasse. Brussel agreed to study the letters to try to deduce the unknown perpetrator's ethnicity, living conditions, skills, educational level, issues, and psychiatric disorders.

Believing there was a method to the bomber's apparent madness, Brussel recognized certain themes in the materials and provided his interpretations. Since the first letter had been sent to Consolidated Edison, he surmised that the offender was probably a former employee with a grudge. Because bombs were the weapon of choice, he thought the perpetrator was most likely a male European immigrant, which also revealed his likely religion: Roman Catholic. His progressively more paranoid messages placed his age between forty and fifty and suggested he was a fastidious loner. Thus he probably lived with an older female—a mother figure—who took care of his basic needs. Because the letters were often mailed in Westchester County, if one considered this to be halfway between his home and his target, he probably resided in an ethnic community not far from the city.

From the letters, Brussel outlined a few more traits and behaviors: The bomber probably attended church and was quiet, polite, and helpful, although he would have difficulty managing his anger. He would also be miserly; hence he would wear an old-fashioned suit, probably double-breasted. And because he was fastidious, as many paranoid people are in their desire to maintain a controlled and orderly world, he would always button it. In addition, although the Mad Bomber had been meticulous in his missives about forming each letter of the alphabet with straight lines, the *W* stood out: It was always rounded. This signaled to the Freudian psychiatrist that the Bomber had sexual issues as well as a strong love for his mother.

Years later, Brussel explained his reasoning in his 1968 memoir, *Casebook of a Forensic Psychiatrist*. His deductions were based on simple probability, flavored by his clinical experience. Records indicate that he did offer erroneous notions about the offender, such as having a facial scar, being of Germanic extraction, and living in White Plains, New York, but having no precedent for such an analysis, Brussel was cutting his own pattern.

He also suggested a strategy for how to use his analysis. Upon completing the profile, Brussel urged the police to publish it in the newspapers, because he was certain from the intense emotional tone in the letters it would draw a response. The Bomber wanted people to see how important he was, which he seemed to measure by newspaper coverage.

Brussel's suggestion worked. Although the profile sparked several false leads and drew an abundance of tips that wasted police resources, the perpetrator did respond as predicted, pointing out Brussel's errors and revealing the date of the incident that had so angered him. With that, it was possible for Consolidated Edison to check through its employee records. Early in 1957, a clerk who had painstakingly gone through the records by hand broke the case when she matched unique phrases the Bomber had used to phrases in written complaints to the company.

When the police finally arrested George Metesky, age fifty-four, in Waterbury, Connecticut, he was in his robe and pajamas. He did live with two unmarried older sisters and he displayed the predicted personality traits. He owned a typewriter, which was matched to the letters, and had a workshop stocked with tools and materials for making the bombs. The police told him to get dressed and he returned (according to Brussel's memoir) buttoning up a double-breasted suit. Nevertheless, it was not the profile's details that had assisted the police, but the way it had provoked Metesky to reveal himself.

Despite Brussel's warning that a psychiatric analysis might influence tunnel vision, which could mislead rather than lead, he continued to be in demand for similar consultations. He believed he was always right, but in light of what we now know about criminal behavior, his analysis of the series of eleven murders in Boston from 1962 to 1964 seems unsophisticated, even amusing.

The first victim, on June 14, 1962, was Anna Slesars, found in her home with the cord from her bathrobe wrapped around her neck. She had been sexually assaulted. Two weeks later, sixty-eight-year-old Nina Nichols was strangled with two nylon stockings, the ends of which were tied in a bow. On the same day, Helen Blake, sixty-five, met a similar death. Soon, two more elderly women were strangled in their homes.

Then the assault pattern shifted to young women, killed in their apartments: Sophie Clark, a twenty-year-old student at the

Carnegie Institute of Medical Technology, and Patricia Bissette, twenty-three, who had resided near Anna Slesers and Sophie Clark. Although Clark was African American, in contrast to the others who were all Caucasian, the way she was killed linked her to them. Four months after Bisette, sixty-eight-year-old Mary Brown was found beaten, strangled, and raped. But then came graduate student Beverly Samans.

Boston was in turmoil. Massachusetts Attorney General Edward Brooke took charge as he set up a "Strangler Bureau" to collect, organize, and assimilate over thirty-seven thousand documents. Hundreds of suspects were fingerprinted and more than three dozen given lie-detector tests. Every known sex offender was tracked down, while patient leaves from mental institutions were checked, but the police were so stymied they even resorted to consulting a nightclub psychic.

On September 8, Evelyn Corbin, a fifty-eight-year-old divorcee, was strangled with two nylon stockings two months before a younger woman, Joann Graff, was raped and murdered in her apartment. Two brown nylon stockings and a black leotard were tied in an elaborate bow around her neck. The final victim was nineteen-year-old Mary Sullivan, murdered in an apartment into which she had recently moved. The killer had thrust a broomstick handle into her vagina and propped a card against her foot that said, "Happy New Year."

Several psychiatrists, including Brussel, were consulted for personality assessment. Given the diverse victimology, quite a few of these professionals believed there was more than one killer, but Brussel insisted that one man had committed all the crimes. To explain the shifting patterns, he suggested that the man had gone through a series of life upheavals.

"What has happened to him, in two words," Brussel recalled saying, "is instant maturity. In this two-year period, he has suddenly grown, psychosexually, from infancy to puberty to manhood." That is, the Strangler had struck out at his mother, symbolized by the elderly women. Once he came to terms with his Oedipal complex, he was able to sexually respond to younger women, as evidenced by semen at those scenes. But he was still angry, so he continued to kill. "He had to commit these murders to achieve his growth. It was the only way to solve his problems, finding himself sexually, and to become a grown man among men." However, Brussel did not explain why the offender had killed two older women in the midst of his attacks on the younger women. He did believe that, with the over-the-top sexual treatment of Mary Sullivan, the killer was finished— was even triumphant. He had been cured of his aberrations. And the murders did appear to stop.

On November 5, 1964, Albert DeSalvo was arrested for a series of rapes. He soon confessed to being the Boston Strangler, and his attorney, F. Lee Bailey, worked out a deal that would send him to trial for only his sexual offenses but including details from the murders to support an insanity defense.

Brussel was proud to have been among the few who "knew" that the murders were the work of a single perpetrator. To his surprise, Bailey invited him to join the defense team, which gave Brussel the opportunity to interview DeSalvo. He conducted two long sessions, whereupon he learned something that contradicted his theory. DeSalvo had never been impotent. Quite the opposite. He'd been sexually insatiable and claimed to have committed over a thousand rapes. He certainly had dozens of rape charges on his record.

Nevertheless, Brussel believed they could prove that DeSalvo was mentally ill and unable to control himself during the commission of each crime. The psychiatrist readily agreed to serve as an expert witness, hoping to help DeSalvo avoid incarceration by getting treatment instead in a psychiatric institution. Yet Brussel conducted only two interviews with the notorious defendant and undertook no standardized assessment; he appears to have accepted whatever De-Salvo told him. Despite Brussel's optimism, DeSalvo was convicted and sent to prison for life. He was murdered there six years later, some believe because he was planning to reveal the real killer.

It remains unknown whether physical evidence would have corroborated DeSalvo's confession (for which he believed he would be paid a substantial reward), and he eventually recanted, putting into doubt not only that he was the Strangler but also that a single perpetrator had committed all the murders. (A recent exhumation of the final victim, Mary Sullivan, cleared DeSalvo of her murder with a DNA analysis, and this finding raised doubts about the rest of his confession.)

In retrospect, with more now known about the motives and behavior of predatory serial killers, it seems naive to theorize that murdering older women would "resolve" a predator's "mother issues" and "graduate" him to younger women. In addition, Brussel had concluded that with Mary Sullivan the Strangler was finished. This prediction, too, is undermined by probability. Crime does not cure killers, and serial murderers rarely just stop, especially when their crimes have grown more frequent and brutal. Even if Brussel was correct about DeSalvo being the killer, DeSalvo's own sexual history defies any notion that he could so decisively control his criminal acts.

The point of Brussel's work is that he used keen observation and probability analysis, which is the basis for criminal profiling today. Whenever asked by reporters what proportion of his assessments were based in science, he would tell them he always began with science but then intuition and imagination would take over. Even so, he'd check his hunches against research data, and he trusted the law of averages. Mostly, he used mental immersion, believing that pondering the gathered facts about an unknown criminal long enough allowed him to envision the man. These notions impressed someone at the FBI: Special Agent Howard Teten. As he read Brussel's *Casebook*, he knew he had to learn more.

PROFILING GOES TO QUANTICO—

With rising murder rates during the 1950s and 1960s, the FBI had been granted expanded jurisdiction, especially for serial crimes. Notorious killers such as Ed Gein, Charles Schmid, John Norman Collins, and Harvey Glatman had been caught by 1970 and all were either convicted of, or suspected in, numerous murders. Something had to be done to catch these killers earlier in their criminal careers.

> The Federal Bureau of Investigation was founded in 1908 but was poorly managed until 1924 when J. Edgar Hoover became its director. In 1935, he set up the FBI Training Academy in Washington, D.C., which was eventually moved to the Marine base at Quantico, Virginia. As the FBI's jurisdiction increased in variety and scope, there was more demand for its resources, and the agency soon developed into an elite law enforcement organization. Greater coordination occurred during the 1950s with the Ten Most Wanted program, and in 1967 with the National Crime Information Center (NCIC), with access for state and local agencies.

At the FBI Training Academy, several agents were teaching ideas from psychology and sociology—disciplines routinely snubbed by law enforcement. Howard Teten was among them, offering a course as early as 1970 titled "Applied Criminology." A former crime scene investigator, he'd developed a method of basic behavioral analysis that he'd tested successfully on already solved cases. He'd even asked several psychiatrists to check his work to ensure he was correct about the characteristics of various mental disorders, and when he read Brussel's 1968 memoir, he thought the psychiatrist's approach provided another insightful layer.

In 1973, Teten met Brussel, then retired, and they struck up an association. Over the course of that year, Teten learned Brussel's method for analyzing unknown offenders from behavioral manifestations ("psychological impressions") at a crime scene. He thought Brussel's approach offered more detail from psychological analysis but believed his own ensured fewer errors. He was also uninterested in Freudian explanations. "His approach was to seek specific areas of psychiatric potential," Teten said in an interview, "and then to combine them to form a profile. This is somewhat different from my approach, which was to derive an overall impression of the gross mental status based on the crime scene as a whole."

Teten blended the two methodologies and applied them to unsolved cases, developing criminal profiling for the fledgling Behavioral Science Unit. Brussel's unique tool was now in the hands of an agency that could "spread the wealth."

Robert "Roy" Hazelwood and Richard Ault, two of the earliest BSU members, co-wrote an article to describe how law enforcement to that point had distrusted psychology, yet they confirmed that "investigators can and should make use of advances in the behavioral sciences." Unlike detectives who looked for physical clues at a crime scene, members of the BSU viewed a crime scene's appearance and the way the crime was committed as symptomatic of the offender's unique aberration. John Douglas compared this activity with understanding artists through their art or homeowners through their furnishings.

Initially, the BSU had eleven members and Jack Kirsch was its first chief. A former police training coordinator, Kirsch served for eight months, followed by John Pfaff. Yet Teten and his teaching partner, Patrick Mullany, designed the method for analyzing unsubs.

The initial BSU staff handpicked agents who had a knack for behavioral analysis, and as the demand on their time and the daily exposure to brutal crimes became more intense, they developed a strong camaraderie. With the pressure for greater analytic sophistication, many of them began to specialize. Hazelwood, for example, researched sadistic sexual crimes and autoerotic fatalities, while Ken Lanning focused on child abuse and alleged satanic ritual abuse. As the various members went out to local jurisdictions to teach, they helped solve many puzzling cases. Their first success story occurred in Montana.

Someone grabbed seven-year-old Susan Jaeger from her tent during a family camping trip in Montana in 1974. The site yielded no obvious physical evidence and there was no ransom request, but the police did develop a suspect, David Meirhofer. Since he was well-groomed, courteous, and educated, and he passed a polygraph, he seemed increasingly unlikely. Yet within a few months he became a suspect in the murder of a young woman from the area whom he'd dated. Nevertheless, interrogators got nothing out of him. When detectives called on the BSU, the agents were convinced that, despite appearances, Meirhofer was the culprit for Jaeger's abduction. The profile they devised indicated that her abductor would be young, white, sexually gratified by murder, and a collector of grisly trophies. When the kidnapper called the girl's mother a year after the incident, she recognized his voice and collected enough information for a warrant to search Meirhofer's home. There, the police turned up body parts from both victims, and it appeared as though Meirhofer had kept little Susan imprisoned for a while before killing her. In his confession, he added the murder of two boys and the woman. Then he committed suicide.

Requests for consultations came in to the unit from police departments around the country, so more agents were trained. In 1976, Robert K. Ressler began conducting interviews with convicted offenders to start building a database of information, and by 1977, the unit had a substantial identity with a three-pronged purpose: crime scene analysis, profiling, and the analysis of threatening letters. This became the Crime Analysis and Criminal Personality Profiling Program.

The early profilers—those who entered the BSU during what many refer to as its "golden age"—were bold, innovative, and instinctive. They knew they were pioneering a program that would have to be carefully introduced to law enforcement agencies, because many officers (especially old-timers) would resist change that involved information from a subject area they did not know or trust. The right personalities came together synchronously to produce what many today regard as an important contribution to understanding the most brutal and extreme human behavior. Unlike technicians who could clearly compare fibers or fingerprints, the profilers were evaluating the indirect results of elusive and sometimes clever minds.

Let's see how it's done.

TWO

-Brainstorming-

DEVELOPING A PROFILE

They are obsessed with a fantasy, and they have what we must call non-fulfilled experiences that become part of the fantasy and push them toward the next killing.

—ROBERT K. RESSLER

During the BSU's early days, as its members developed ideas about behavioral profiling, they used several ways to check themselves. Howard Teten spent seven years examining solved cases, without knowing the solution or details about the suspect, to devise "blind" portraits of the unsubs. He would then compare the offenders who'd been convicted for these crimes against his results. This exercise revealed areas to him that needed more work. It soon became evident that the most difficult items to predict were an offender's age and race. (No one back then thought much about the behavioral differences between male and female killers, as the vast majority of serial offenders studied to that point were male.)

Robert K. Ressler and Russ Vorpagel, who were both heavily involved in the BSU's early formation, had a unique opportunity to write a profile of a case actively under investigation in Sacramento, California. They had access to information from the investigation and also managed to interview the offender after he was caught. (This case influenced *CM*'s "Blood Hungry.")

In the middle of the day in January 1978, a strange man entered the home of Teresa Wallin, twenty-two, who was three months pregnant. He shot her twice and then dragged her body to the bedroom. With a knife, he carved off her left nipple, cut open her torso, and repeatedly stabbed her. He also cut out her kidneys and severed her pancreas in two, placing the kidneys together back inside her. Then he used a yogurt container from the trash to drink her blood. Neighbors described a lanky stranger wandering around, and three days later, the same man entered another home and killed Evelyn Miroth, thirty-eight, a male friend of hers, her six-year-old son, and her infant nephew.

Ressler used all the tools available. A former hostage negotiator, he'd developed an appreciation for behavioral analysis for negotiations. From a psychiatric study of the relationship between body type and mental temperament—the one James A. Brussel had also consulted—Ressler believed the offender was probably scrawny. Given the disorder at the scene, it was likely the unsub had no employment that required organized thinking, and little education. He also knew how long it took schizophrenia to develop into extreme violence, so it helped him estimate the perp's age to be in the mid-twenties. As Vorpagel devised a profile independently, he came to similar conclusions.

Both believed the unsub was psychotic. This meant that he'd probably made no plan to kill and had done nothing to hide or destroy evidence. He'd left footprints and fingerprints and had probably walked about with blood from the murders on his clothing. Because personality dictates behavior, the agents said that his domicile would be as sloppy as the manner in which he'd ransacked the victims' homes. He probably was not very mobile and thus lived fairly close to the crime scenes. He was white, unemployed, twenty-five to twenty-seven years old, thin, undernourished, untidy, reclusive, and probably kept evidence from the crimes in his residence. He was likely getting disability payments and probably had been in a psychiatric institution. This composite portrait was developed from known data that such crimes tended to be intra-racial, specific to a certain age range, and similar to what other violent offenders with a paranoia-based mental illness had done. Ressler predicted that if he was not stopped the unsub would continue to enter homes and kill people.

Local detectives soon identified a suspect, Richard Trenton Chase, and closed in to arrest him as he was leaving his apartment. He surrendered, and they found enough evidence to detain him for trial.

Ressler and Vorpagel compared what they'd learned about Chase—a skinny, undernourished man, age twenty-seven—to their profile. They were correct that he'd been institutionalized several times, had been diagnosed with paranoid schizophrenia, and had a history of being preoccupied with signs that something was physically wrong with him. He lived alone, was unemployed, and received disability funds. He had also fatally shot a man before he murdered Teresa Wallin. In prison, Chase told the agents that he had needed blood from his victims because of "poison" that made his blood turn to sand. So, in fact, he *had* planned to kill, and to do so repeatedly. Despite his delusions, Chase was convicted of six counts of first-degree murder and sentenced to be executed. Instead, he died in his cell from a drug overdose.

The case of Richard Trenton Chase was among those that assisted with making a behavior-based distinction between types of offenders that the BSU referred to as "organized" and "disorganized."

THE PSYCHO-BEHAVIORAL CONTINUUM—

Profiling is part of criminal investigative analysis (CIA), which involves four distinct stages. When first entering a case, agents determine whether a crime has actually been committed. In stage 2, they determine what type of crime. During stage 3, they might profile the scene or scenes and offer ideas about the offender(s). If necessary, they advance to stage 4, in which they present evidence from their methods and findings in court. They can also provide investigative strategies and interviewing techniques.

To devise a detailed profile also involves several steps. First, the agents decide the type of crime with which they're dealing and think about what they already know. Then they thoroughly analyze the crime and crime scene (such as weapon used, time of day, number of scenes involved, and type of location). Next comes the victimology and formulating possible motives for what occurred. With all of this information, they'll describe the possible perpetrator in as much specific detail as possible: his or her habits, age, possible employment, marital status, military background, mental state, risk potential, and personality traits. While profiles are most often associated with serial murder, they have been offered as well for product tampering, kidnapping, and serial bombing, burglary, rape, and arson. They can even be done on single crime scenes.

Investigators must learn significant facts about the victims' lives and habits, especially in the days and hours leading up to the incident. A timeline is devised to map victims' movements, and investigators study all recent communications for information about where they may have crossed paths with a viable suspect. It's important to know the victims' state of mind and mental health history as well as their risk level at the time of the crime (for example, being out and about at night versus home behind locked doors).

Once the victim's details are known, the crime scene and offender's methodology are evaluated for how best to categorize him (or her). Based on the idea that personality more or less dictates behavior and that the clues their behavior leaves will reveal their personalities, investigators can assess whether the person planned and arranged a crime or committed an impulsive act of opportunity. (Note: Some researchers dispute that the relationship between behavior and personality traits is as consistent as this profiling method assumes.)

BSU members John Douglas and Roy Hazelwood wrote a significant article, "The Lust Murderer," in 1980, in which they enumerated the distinction between "organized" and "disorganized" homicides. Although other BSUers thought the distinction was too simplistic, Douglas and Hazelwood offered such a solid list of the characteristics that were recognizable to law enforcement officers that the labels proved practical for many applications. The division is still used today, although most investigators recognize that there are no pure types. In broad strokes, the differences between an organized and disorganized offender provides just a basic guideline.

Organized offenders tend to be educated, intelligent, aware of law enforcement, narcissistic, controlled, and prepared. They leave a clean crime scene and often hide a victim's body. They may take a trophy to relive the pleasure of their crime. They often feel no remorse, and they pay close attention to any media reports about their crimes. The most disorganized offenders tend to suffer from a mental illness—especially psychosis—or to be criminally inexperienced. They often use a weapon found at the scene, rather than bringing one with them, and tend to leave evidence behind. With murder, they use a blitz attack and often mutilate a body postmortem. They may feel badly about the crime later and don't pay much attention to media coverage or investigative methods.

Profilers will be interested in other aspects of behavior as well: if the offender used a vehicle, appears to be criminally sophisticated, or seems to be operating within a compulsive sexual fantasy. They consider whether a weapon was brought to the scene or taken away, the state of the scene(s), the type of wounds inflicted on a victim, the risks the offender took, his or her method of controlling the victim, and evidence that the incident may be staged to look like something else. In addition, there may be indications that the offender has one or more partners. On *CM*'s "Open Season," for example, it's clear from tracks that two offenders were hunting down people in the woods who were fleeing for their lives.

Profiles are easiest to work up when an offender displays obvious psychopathology, such as a paraphilia (more about this subject in Chapter 4), the desire to torture, or the need to mutilate. Such offenders generally make a distinct, individualizing impression, called a "signature." The agents refer to this as "personation," because it's a behavioral manifestation of a personality quirk or compulsion and it can take any form. An offender might position a body for humiliating exposure, bite a victim in a specific manner, cover the face, or tie ligatures with a specific type of knot. Personation helps link crime scenes and may flag other behaviors to look for. In "Masterpiece," the fact that all of the female victims were strikingly beautiful and the suspect was obsessed with perfection helped the agents see how he'd used mathematical concepts to select victims.

What a profile offers to local investigators is a set of characteristics that can help narrow the pool of suspects: the offender's likely age range, racial identity, modus operandi, living situation, education level, travel patterns, criminal or psychiatric record, and basic habits. A profile may also describe a fantasy scenario, such as the evidence of cannibalism in "Lucky," that drives the person's offending behavior or pinpoints an area where he or she probably works or resides.

The basics of profiling are spelled out in "Unfinished Business," based on the way the infamous BTK case unfolded in Wichita, Kansas. (A killer surfaced after eighteen years of lying dormant after a profiler published a book.) A profile can predict future possible attacks; offer a general and specific background of the perpetrator; and provide creative thinking on aspects of the crime from a combination of intuition, comparison, and experience. For example, the series of shootings in broad daylight in "LDSH" is similar to the actual profiling of a serial sniper in Phoenix, Arizona, in 2005.

There are offsite and onsite procedures for profiling. Both require data from the crime scene, such as physical evidence, location, accessibility, body position, patterns of evidence, and whether or not a weapon was left at the scene. There are also significant factors that must be established from the crime scene such as time of the crime, duration, weather conditions (if outside), if the body was moved, and the social environment. In one case on *CM* ("The Tribe"), Native American rituals were involved but performed incorrectly, so it was clear that the perpetrators had staged the crime to try to implicate residents on the nearby reservation. Certain critical factors in a crime scene help clarify how offenders think and thus how they make choices that direct their behavior. The type of wounds made and the evidence of sexual behavior—especially deviant—offer many clues. (Wind chimes fashioned from victims' rib bones, for example, shows an especially depraved, remorseless, and dangerous individual.)

Onsite analysis involves going to the crime scene. Offsite requires collecting detailed photographs and reports, including lab reports from processing evidence, such as toxicology and serology analysis, and autopsy details on the cause of death and the sequence of wounds. This also includes police reports, witness statements, and any other avenue of information gathered beyond the actual crime scene.

From scene elements, profilers can deduce aspects of the offender's behavior that could inspire crime: whether he has been snubbed or has a deformity, is recently unemployed or separated from a significant person, abuses drugs or alcohol, has access to firearms, is physically strong, or has served in the military. Each aspect of the crime is studied to determine how the offender viewed it. The murders of several elderly women in Mexico—a case on which "Machismo" was based—turned up a surprise female serial killer who hated her mother. At first, investigators believed that a male offender was committing these crimes, but viewing them from the perspective of an angry female with mother issues gave it a different cast.

The profiler is looking for evidence of whether the offender approaches victims by cunning and manipulation ("P911"), as the result of mere opportunity ("Plain Sight"), or with a blitz-type of attack. It is also important to know if the offender commits a crime via contact with the victim or from a distance, with a knife, blunt force, or a gun. After subduing a victim, the offender's method of controlling that person is instructive: He might bind her for torture, kill her immediately, knock her unconscious, or gag her but let her experience whatever he's doing.

Brussel had used psychological studies to derive his deductions, and the BSU agents did the same. However, when the unit first formed, there were no dedicated studies specific to serial murder. What they needed was a way to do statistical analyses and comparisons on this population, so they decided to start a specific database. This meant meeting the perpetrators face to face.

THE PRISON INTERVIEWS—

In "Riding the Lightning," the female partner of a serial killer submits to an interview while awaiting execution. Her reasons for participating, her pre- and post-crime behavior, and her experience of the crimes are all subject to study. In reality, women like this were part of a study of compliant accomplices undertaken by Hazelwood and Janet Warren. However, several years before that research, Ressler started the initial prison interviews with convicted offenders that would lay the foundation for both a comprehensive manual on crime and a computerized database.

"All we had to go on," Ressler writes in *Whoever Fights Monsters*, "was what everyone else had." He was aware of a few books, such as Dr. Marvin Ziporyn's account about mass murderer Richard Speck and James Melvin Reinhardt's *Sex Perversions and Sex Crimes*, a collection of cases similar to those of von Krafft-Ebing. Reinhardt was a professor of criminology at the University of Nebraska, and he'd spent a considerable amount of time interviewing and writing about spree killer Charles Starkweather. In 1957 and 1958, Starkweather and his fourteen-year-old girlfriend had driven across Nebraska, killing eleven people in the process. Reinhardt had just published his study of sexual perversion, and he was given privileged access to Starkweather. One chapter of his perversion book was devoted to the "remorseless ego," so he offered a theoretical framework for thinking about the type of offenders the agents would one day be tracking. He also described lust murders, fetishism, "sex fiends," and the "role of fantasy in crime." Ressler studied this text so that he could "better understand the mind of a violent criminal." He was aware that fantasy played a role in how killers behaved, but no one had yet made a systematic study.

The prison studies came about from an idea Ressler had while on the road teaching local jurisdictions about behavioral analysis. He decided that since he was going all over the country it would be productive to visit some of the nearby prisons, many of which held the country's most dangerous criminals. He reasoned that acquiring information from known offenders about motives and other aspects of their criminal activity would help educate the BSU agents and make them better at profiling unsubs. Rather than going through time-consuming formal routes and asking permission, he went right to the prisons and used his FBI credentials to gain access "for research."

His initial interviews failed to deliver much in the way of results. John Linley Frasier, who had slaughtered a family in Santa Cruz to punish their "misuse" of natural resources, was still more or less psychotic. Sirhan Sirhan, the convicted assassin of Robert F. Kennedy, was delusional. Herb Mullin, who'd "sacrificed" thirteen people on a murder spree, lacked insight, and Juan Corona, killer of twenty-five migrant workers, refused to talk. Ressler decided to seek out killers who had shown intelligence, planning, and cunning. There in California, he had an infamous mastermind of mass murder, Charles Manson, as well as a notorious serial killer with a genius IQ, Edmund Kemper III.

Edmund Kemper III murdered his grandparents at the age of 15 in 1964. His grandmother had made him angry, so he'd shot and stabbed her to "see what it felt like," and then eliminated his grandfather. He was placed into the California juvenile system, but released in 1969. Soon he was ready to kill again.

In 1972 and 1973, Kemper noticed young females out hitchhiking and envisioned things he could do to them. He picked them up, sometimes two at a time, and shot, stabbed, or strangled them. Then he shoved them into the trunk of his car. "I'm picking up young women," he stated in an interview, "and I'm going a little bit farther each time. It's a daring kind of thing. . . . We go to a vulnerable place, where there aren't people watching, where I could act out and I say, 'No, I can't.' . . . And this craving, this awful raging eating feeling inside, this fantastic passion. It was overwhelming me. It was like drugs."

At his apartment or his mother's house, Kemper brought the bodies inside to behead and dismember. He admitted to police later that he'd also had sex with the parts. After killing six young

THE FORENSIC PSYCHOLOGY OF CRIMINAL MINDS | 41

women, the six-foot-nine giant murdered his mother and her best friend before fleeing to Colorado. From there, he called the police in California to turn himself in. They found his mother's decapitated body in a closet, battered and used for dart practice. Her tongue and larynx were chopped up beside the garbage disposal. Her friend was there as well, also beheaded and stuffed into a closet. After the police brought Kemper back, he described his activities in meticulous detail.

On November 8, 1973, Kemper, 24, was found guilty of eight counts of first-degree murder. Although he'd hoped to receive the death penalty (with torture), he was convicted during a time when the U.S. Supreme Court had placed a moratorium on capital punishment, so all death sentences had been commuted to life.

To acquire consistent information across cases, Ressler devised a standard questionnaire and interview protocol, and John Douglas soon partnered with him. The initial plan was to interview one hundred incarcerated individuals from around the country.

Initially, Ressler and Douglas contacted different types of offenders, from mass murderers to assassins to serial killers. Data were also collected about 118 victims, including some who had survived an attempted murder, and eventually the team worked up an assessment routine that covered the most significant aspects of the offenses. The goal was to gather information about how the murders were planned and committed, what the killers did and thought about during and afterward, what kinds of fantasies they had, and what they did before the next incident (where relevant). The agents believed it was important to learn if the offenders had felt depressed, angry, remorseful, energized, or nothing at all during each stage of their crimes, and whether the criminal acts affected their routines in ways that people who knew them might notice.

Among the interviewees were Edmund Kemper; Jerry Brudos, a foot fetishist who had killed and mutilated several women in Oregon; Richard Speck, who'd strangled eight nurses in their shared residence in Chicago; Charles Manson, who'd led the 1969 Tate-LaBianca slaughters in Los Angeles; and John Wayne Gacy, who'd raped and killed thirty-three young men, burying most of the bodies in the crawl space beneath his home. Other offenders who were not killers were interviewed as well, but the database was primarily for organizing information about extreme crimes like serial murder. When pressed by his superiors about what he was doing, Ressler thought quickly and named his research project the Crime Personality Research Project.

One of Ressler's interests was William Heirens, the Lipstick Killer, whom he made a point of interviewing when he was in the Chicago area. Heirens was just seventeen when he began his crime spree. One of his behaviors—leaving a desperate message—has shown up in several episodes of *CM*.

During the summer of 1945, Heirens burglarized the apartment of Josephine Ross, and when she surprised him, he bludgeoned her and cut her throat. Then, oddly, he washed her body in the bathtub and taped her wounds with adhesive tape. Six months later, in December, Heirens broke into an apartment on Chicago's North Side. He shot and stabbed Frances Brown, 33, leaving a bread knife in her chest. Then he washed himself off in her bathtub, and before he exited, he used her lipstick to scrawl on a wall, "For heaven's sake catch me before I kill more. I cannot control myself." The police believed the two fatal break-ins were related.

A month after the Brown murder, a six-year-old girl disappeared from her bed and a ransom note was left in the room, but her head and body parts were found in bags in the sewer.

The police increased their vigilance, and in June 1946, an off-duty cop caught Heirens. Under truth serum and a spinal tap, Heirens was confronted with the similarity between his writing and that of the "Lipstick Killer," so he confessed. A psychiatric examination found that entering apartments sexually excited him, making him urinate or defecate. In his defense, Heirens blamed his criminal behavior on an alter ego. Pleading guilty, he received three life sentences.

The BSU agents kept refining their methods and often had to be creative to get the information they sought. They soon realized that self-report interviews with offenders did not necessarily yield the truth. Psychopaths, playing the victim card, often exaggerated or made up their personal stories, and they invariably blamed circumstances or other people for what they had done. They also liked to brag, whereas psychotic individuals did not necessarily make much sense. Nevertheless, these men were present when the crime was committed, so they were considered the best interview subjects.

To get as much information as possible, the agents did extensive research beforehand. Armed with facts, they believed this preparation would show the respect the killer might enjoy, but it also allowed them to spot whenever an interview response deviated into exaggeration or outright fabrication. Despite the brutality of many of the crimes, the agents realized how important it was to convey nonjudgmental interest, and the first interviewers passed along this insight to those who took up the task later.

Although the plan was to interview a hundred offenders, the agents compiled data from only thirty-six men. Of those, only twenty-five were serial murderers, and not all of them agreed to an interview. At times, the agents had to resort to data on file in prison records. From this initial group, a number of agents performed statistical analyses and published articles. They found that one-third of the offenders were white, nearly half had a parent missing from the home growing up (usually the father), three-fourths reported having had an indifferent or negligent parent, a majority had a psychiatric history, most had spotty employment records, their mean IQ was bright normal, three-fourths had sexual paraphilias, and the same portion reported an experience of physical or psychological abuse. While the sample was too small to draw significant conclusions, and was clearly not a scientifically gained random sample, the unit thought it was a good start for the database.

Over the years, more agents have conducted these interviews. However, because they depend on voluntary and articulate subjects, the studies are still not scientific. In other words, they cannot serve as the basis for generalizations about all serial killers or mass murderers. Their purpose was largely to provide information that could assist in the activity of profiling.

From compiling the data, the interviewers learned about offenders' values, homicidal fantasies, thinking processes, levels of post-crime recall, sense of responsibility for a crime, factors in changing the MO, substance abuse levels, and specific crime-scene rituals. Over the course of a decade, several agents used these data to write a comprehensive manual for law enforcement, which they called the *Crime Classification Manual*. With the intent of providing for the investigative world an equivalent of the *Diagnostic and Statistical Manual of Mental Disorders* (DSM) for psychiatrists, they focused on categorizing areas for three major felonies—murder, arson, and sexual assault—describing within each category the offender's typical motivation and behavior. The manual provides police officers and other law enforcement personnel as well as forensic mental health professionals access to the same information used by the FBI to coordinate its investigations. (In the second edition, they added more crime classifications, such as stalking and cyber crimes.)

WHAT IT TAKES—

A profile is as good as the information acquired and the person devising it. Like any other field, there are skilled profilers and unskilled ones. The early agents in the BSU, when looking for their successors, had to ponder what the unit needed (as do the agents on *CM* when they must replace BAU members).

A common phrase is "There's no *I* in team," and the BAU characters make this clear to SSA Rossi when he rejoins the team, post-retirement. In his day, the agents often worked alone on cases, and he must get used to the ensemble approach (although it's unlikely that the FBI would send out half a dozen top BAU agents to every case). Thus the first requirement for a good profiler is the ability to work with others: to respect their talents and learn to make his or hers count at the right time, in the right place.

The best profilers have gained their knowledge from experience in the field with crime scenes and criminals. They have developed a strong and accurate intuitive sense about certain types of crime, with a knowledge base developed from both physical and non-physical evidence. Generally, profilers employ psychological theories that provide ways to detect mental deficiencies, spot imprints from hostility, recognize criminal thought patterns, and predict the right character defects. Thus they need to study criminal psychology. They must also know about how data have been analyzed into trends and predictions, such as the age range into which offenders generally fall and how strongly related an unstable family history is to criminality.

Good profilers have an eye for patterns, an ability to synthesize disparate information, the capability to take charge, the skills for solid communication, and an awareness of personal and technical limitations. They will have support systems in place, be able to maintain role boundaries on a team, and be versed in the latest technology of crime detection. For collecting data, profilers must be good at listening, spotting deception and manipulation, and staying focused. They also need to possess good critical reasoning skills. Each profiler on the *CM* team has strengths in these areas, and one is a genius with a photographic memory who can absorb and retain large amounts of information. Others know when to rely on him as well as when to engage their own strengths (e.g., empathy, authority, physical strength).

Former BSUer Hazelwood offers his own list of preferred traits, starting at the top:

Common sense, practical intelligence. They also need to have an open mind—you have to be able to accept other people's suggestions. Number three is life experience. Number four is an ability to isolate your personal feelings about the crime, the criminal and the victim. Number five would be an ability to think like the offender thinks. All you have to do is reason like he does. You don't have to get into his mind.

In the early days, Hazelwood and Douglas used their respective abilities on a case that gained the unit its widest renown: a string of deaths of African American children in Atlanta, Georgia, that was making national news.

From 1979 to 1981, more than twenty-five black males (some as young as nine) had been strangled, bludgeoned, or asphyxiated in Atlanta. The only solid clue was the presence on several bodies of yellow-green fiber threads and some strands of dog hair. Douglas and Hazelwood arrived to assist after a number of the murders had been committed, and their first act was to walk around the neighborhoods where many victims had lived. They realized at once that the killer was not a white man committing hate crimes. Because no one in these neighborhoods had noticed someone who stood out as a stranger and who did not belong there, the chances were high that the children's abductor and killer was black. The agents also predicted from the pattern they spotted that the next victim would likely be dumped in the Chattahoochee River.

In response, local detectives set up a stakeout. On May 22, 1981, during the early morning hours, the stakeout patrol heard a loud splash. On the James Jackson Parkway Bridge, they saw a white Chevrolet station wagon. When they stopped it, they learned that the driver was Wayne Williams, a twenty-three-year-old black photographer and music promoter. He said he'd just dumped some garbage, so they let him go. When the body of Nathaniel Cater washed up—the twenty-eighth victim—investigators remembered Wayne Williams. The police got a search warrant for Williams's home and car, and turned up valuable evidence: The floors of the house were covered with yellow-green carpeting like the fibers found on Cater and other victims, and Williams also had a dog. Comparisons from the samples removed from the victims showed consistency with Williams' carpet, while three polygraph tests indicated deception on Williams's part.

The prosecution relied on two of the murders to make the case, along with assistance from John Douglas. Williams was convicted, receiving two life sentences.

"That was good for our program," Douglas said afterward. "We'd proven that a psychological profile can help convict a killer."

THE NATIONAL CENTER FOR THE ANALYSIS OF VIOLENT CRIME—

One other figure from the early days deserves mention because he was instrumental in one of the most important developments for the BSU. To bring him into the picture, we must return to the decade of the Mad Bomber but to the case of another offender, this one a serial killer.

Harvey Glatman was intelligent but homely and socially malad-justed. He had trouble getting dates. He also had trouble with petty crimes, getting himself arrested for robbery. Emerging from prison, he learned photography. When he met a woman in 1957 who told him she modeled, he said he needed a model for photographs for a detective magazine. Believing him, she agreed to be tied up and gagged. After Glatman kept up the pretense for a while and took a few photos, he put a gun to her head and raped her. Then he drove her into the desert east of Los Angeles and killed her. He buried her body in a shallow grave. His next victim came via a "lonely hearts" ad, and he killed her in the desert as well. Glatman took pictures of her and left her unburied. The third victim was also a model, and he spent the day photographing her, bound with rope, before he ended her life. But his fourth victim was his downfall. In the car on the way to the desert, she sensed something wrong and as they struggled over his gun, a patrol officer drove up, saving her and arresting Glatman.

A detective in Los Angeles named Pierce Brooks, commander of the Robbery-Homicide Division, was already investigating one of the murders. As he studied it, he believed the offender had killed before. Then he investigated an unrelated case that struck him the same way. Brooks initiated a search, spending off-hours in the evenings and on weekends in the library looking for similar incidents as a way to link these crimes to a repeat offender. He started in Los Angeles and then began to go through articles from other major cities. The task seemed hopeless, but finally he found a murder that was similar to one of his. He made a fingerprint match between the two cases and identified a solid suspect. But the process had been time-consuming and painstaking.

When Glatman was brought in for assault and attempted murder, Brooks interrogated him, getting a detailed and remorseful confession about the desert murders. He realized how easy it was to overlook how several murders were connected, so he asked his chief for a computer with which to collect and speedily analyze the details from different cases. The chief scoffed at the idea, because the cost of a computer at that time was exorbitant, not to mention that a mainframe took up a lot of space. The request was impossible to fulfill. Brooks (who became a consultant for the television show *Dragnet*) knew that investigators around the country needed a centralized database, and he never stopped pushing for it. However, he'd be retired before he saw his plea come to fruition.

In 1983, as the murder rate rose, especially fatal assaults committed by strangers, politicians took a hard line on crime, and in October, the FBI provided several disturbing estimates: some five thousand people had been victims of strangers the previous year, and most of those cases remained unsolved. There could be as many as thirty-five to fifty serial killers roaming around the country. Roger Depue was head of the BSU, and he called attention to the fact that there was as yet no reliable means for connecting the crimes of mobile serial killers. He was now listening to Pierce Brooks's idea about a national database for violent crime and he helped establish the Violent Criminal Apprehension Program (ViCAP) Task Force to study its viability. The BSU fully participated, as did investigators from nearly half of the states. It was time to get funds to make the idea a reality.

At a Senate subcommittee meeting for the U.S. Congress, Brooks and many others presented a case for a computerized system. John Walsh was among them, testifying about his murdered son, Adam. True crime writer Ann Rule also testified, and she pointed to a large group of serial killers who'd been sufficiently mobile to travel from state to state: Ted Bundy, Kenneth Bianchi of the "Hillside Stranglers," Gary Addison Taylor, and Harvey Louis Carnigan. She said that in Bundy's case, a system like ViCAP might have saved as many as fifteen lives. Brooks said that his own method of looking up linked crimes had remained the same for a quarter of a century, which he considered shameful in light of computerized technology. Roger Depue supported him, as did Senator Arlen Specter.

The program was approved and set up, to be run by the FBI out of Quantico. In 1985, under the auspices of the newly formed National Center for the Analysis of Violent Crime (NCAVC), Pierce Brooks was rightfully named ViCAP's first director. The BSU became part of this operation.

Using standard ViCAP analysis report forms, investigators collect data from police departments around the country on solved, unsolved, and attempted homicides; unidentified bodies in which the manner of death is suspected to be homicide; and missing-persons cases in which foul play appears to have been involved. In other words, thanks to the program, a homicide in Los Angeles may be linked to one in Florida or New York done by the same person; a murdered John Doe in Missouri can be identified as a runaway from Boston.

In May 1985, a gratified Brooks oversaw the processing of the first form by the new computer. Ressler was appointed as ViCAP's manager from the BSU, and now all the agents set about learning computer processing. While profiling itself was not a computer program, the use of ViCAP assisted in getting more reliable—and faster—results.

To devise a profile via ViCAP meant collecting pages of data for the report, organizing them along several dimensions, reconstructing the crime, devising an offender profile, and writing a report for the requesting jurisdiction. With new information, the profile could be adjusted and revised.

Yet behavioral analysis is not just about profiling. There's another area of forensic psychology that the agents on *CM* often use. Because CIA involves first determining that a crime has been committed and then what type of crime it is, a specific type of death investigation may be required. Let's return to the victimology.

THREE

−Psychological Autopsy and Victimology−

When you think about an unknown criminal long enough, when you've assembled all the known facts about him and poked at them and stirred them about in your mind, you begin to see the man.

−JAMES A. BRUSSEL

In 1984, eight women were successively murdered and dumped along highways outside Tampa, Florida. Most were nearly nude and bound with their arms behind their backs. Some had nooses draped two or three times around their necks and all were badly bruised, which raised the probability of a single offender. When investigators looked into the victims' backgrounds, they found that most had some association with a specific Tampa neighborhood, as dancers, drug addicts, or prostitutes. All had been in a position to accept rides from people they didn't know, raising their risk for being victims of violence, and whoever had picked them up had brutalized them before killing them. He'd raped and strangled each one.

For physical evidence, police had tire tread impressions, red carpet fibers that were consistent across victims, brown Caucasian hairs, and semen that indicated type AB blood. (This case occurred before DNA analysis was available.) Although this collection provided no leads, it would help if a suspect was caught.

The BSU received the case reports after the third or fourth murder, and the agents worked up a profile of the killer's probable background and personality traits. They first focused on certain factors about the victims, deciding that the killer was mobile and probably owned a vehicle—a flashy red one that would have red floor carpets. The leash-like ropes circled around the victims' necks and the brutal beatings that exceeded what was necessary to kill showed a sadistic sexual deviance and the need for control. It seemed likely that each victim had been randomly selected because they were all easy, available prey, out in the open at night. Given the known facts, the profilers believed that the unsub was a white male, in at least his mid-twenties, who was gregarious, extroverted, and manipulative. He seemed "organized," operating normally in society, yet was also self-centered, demanding, and impulsive but not to the point of risking capture. Even so, it was likely that he'd eventually make a mistake. He liked to brag and had a macho self-image. He might even have tattoos and carry a weapon to prove his manhood. At best, he had a high school education. He had issues with authority and may have been truant as a child. In keeping with his self-image, he'd take up masculine-type employment but would not have a regular job or career. If he'd ever served in the military, he would have joined a macho unit, such as the Marine Corps, but his authority issues would have caused confrontations.

He dated regularly but did not have long-term commitments. He bragged about his sexual exploits and probably dated subservient women. If he was married, he cheated easily and often. It was likely he had a prison record, or some encounter with law enforcement. Before these murders, he may have committed neighborhood crimes, such as voyeurism or burglary. He probably used some scheme to lure women into his car and then tortured them mentally and physically. He would leave little or no evidence behind, and he'd kill again until caught.

This prediction proved to be correct for a number of similar murders over the next few months, but then the unsub released a girl whom he'd impulsively abducted and repeatedly raped. She led the police to the door of Bobby Joe Long, a white, divorced male, thirty-one, who drove a maroon Dodge Magnum. He did have a criminal record and was currently on probation for an aggravated assault. During his interrogation, he admitted he had raped at least fifty women, using the ruse of a clean-cut man to get through their doors. He'd enjoyed seeing himself described in the newspapers as the Classified Ad Rapist. He also added another murder to the list that the police had not yet discovered.

Long was charged with nine counts of murder and sexual battery, nine counts of kidnapping, and one count of probation violation. Convicted, he received two death sentences and thirty-four life sentences, plus an additional 693 years. He is still appealing.

To devise the profile on Long, the agents had relied on the victimology: who each woman was; where she had likely met her killer; and how he had treated her before, during, and after the crimes. Most had been in high-risk occupations (dancer, prostitute) and had either depended on others for rides or were willing to get into a stranger's car. Long had an easy manner and knew how to be disarming. While the profile had not led to his arrest, and probably never would have, in retrospect its details were accurate, and it had given local investigators an idea of the type of offender they were looking for and where he'd probably turn up. The FBI's prediction of escalation had also motivated them to be vigilant.

Complete background on victims is vitally important to devising a profile. Risk factors must be identified as well as potential relationships with an offender. Where the victim was assaulted, abducted, and/or killed determines the degree of risk for both parties, as do the victim's age and occupation. Among low-risk victims are those who live fairly normal lives and are assaulted during daytime hours or in their homes ("What Fresh Hell?"). High-risk victims include prostitutes ("Sex, Birth, Death,"), exotic dancers, women who travel alone, substance abusers, and people who work nightshifts where few others are around. Medium risk is somewhere in between, such as when a normally low-risk person goes out alone one night to a club in a crime-ridden neighborhood. Whether the victim was killed at home, was involved in drugs, was having an affair, had a criminal history, was employed, had domestic problems, or was associated with certain social groups are all relevant factors to developing an understanding of how the crime could have occurred. If a victim is still alive, as in the Long case (and several episodes of *CM*), he or she can help with details.

Profilers lay out a timeline of the victim's known movements up until the point of the crime ("Scared to Death"), relying on victim diaries, eyewitness statements, phone or e-mail messages, recent purchases, and whatever the victim's acquaintances may know. A timeline may cover a single day or several weeks, depending on what's needed and what's actually known about the victim. It may be that she met a rapist or killer at a place where they were seen together, or that she purchased something where he worked. Perhaps he was a former boyfriend who was stalking her, or they'd once worked together. Any communications that establish the victim's frame of mind are significant, especially if there was any anxiety about another person ("Somebody's Watching.") Whether there was any degree of victim compliance is noted, because it implies a violent acquaintance. Another source is the victim's mental health history, criminal history, and any record of substance abuse.

It is important to try to determine why that particular person was targeted—whether it was from a spontaneous opportunity or involved some relationship or some fantasy that implied preselection. Then the profiler determines how the victim was approached. It is also important to note the time of day an offense took place, because that may indicate something about how the victim knew the offender—possibly via employment or mutual membership in a club. If there was transportation involved, it can mean the possibility of a broader geographic area involved than just the victim's neighborhood.

EQUIVOCAL DEATH INVESTIGATION—

Victimology plays a significant role in another type of death investigation as well: a psychological autopsy. In the episode "Higher Power," the agents examine a number of alleged suicides in a small geographical area near Pittsburgh, specifically recognizing that they will undertake the method of psychological autopsy on each victim. In real life, the BSU was involved in a highly visible psychological autopsy for the government, and the findings proved controversial.

Forty-seven sailors were killed aboard the battleship *USS Iowa* on April 19, 1989, and the navy invited the BSU to offer a profile. During a training in the Caribbean, an explosion had occurred in one of the gun turrets, sparking a series of deadly fires, and after a five-month investigation, the navy identified its chief suspect as Gunner's Mate Clayton Hartwig, who was among the dead. The Naval Criminal Investigative Service (NCIS) ruled out accidental causes, and investigators found that Hartwig allegedly had made a statement about dying in an explosion in the line of duty so he could be buried in Arlington National Cemetery. In part, the NCIS's conclusions derived from the psychological autopsy performed by experienced members of the BSU, who were hired to assist from an impartial perspective.

Special Agents Roy Hazelwood and Richard Ault were involved, describing their work as an "equivocal death analysis." They had relied on the navy's stash of letters, journals, reading material, song lyrics, and bank account balances associated with Hartwig as well as interviews the navy had conducted with Hartwig's friends, relatives, and fellow sailors. It seemed that Hartwig had an interest in explosives and that he'd possibly been depressed over a failed relationship with another sailor. He had taken out a life insurance policy, naming this man as a beneficiary (although this person claimed there had been no relationship). Unfortunately, the best eyewitnesses to the central incident had perished in the blast. In addition, the agents were limited to materials the NCIS handed over. From the start, it was clear that the agents were there to consider only the NCIS's hypothesis about an intentional act and then to decide on a finding of suicide, homicide, or a combination of the two.

The ship itself had had its problems, having been through two wars, and some conditions on it were dangerous, but the agents did find that Hartwig had exhibited a certain amount of emotional instability. Hazelwood and Ault concluded that there was good evidence that Hartwig—whom they considered an angry, suicidal loner who had been concealing a history of lies—had acted intentionally, killing himself and the other men in a suicide/homicide. He had motive, knowledge, and opportunity to commit the act.

Hartwig's family was horrified by this conclusion and they mounted a campaign to clear his name. The man who had supposedly rejected Hartwig brought a civil suit as well. Congress took up the challenge, organizing a subcommittee for the Armed Services to look into the case. Twelve psychologists from the American Psychological Association and two psychiatrists were asked to review the FBI profile. The panel included experts in suicidology, forensic psychology, personality assessment, psychopathology, and risk assessment. They examined the validity of the report's conclusion, how exhaustive the investigation had been, viable alternative conclusions, and the limitations of a postmortem analysis of personality and motives.

Ten of the professionals stated that the method of a psychological autopsy had no basis in science. Thus, they could not support the degree of confidence with which the agents had filed their report, although four of them accepted the navy's conclusions about Hartwig's suicidal state of mind as appropriate. Even so, it did not support an intentional act of homicide. In addition, they noted that a serious flaw arose from how the BSU agents had used only what the navy had collected, rather than conducting independent interviews—a direct contradiction to their supposed independent function in the investigation.

Ault and Hazelwood testified before the Armed Services Subcommittee hearing at the end of 1989, at which time the work of the NCAVC was described and defended. Ault indicated that an equivocal death analysis uses all possible resources and generates a number of hypotheses before deciding on the one that best encompasses the evidence. Hazelwood testified about how they'd applied these principles to the USS Iowa case. They were challenged on their degree of confidence at offering their findings, and Ault took issue with the academic analysis, because the psychologists who'd offered their opinions did not work in the field and therefore could not draw solid conclusions about investigations. "We don't keep research records with great internal validity," he said, "because we're not oriented that way." Nevertheless, he assured the committee members that he and Hazelwood had often been correct in their evaluations.

Given the diversity of opinion among the experts, the House Armed Services Subcommittee faced an overwhelming task. Aside from the BSU agents, nearly every expert had been tentative—the typical manner of a social scientist who relies on probability assessments. Nevertheless, it did become clear that, as these professionals had stated, there was no scientific validity backing up a psychological autopsy. Thus, the subcommittee decided, until such time as this procedure had better confirmation, its use in a forensic setting was deemed inappropriate. In the end, the members found that the evidence was insufficient to draw a definitive conclusion about the cause of the explosion. Thus, more than two years after the blast, the navy issued a public apology to Hartwig's family.

It is true that little research has been done to confirm psychological autopsy as a reliable scientific method. Also called "psychiatric autopsy," "retrospective death assessment," "reconstructive evaluation," and "equivocal death analysis," the term refers to a specific method used for examining a person's life—that is, the life of a dead person. It is designed to assess the behavior, thoughts, feelings, stress factors, and relationships of a deceased individual whose manner of death is questionable or complex.

In death certifications, there are three important matters: the cause, the mechanism, and the manner of death. The cause is an instrument or physical agent used to bring about death (a bullet or blow to the head), the mechanism is the pathological agent in the body that resulted in the death (excessive bleeding), and the manner of death is determined by means of the NASH classification: natural, accidental, homicide, or suicide. In an estimated 5 to 15 percent of cases, while the cause and mechanism of death can be determined, the manner cannot. Thus, it becomes an "undetermined" death or, if still under investigation, "undetermined, pending." (Some jurisdictions add "suicide by cop" as a special category, because such incidents have increased in recent years.)

A medical autopsy determines the cause of death by examining the physical condition of the body. In cases in which the manner of death is unexplained, a psychological autopsy may assist the coroner or medical examiner in clearing up the mystery. The idea of a psychological autopsy is to discover the state of mind of the victim preceding death because the results may be needed to settle criminal cases, estate issues, malpractice suits, or insurance claims. When the circumstances surrounding a death can be interpreted in more ways than one, psychological investigators or consultants can use their behavioral expertise to compile information retrospectively about mental state and possible motive.

Most equivocal deaths are either accidents or suicides, and the potential for homicide is less frequent. Thus experts in suicide have provided some of the most common red flags for a determination of suicide—for example, a past history of suicide or a sudden change in a person's religious habits. It helps to know some statistics about certain populations. Among teenagers, for example, accidents are the leading cause of death, with homicide second and suicide third. Yet it has also been noted that to save families grief, suicide in teenagers has been underreported.

The practice of psychological autopsy began with the systematic examination of ninety-three deaths among New York City police officers during a six-year period that were determined to be suicides. This occurred during the 1930s. However, it was in Los Angeles that the phrase *psychological autopsy* was coined. In 1958, the L.A. County Chief Medical Examiner, Theodore Curphey, was overwhelmed by cases of drug-related deaths. It wasn't always clear whether they were suicides or accidental overdoses, so he enlisted Edwin S. Shneidman and Norman Faberow, co-directors of the Los Angeles Suicide Prevention Center, to assist. Shneidman called this work *psychological autopsy* in a 1961 article, in which he listed sixteen formal categories for the process. Among them were to look at the history of substance abuse, look for suicide notes, review the deceased's recent writings, assess his or her close relationships, identify mood fluctuations, and make note of vague references interpretable as suicidal depression. Yet even today there are no standard procedures, although psychologists have developed a guide that lists twenty-six separate areas for focus. Nevertheless, the process of interpretation is largely subjective.

In a 1986 study, nearly half of the country's medical examiners (195 out of 400) participated in a standardized comparative analysis of both typical and equivocal death scenarios. Half of them received information from a psychological autopsy in addition to standard information about the death scene. In typical cases, this additional information failed to influence decisions, but in the equivocal cases it had a significant impact on the determination of the manner of death. This result underscores the importance of gathering psychological information that could shed light on the circumstances surrounding an ambiguous death. (If more such experiments were performed, a strong body of research could provide the scientific underpinning that's still lacking for this method.)

However, there are also autoerotic asphyxiation (AEA) incidents to consider during equivocal death investigation, because they are dangerous enough to accidentally cause death. These incidents, designed to cut off oxygen or apply unusual pressure for sexual gratification, often appear to be suicides and many have been mistakenly labeled. Hazelwood made a study of 132 such incidents for the BSU and became an expert in identifying when a death that appeared to be suicide was, in fact, an accident. The majority were male, mostly adolescents or lonely adults. Hanging was the method most frequently used, although some flirted with electrocution. One young man had somehow found sexual gratification by fitting himself into a garbage can, and he died when his plan for escape failed to work. Another submerged himself underwater in a specially designed suit that did not work as he'd expected.

One of the most important aspects of a psychological autopsy is to identify a homicide when an incident initially appears to be a different manner of death. One incident in Cannon Beach, Oregon, was variously determined to be a suicide, an accident, and a homicide.

On November 12, 1995, David Wahl, twenty-seven, and Linda Stangel, twenty-three, went drinking and then for a drive. They ended up in Ecola State Park, a rugged area with trails going up to high cliffs. David disappeared and Linda reported that he'd gone for a walk on the beach but never came back. She'd finally just left the area to wait for his call. However, their relationship had been in trouble, so this disappearance was suspicious to David's family. The police, volunteers, and relatives searched the park, but found no sign of David. Finally they had to give up. A month later sixty miles north, a headless male corpse washed ashore. A fingerprint and partial jawbone were matched to David Wahl, so his death was declared a suicide, with the assumption that, despondent over his crumbling relationship, he'd jumped into the ocean, either from the cliff or from the beach.

The Wahls insisted that David would not have killed himself and they demanded a full investigation. Detectives brought Linda in for further questioning, although she'd already passed a polygraph. This time, however, they took her out to the park and up the precarious trail to the edge of the cliff to get her to help them reconstruct the incident. They thought they might be able to spot if she'd been deceptive, and once on the cliff, she offered an entirely different scenario.

David had actually returned to the car that morning, she admitted, and they'd gone up the trail together to see the cliff. He'd "fake-pushed" her to playfully scare her and she'd pushed him back, inadvertently causing him to lose his balance in a precarious place. To her horror, he'd fallen to his death on the rocks below. Fearing that she'd be blamed, she kept the incident to herself. Back at the police station, Linda repeated this new version of the story on tape, and told it later to the DA. So, she offered it three times without coercion. Each time she was read her right to remain silent.

Now David Wahl's death was being considered accidental. However, the DA had different plans, in light of Linda's earlier lies. He charged her with first-degree manslaughter. But at her trial, Linda changed her recollection once again. With backup from an expert in coerced confessions, she now stated that she'd fabricated the story about pushing David because she was afraid of heights and she'd wanted to get off the cliff. She continued to repeat it once she was off the cliff because she'd thought she had to stick to the story. The jury did not accept her new explanation, especially after seeing evidence that she was not afraid of heights. Linda was convicted of second-degree manslaughter.

Such stories demonstrate how ambiguous evidence can be. A close examination of a death scene that's a suspected suicide may help establish the degree of intent and lethality, which could be the difference between a suicide and an accident. Secluded places, with messages left to deflect people from looking for the person, would be a suicide flag. (An example is the deceased alcoholic found in a hotel room near his home, surrounded by empty bottles of alcohol, who'd told family and friends he was going on a vacation.) It may also be true that people who knew the deceased have motives for concealing what may have happened, so the investigator must watch for potential deception. At times, the results will be clear, while at other times, the deceased's state of mind before death cannot be known with certainty. In such cases it's often the psychological factors that assist with making the final assessment. (Even so, there are times when a body is exhumed for reexamination because new evidence shows that the manner of death was in error.)

The methods of psychological autopsy are similar to writing a biography, because the information gathered is generally both personal and extensive. Some mental health professionals estimate that a comprehensive psychological autopsy could take around twenty hours to complete, as long as sources are available and people are talking. The amount of time it requires depends on the goal, the funds available, and on its ultimate purpose. A few have been done out of sheer curiosity.

In 1973, Edwin Shneidman undertook the psychological autopsy of a historical figure: the eighteen-year-old son of Herman Melville, author of Moby Dick. Malcolm Melville had died in 1867 from a pistol wound to the head. At the time, his death was thought to be, alternatively, a homicide, suicide, and accident. Since the manner of death was never definitively settled (specifically between accident and suicide), Shneidman decided to apply modern methods to try to decide what had occurred. He offered the account as an "open case" to his colleagues at the Los Angeles Suicide Prevention Center, to get their input. Part of the procedure was to examine Malcolm's family life, and toward that end Shneidman decided that Herman Melville had been "suicidogenic," i.e., he was prone himself to suicidal depressions that could have affected his son; he also wrote about suicide as a repeated motif. Herman Melville was self-centered and monomaniacal about his writing, neglecting his four children and even rejecting them outright—especially his firstborn, Malcolm. This boy may have come to feel as if he should never have been born and would be better off dead; his options for peace of mind were parricide or suicide. Melville himself had been a battered child and thus psychologically battered his own children with indifference and outright hostility. Most of the 18 members on Schneidman's staff believed that Malcolm's death was suicide or probable suicide. Since the young man had known how to handle a weapon, they ruled out the next best option, an accident.

To put together a sense of a deceased person's final days and hours, a psychologist might use any number of sources, with the awareness that anyone he or she interviews could contaminate as easily as facilitate the process. Among the most productive sources are interviews with eyewitnesses and the first responders; autopsy reports; an examination of the death scene (or photographs); journals, e-mails, correspondence, social networking pages, and suicide notes associated with the victim; the victim's preferences in books, music, television shows, or video games; recent changes in behavior patterns noted by others, especially that signal depression; school, military, employment, medical, or psychiatric records; acquaintance reports; comparisons against archival data, such as suicide studies; reports about conflicted relationships or other stressors; and death history or mental illness in family—especially a history of suicide. It's also helpful to know how the individual coped with stress.

The goal is to compose a report that will include basic biographical information and the details about the death incident. The psychologist may attempt an incident reconstruction or simply address living circumstances and possible motives. Any signs of preparing to terminate life will be highlighted, as will the presence or absence of support systems and the relationship histories. The final result should be a fairly accurate sense of the victim's personality, habits, and behavior patterns, specifically including any recent changes. Often the likely manner of death will emerge from these facts.

Aside from determining the manner of death, psychological autopsies may serve other purposes as well. If suicide is established as the manner of death, the analysis can clarify its triggers. In the event of homicide, psychological investigators can contribute what they deduce for a crime reconstruction. They can also offer grief counseling for survivors, which will differ depending on whether the deceased was a homicide victim or a suicide. Investigators may gain data about behavior that can also assist with future such investigations. In addition, psychological autopsies, such as a famous one performed postmortem on Howard Hughes, might clarify a person's state of mind just before death when financial decisions are questioned.

Testimony from a psychological autopsy is not yet accepted in court as direct evidence, but it has helped in legal appeals. The lack of standards has been noted, and a U. S. Supreme Court decision in 1993 to screen out poor methods and "junk science" imposes an additional hurdle in federal courts and those state courts that use the standards. However, because psychological autopsy relies on clinical information and clinicians often testify in court on state of mind, the future for this type of testimony in a forensic context is unclear. Better studies might make it a more viable method.

Another use of psychological autopsy is to examine an event after the fact to determine the red flags that led up to it. The manner of death might be clear, but the reasons still unknown. For example, a psychiatric autopsy was performed in the aftermath of a mass murder at a high school. The two shooters had committed a suicide/homicide, and the psychological postmortem was done to try to determine the motives and the risk factors for similar such incidents.

Dylan Klebold, seventeen, and Eric Harris, eighteen, were obsessed with violent video games, a fascistic subculture, and paramilitary techniques. They had collected an arsenal of semi-automatic guns and homemade bombs to commit a crime they hoped the world would never forget. If everything went according to plan, they would cause a lot of death and damage at Columbine High School in Littleton, Colorado. Members of the "Trench Coat Mafia," dubbed for their habit of wearing black trench coats, the two boys had long been bullied by classmates. One day in April 1999, they sent an e-mail to the local police declaring that they were going to do something at the school. They blamed parents and teachers in their community for turning their children into intolerant sheep and then announced their own suicide. Then, at 11:30 A.M. on April 20, the boys hid weapons and bombs under their long trench coats and ran amuck through the school, yelling at teachers and students, and shooting at random. When they reached the library, they cornered and killed most of their victims before turning their weapons on themselves. Once the police entered the building, they counted thirty-four casualties, with fifteen dead, including the shooters.

Then Harris's diary turned up, confirming the deadly plan. For over a year the boys had been drawing maps, collecting weapons, and devising a system of hand signals for coordinating their moves. Behind closed doors, they'd spoken of their lone-wolf vision. Yet the fact was that they were just angry, bitter kids with access to guns, who were inspired by images of grandiose violence to harm people they blamed.

In September 2001, five members of the Threat Assessment Group (TAG), headed by forensic psychiatrist Dr. Park Dietz, performed the psychiatric autopsy. They interviewed the shooters' friends and teachers and read through relevant documents to try to learn why Harris and Klebold had acted in this manner. The team was made up of experts in risk management and violence prevention who had worked with many companies on workplace violence.

TAG examined the diaries and the "to do" list for the day of Ground Zero. At the end of this list, after the items for setting off the bombs, one of the shooters had written, "Have fun." TAG also went to the scene, examined the type of weapons used, and watched films that had obsessed the young men. The team looked over the mental health records for both boys, noting that they'd been in trouble before in a minor way and had been ordered to go through an anger management program. Harris was taking Luvox, an antidepressant, and changes in Klebold's outlook over the two years before the incident indicated depression as well. They were both quite cynical, with an apparent high level of anger. While TAG did hear about a recurring dream that Harris had told a class about shooting teachers and students, and about Harris's breakup with a girl, the team was denied access to the tapes that the boys made.

Due to pending lawsuits, many key people did not respond to TAG's requests for interviews—notably members of the Harris and Klebold families. This would prove to be a serious gap in their analysis. Yet there were over fifty people who did agree to talk about that day or about the mass murderers, which helped to fill in the psychological details.

In many ways, Klebold and Harris appeared to be typical kids growing up, without any outstanding problems. Their families, from the appearance of the homes and from reports of friends, seemed to be normal. The town was upper middle class. Without all the facts, TAG could only hypothesize that the boys' anger had grown from resentment, and their depression from sadness or disappointment, reinforced with immersion in violent imagery. That had helped to raise the emotional tone to rage and thoughts of suicide. They'd even made a video, "Hitmen for Hire," starring themselves, which appeared to be a rehearsal for their final plan. TAG considered the fact of bullying to be insufficient to explain the level of violence displayed. Rather, the way the two angry young men had reinforced each other appeared to be a more striking factor. Each time they had worked on their plans, laughing over who might die and envisioning their "fame," they had taken ever more certain steps toward enacting the violence. A date, a purpose, access to the weapons, and a sense that they had no other future ensured that they'd play out the scenario the way they'd rehearsed it.

Understanding the motives leading to extreme acts of murder—mass or serial—has been the primary purpose of the BSU/BAU. With that in mind, it's time to fill in the details with the types of deviance and perversion that fuel violent fantasies.

FOUR

–Varieties of Deviance–

What I needed to have was a particular experience with a person, and to possess them in the way I wanted to I had to evict them from their human bodies.

–EDMUND KEMPER III, SERIAL KILLER

Author Robert Block immortalized one of the most deviant killers ever to inspire fiction, the psychotic Wisconsin killer Ed Gein (mentioned on "Cold Comfort"). His bizarre activities helped form characters in such books and films as *Psycho*, *The Texas Chainsaw Massacre*, and *The Silence of the Lambs*. The very existence of such a person sent shock waves through the nation, with barely anyone able to comprehend how an ordinary man could have developed into such a monster, and because he'd been studied in-depth Gein was among the killers known to the behavioral analysts who developed the profiling program.

When the police went to Gein's farm in Plainfield on the cold evening of November 16, 1957, they were searching for evidence that he might have robbed a store. He didn't answer the door, so they looked around. Inside a dark summer kitchen, the search party found a dressed carcass hanging from a hook in the rafters, but then they noticed that it did not seem to be a deer carcass. On closer inspection, they realized that it was the headless, nude corpse of a woman, upside down, with the belly slit open from the genitals to the neck. The victim was Bernice Worden, a local storekeeper who'd gone missing that day. On a pot-bellied stove nearby was a pan that held a human heart. The stunned searchers called for backup and prepared to enter Gein's house.

Amid a disgusting and smelly array of clutter, their flashlights picked out several unbelievably grotesque items: chair seats woven from strips of human skin, a box of preserved female genitalia, a box of human noses, skin bracelets, the sawed-off crania from skulls, ten female heads with the upper part missing, refrigerated intestines, nine death masks made from skin (mounted on walls), a skin vest with breasts, a pair of skin leggings (from legs), a drum made with skin, a bowl made from part of a skull, a female scalp with black hair, and a pair of lips on a string. The officers couldn't imagine where Gein had found all his victims, but they estimated that the remains of some ten to fifteen women were present. It was stunning.

Located and arrested, Gein admitted to digging up the graves of freshly dead bodies to steal the parts. He also said he'd killed Bernice Worden and Mary Hogan, a woman who'd been missing for three years.

The startling case drew international attention, and those who studied criminal psychology made much of the fact that Gein had been raised by a Puritanical, domineering mother, with whom he'd shared a home after his father and brother died. She had taught her sons that sex was wicked, and psychiatrists who later studied Gein believed he'd come to despise himself and the female suit of skin was his attempt to change into a woman. Since his mother was dead, no one had been around to notice how weird he was getting (not that she would have, anyway). In his privacy, he'd devoured books on human anatomy and Nazi experiments, even purchasing mail-order shrunken heads.

One day, Gein had spotted a newspaper report about a woman recently buried, so he decided to dig her up to see a female body up close. For a decade, Gein continued with this sinister habit, with the help of an equally odd friend. Sometimes he took the entire corpse for dissection and sometimes just certain parts. He later claimed that he'd dug up nine separate graves in three different cemeteries. When his ghoulish associate was taken to an asylum, Gein could no longer dig graves alone. But there was another way to acquire fresh bodies: murder.

Storing the organs in his refrigerator, Gein made things out of the bones and skin, including a female body suit and mask to wear as he danced in the moonlight or dug up more graves. It was difficult for investigators to listen to Gein's accounts, because he failed to comprehend the moral enormity of what he'd done. Found insane, Gein was incarcerated for life in an institution, where he eventually died. But other killers have been equally perverse, and often with their wits intact.

Crime scenes reveal quite a lot about personality types and preferences in terms of showing an orderly, overcontrolled, socially competent, or intelligent personality vs. a disorderly or socially immature personality—or elements of both. The type of crime depends on such factors as how a victim was handled, how a victim was selected, whether there were postmortem acts, and how the crime occurred. Using such categories can pinpoint where a suspect might live and what his vehicle or living quarters might be like as well as the type of employment in which he might be engaged.

Then there's the signature: an offender's method of perpetrating a crime shows his degree of planning, but what's left behind as a personal stamp reveals his needs and compulsions. A serial killer in India always left beer cans next to victims, while in Greece, another killer stabbed each of four elderly prostitutes exactly four times in the neck. Signatures are often compulsive, but some are done for effect. Many offenders have posed a corpse in a provocative sexual position, carved something on a body, or taken a souvenir to aid in reliving the thrill of murder. One killer on "Cold Comfort" embalms his victims to spend more time with them, similar to what an actual female serial killer had once done.

During the early twentieth century, the husband of Hungarian Vera Renczi disappeared, leaving her alone with their son, Lorenzo. She told people she'd heard that her husband had been killed in an accident, and then she married again. However, this husband was a philanderer, and suddenly he was gone, too. Several years went by, with Renzi openly carrying on with numerous men, single and married, and then one inexplicably vanished. His wife took up the search. Sending the police to Renczi's estate, the woman insisted her husband had gone there. They searched the rooms and then entered the cellar, where they were stunned to discover thirty-two zinc-lined coffins, each containing a decomposing adult male. Under arrest, Vera offered a confession. The victims, killed with arsenic, were former lovers whom she'd feared would leave her; she added that she'd also poisoned both of her cheating husbands and even her grown son. Lorenzo, she explained, had threatened to expose her. When asked why she kept a chair among the coffins, the so-called Vampire of Berkerekul reportedly admitted that she'd enjoyed sitting among her men to gloat. Renzi died in prison.

The modus operandi, or the way a perpetrator decides to commit a crime, may change as the offender learns and perfects his crimes or as different circumstances dictate. However, the core motivating structure of a signature tends to remain fairly static, because it arises from personality factors rather than from what's needed to kill. Signature crimes have not had many systematic studies, and the myth has arisen that the "ritual" at the basis of personation always presents in the same way, but in fact, as many as 50 percent of offenders will experiment with their rituals. Thus, there might be differences in the behavior from one crime scene to another. What drives the ritual might be a primal compulsion, but different victims and different situations present new opportunities for the offender to tinker and play. Among the most influential factors in the development of a signature is an offender's fantasy life, which can shift and change with experience and circumstances.

MOTIVATING FACTORS—

Fantasy appears to be central to the motivation of many crimes, particularly sadistic sexual murders ("Lucky"). Examining the crime scene and victimology can help discern the type of fantasy that inspired the crime and whether there is likely to be a repeat offense or escalation. In "True Night," for example, a cartoonist suffering a severe form of post-traumatic stress disorder (PTSD) after being victimized incorporates his own characters into his escalating vigilantism. Violent fantasies often involve associating pleasure with torture or death and the way the crime plays out indicates the fantasy's deviant pattern. Once successfully acted out, it becomes a strong motivator to repeat it, often with embellishments. Some victims are selected by virtue of having traits that fit the offender's fantasy scenario ("P911"), while others might be merely victims of opportunity ("Last Word").

Al Carlisle, a psychologist who worked with inmates at Utah State Prison, describes serial killers as having a "compartmentalized" self. They offer a socially correct facade, but they can simultaneously and covertly nurture a darker side through their fantasies. Because they harbor painful memories, disappointment, or frustration, they've exploited their imagination to create a more comfortable internal world for themselves. Yet such fantasies can turn violent and demand release. The expression of unacceptable impulses, desires, and aspirations gradually gains equal footing with the "prosocial" persona and, through rehearsal, can gain substance. It's but a short step toward acting them out.

As the killers get away with murder, they learn how to deflect others from discovering their secrets, and they devise different sets of values for different life frames. Their secret lives grow more perverse because the killers' self-interested values justify them. Carlisle proposes that the ability to repeatedly kill while functioning as a "normal" person occurs via three primary processes: fantasy, dissociation, and compartmentalization. Through imagined scenarios that create an alternate identity, killers can distance themselves from uncomfortable feelings and create a persona that lacks accountability and feels more powerful. As infamous serial killer Ted Bundy once described it, this private arena is entirely separate and controlled. He was not alone with this notion. Many killers with a dark inner life and murderous habits manage to pass as ordinary individuals.

Jeffrey Dahmer burst into international prominence in the summer of 1991. He murdered seventeen men in Milwaukee, Wisconsin, without detection before one escaped and brought back the police. Around the apartment they found skulls, bones, rotting body parts, bloodstained soup kettles, complete skeletons, and three human torsos. Dahmer was killing men and preserving their parts, or cutting off pieces and dissolving them in acid. In all, investigators counted the remains of eleven different men. When Dahmer confessed, he added six more who'd been killed and dismembered in other places.

Dahmer was only eighteen when he first killed someone. His parents had abandoned the family home, going their separate ways, so Dahmer lived alone for a few weeks. When he spotted an attractive hitchhiker, he lured the man home with the promise of getting high. They had a good time together, but when his guest decided to leave, Dahmer smashed a barbell against the back of the man's head and strangled him. He was aroused by the idea that he had a captive and when he cut the body into pieces for disposal, he was excited all over again.

Dahmer soon moved in with his grandmother, where he killed more young men, and continued this activity after he moved into his own apartment. What he wanted was a zombie, a sex slave to do his bidding, so he tried drilling holes into the heads of his unconscious victims to inject acid or boiling water into their brains. Even more macabre, he designed an altar made of skulls, which he planned to build when he'd killed a sufficient number of men.

At Dahmer's trial, psychiatrist Park Dietz testified that Dahmer had been conditioned toward sexual excitement over corpses from early sexual fantasies that centered on the mutilation of animals. What might have started as a boy's curiosity about roadkill became a young man's obsession with bodies and offal. For him, killing became a form of bonding, a comforting behavior for a lonely prepubescent boy. Even those closest to him failed to notice just how deviant he was.

On *CM*, "Blood Hungry" depicts a killer with a similar cannibalistic compulsion, and some offenders like Dahmer actually view consuming the flesh as an act of love toward the victim. Some aberrations are even worse.

As much as we've learned from killers about their motivating fantasies, thanks to how widely the human imagination can range there is no profile of a serial killer, no single factor that sets them apart, no blueprint by which to construct a one-size-fits-all theory.

This fact makes the method of profiling both complicated and difficult as well as prone to errors. It's important for profilers to have a working knowledge of abnormal psychology, and it was on this foundation that Howard Teten developed the BSU. Those who familiarize themselves with personality theory and the various ways in which offenders actually operate are better prepared to interpret crime scene behavior and to assess the behavior of potential suspects for the right fit to the crime. The more knowledge and experience, the better. In the following case, a profiler contradicted a mental health professional, and the profiler turned out to have the most informed perspective.

On February 11, 1987, in Fort Collins, Colorado, the police discovered a body in a frozen field at the end of a trail of blood. The victim was thirty-seven-year-old Peggy Hettrick, who was last seen six hours earlier leaving a bar. She'd been stabbed once in the back and her vaginal area had been surgically mutilated with two different knives.

Clyde Masters and his fifteen-year-old son, Tim, lived nearby in a trailer. When questioned, Tim admitted he'd seen a body that morning, but the fact that he hadn't reported it made police suspicious, so they searched his room. They located several knives, although none could be linked to the murder. But there was something else: fifteen notebooks full of Tim's writings and sketches depicting decapitation, death, and dismemberment. Hidden in a closet was a homemade female mannequin, used for sexual purposes. Tim was brought to the police station for questioning and he failed a polygraph. The facts were disturbing but not probative, so no case could be made. Because no other suspects were identified, the murder went unsolved.

Nine years later, a detective looked through the file with a psychiatrist, an expert in the pathology of sexual homicide. He reviewed over two thousand sheets of paper containing narratives or drawings depicting sexual violence, although he never interviewed Tim Masters. The expert said that he'd never seen such a voluminous production by a suspect. In fact, he began referring to Tim as a perpetrator and thought the psychological evidence was solid.

However, BSU Special Agent Roy Hazelwood looked at the drawings, too, and said the doodles did not resemble the crime scene. He insisted that fantasy was not the same as motive and thought that trying to link Tim through these drawings to the crime was "overreaching."

The prosecutor decided to go with the psychiatrist's interpretation, and in 1999, Masters was brought to trial. For the jury, the psychiatrist focused on two specific sketches. The first depicted a figure being dragged across the ground—just as the victim had been—and Masters had admitted to drawing it the day after Hettrick was killed. The second drawing, dated the month before the murder, was of a woman who had been sexually mutilated—also like the victim. The expert called it a "rehearsal fantasy" of what Masters wanted to do. He explained that many rapists and killers mentally act out a fantasy, which then guides their subsequent actions. The prosecutor placed a photograph of Peggy Hettrick's mutilated vaginal area next to Masters's drawing. On March 26, 1999, Masters was found guilty of first-degree murder.

However, in 2008, new evidence emerged, including the fact that a sex offender had lived close to the murder scene who'd had a fetish for the very things that had been done to Hettrick. Yet no one had investigated him. There had also been footprints around the body from a type of shoe that Masters had not owned, and it had been clear to investigators that moving the body to this spot would have required the efforts of two people. A DNA analysis excluded Masters and indicated that an ex-boyfriend of the victim's had pulled down her underwear. So Masters went free and many people questioned how testimony from a psychiatrist who'd never even questioned the suspect could have been so influential. As Hazelwood had noted at the time, psychological evidence is ambiguous and highly interpretable and should, therefore, be used with caution. Fantasy, while often an ingredient in criminal acts, is not the same as motive and doesn't always compel action.

CM refers to many different types of killing motives, so we'll now examine a range of deviance and depravity. Quite a few serial killers were influenced by the way a 1963 novel depicted total control over another person.

COLLECTORS–

The Collector, by John Fowles, features Frederick, a lonely entomologist who stalks and abducts a beautiful woman named Miranda. This story was offered as a clue in "The Fisher King," and Reid puzzled it out in time to save a real-life captive. The gruesome tale features a locked dungeon on Frederick's large, secluded property, where he knew he could hold Miranda indefinitely until he was able to make her love him. He treats her like one of his butterfly specimens—a thing he can do with as he likes.

Miranda initially resists, begging him to free her and then threatening him. Finally, she tries starving herself, but nothing works. At this point, the story gets more interesting for people who view Frederick as a role model, because Miranda grows used to her monotonous captivity and even begins to look forward to seeing Frederick. Yet, eventually, she becomes ill and dies. Frederick quickly dismisses this unfortunate "accident" and looks for another captive—a submissive woman who will yield more readily.

The message to some predators is that captives can be broken and remade into slaves who will do exactly what they want. Dahmer had such a plan when he tried creating zombies. Psychopathic individuals have little to no empathy or sympathy because, to them, other people are merely objects for their gratification. They have no appreciation for the terror and pain another person might experience, except that they're narcissistically pleased to know they can elicit this response. It makes them feel in control.

The idea of having slaves indicates weak or inadequate personalities who feel an extreme need for power over someone, yet there's clearly a delusional quality to it. Some "masters" believe they're entitled to do whatever they want with another person. Others have expressed a belief that they're "benefiting" their abductee—introducing him or her to sexual pleasure, for example, or saving them from a terrible world. Sometimes people survive such captivity, but often they die from the treatment or are killed to prevent them from talking.

On *CM*, "Identity" features two males trying to catch women to keep as sex slaves. As the police chase down one, he commits suicide, and the other one—who was weaker—continues committing the crimes as if he were now his former partner. This episode is reminiscent of California team killers Leonard Lake and Charles Ng.

Lake, thirty-nine, was arrested on June 2, 1985, whereupon he swallowed a cyanide capsule to kill himself. He owned property on which stood a cinderblock bunker, and investigators soon learned that this is where he and Ng, twenty-four, brought as many as twenty-five people to kill. Lake was supposedly involved in satanic cult meetings, masterminding the gathering of female slaves, and these two men had sexually assaulted and tortured many women in their quest to find the one beautiful woman who would be perfectly submissive. Lake and Ng raped and sodomized their victims before shooting or strangling them. Often, they dismembered or cremated the bodies, and searchers found forty-five pounds of bone fragments and teeth on the property. After Lake's demise, Ng fled to Canada but was extradited for trial. He was convicted of eleven murders, including two babies, and sent to death row.

This behavior is an illegal extension of the practice of dominance and submission—even sadomasochism (S&M)—which involves intense sexual rituals into which many people enter voluntarily. Serial murderer John Robinson was a participant. He called himself "Slavemaster" in various Internet chat rooms devoted to S&M, easily luring willing women who expected only to become compliant partners; some left homes and families, and a few even signed contracts that gave Robinson total control. None realized that, for him, this meant killing them. It was more than just sexual games; it was life or death.

To affirm their sense of control, men interested in sexual slavery often keep a meticulous log as a record of their mastery as well as a means of reliving what they've done. An examination of these logs typically shows minute details of their slaves' daily routines and experiences. Robert Berdella, for example, recorded each reaction and each word his unwilling male captives said whenever he applied his fiendish tortures. He noted the exact amounts of the injections he gave, along with the times he gave them; when he used electrical currents on sensitive areas, he documented the victims' responses in his journal. Adding an additional layer of torture, he showed them pictures of those he'd already killed and when each man died Berdella recorded the date. He placed the parts of one victim in his curbside trash and kept the skull in his home. Had another imprisoned man not managed to escape, run naked to a neighbor, and alert the police, Berdella might have had more victims.

Captivity is one thing, but sometimes helpless people are forced into a more dangerous game. That brings us to another fictional tale popular among serial killers, some of whom have tried to pattern themselves on it.

THE THRILL OF THE CHASE—

The award-winning tale by Richard Connell titled "The Most Dangerous Game" was first published in *Collier's Weekly* in 1924. While engaging as fiction, the short story was also a cynical commentary on callous big-game hunts that were fashionable among the wealthy class during the 1920s.

In the story, Sanger Rainsford is an arrogant New Yorker, renowned for his skills as a hunter. While traveling by ship to Brazil, he gets stranded on an isolated Caribbean island, where he encounters its lone inhabitants: a Russian aristocrat, General Zaroff, and his deaf-mute Cossack slave, Ivan. Zaroff, himself a big-game hunter, is familiar with Rainsford's reputation, and he's delighted to have the company of a kindred soul. Over dinner, Zaroff describes his boredom with hunting animals and confesses that he's been luring ships into dangerous waters to acquire more enterprising prey. He forces surviving crew members to play a "game"—*as* game. To earn their freedom, they must survive for three days while he hunts them with a pack of vicious dogs. Rainsford realizes that Zaroff expects to experience the supreme thrill: to hone his skill against a master hunter—him.

The story's central tenet—hunting humans—has inspired real-life psychopaths who fancy themselves "above the herd." Among them was the infamous Zodiac, who seemed to have read Connell's story or seen one of its film renditions. Having killed at least seven people in the San Francisco area during the late 1960s, Zodiac aggressively sought public notoriety. As he claimed responsibility for a double homicide and threatened more, he sent a cryptogram to three local newspapers. Part of the message echoed Zaroff: "I LIKE KILLING PEOPLE BECAUSE IT IS SO MUCH FUN IT IS MORE FUN THAT KILLING WILD GAME IN THE FORREST BECAUSE MAN IS THE MOST DANGEROUS ANA-

MAL OF ALL TO KILL" (*sic*). In addition, in one film version, Zaroff dresses in black, wears a knife in a sheath on his left side, and keeps a rifle in his right hand—precisely how Zodiac looked to a surviving victim.

Serial killer Robert Hansen also seemed to replicate Zaroff's agenda. In 1980, he flew prostitutes into wilderness areas in Alaska to turn them loose without resources and hunt them down with a high-powered rifle. The BSU finally brought him to ground, and he confessed to the captivity and torture of seventeen young women, whom he then murdered for his pleasure. This type of person is almost off the scale in terms of depraved indifference to human suffering.

Michael Welner, MD, has been chair of the Forensic Panel since its 1998 inception and is a clinical associate professor of psychiatry at New York University School of Medicine. He has developed the Depravity Scale to standardize courtroom qualifiers such as *extreme*, *wanton*, and *vile* that can influence the severity of a sentence. These imprecise labels often blur the true nature of the actions in question and encourage juries to make emotion-based judgments.

For the Depravity Scale, Welner examined more than a hundred court cases involving aggravating factors to provide an itemized list of actions, attitudes, and indicators of intent that can help courtroom fact-finders evaluate the heinousness of a crime. With emphasis on the capacity of the offender to make a deliberate choice, he asked a wide range of respondents to rate these factors in terms of degree of depravity. For example, did the offender intend to cause emotional trauma or physical disfigurement? Was the attack prolonged? Does the offender blame the victim or express satisfaction with the crime?

In an attempt to offer courts across the country an objective instrument for weighing an act's degree of depravity, Welner uses a numerical scale to grade crimes according to whether they are more or less depraved. People who score high deserve tougher penalties. At the same time, the assessment device provides researchers with a more precise operational definition for clarifying the underpinnings of exceptional crimes, such as those committed by offenders depicted in the following section.

THE KILLING MACHINE—

In "Natural Born Killer," the *CM* team refers to one of the coldest, most dangerous men they'd ever faced, and it's clear that the inspiration for this killer was Richard Kuklinski, the so-called Ice Man. Most people who have dealt with Kuklinski have called him a psychopath, so let's examine the term.

Psycho is slang used to designate both a psychotic individual and a psychopath, but there's quite a significant difference between the two. People who live within a delusional world and experience a break with reality such that their ideas make little sense to others are considered psychotic. They may manage to carry out a plan and can even give somewhat logical reasoning for their behavior ("I thought a demon was inside my mother, so I stabbed her"), but they have trouble controlling all the factors. Communicating with them requires patience, focus, and the ability to avoid triggering the aspects of their delusion that frighten them.

A psychopath is something else. He (or she) is fully aware of what he's doing but suffers no pangs of conscience over it. Psychopaths behave from a personality disorder that involves narcissism, lack of remorse, impulsivity, and manipulative tendencies. Those who commit crimes seem to be more brutal than other criminals, more aggressive, and more varied in their routines. They also represent a high percentage of repeat offenders. They are callous, resistant to therapy, and intolerant of frustration. It doesn't matter to them whom they hurt or frighten; what matters is that they get what they can for themselves. Psychopaths possess their own inner logic, as they calculate the world around them in terms of self-gain. They are society's vampires, and their agendas have no socially acceptable framework in the normal world.

Psychopathy was among the first psychiatric diagnoses, although its history is replete with confusing definitions. Currently, American mental health professionals use the parameters of antisocial personality disorder for diagnosis, but that classification is not equivalent to the list of traits and behaviors that help to designate someone as a psychopath. Neither is the classification of a sociopath, although many people believe the three terms are interchangeable. Most of the early work done to crystallize the idea of psychopathy was initiated by Dr. Robert Hare in Canada. He and his colleagues devised the Psychopathy Checklist, and in 1985, he reworked it, so it's known as the Psychopathy Checklist-Revised (PCL-R). "Psychopathy is a personality disorder," Hare writes in *Without Conscience*, "defined by a distinctive cluster of behaviors and inferred personality traits, most of which society views as pejorative." He points out that among the most devastating features of psychopathy are a callous disregard for the rights of others and a propensity for predatory and violent behaviors. Without a second thought, psychopaths charm and exploit others for their own gain. They lack a sense of responsibility, and they manipulate, lie to, and con others without regard for anyone's feelings.

The combination of these individual personality traits, interpersonal styles, and socially deviant lifestyles are the framework of psychopathy and can manifest themselves differently in individual psychopaths. However, not all violent offenders—including serial killers—are psychopaths and not all psychopaths are violent offenders. If violent offenders are psychopathic, they're able to assault, rape, and murder without concern for legal, moral, or social consequences.

The crime scene behavior seen with psychopathic offenders is often distinct from that seen with other offenders. Clarifying this distinction can assist law enforcement in linking serial cases, so in recent years the BAU has worked with Hare to view crime scene behavior via characteristics of psychopathy. Identifying a homicide series is easier in rapidly developing, high-profile cases involving low-risk victims, but in general, psychopathic crime scenes reveal whether an offender tends toward being a fatal, manipulative charmer; a callous, remorseless killer; an impulsive thrill-killer; or a criminally versatile psychopath with a long record. "When a psychopath commits a violent crime," says former BAU member Mary Ellen O'Toole, "he leaves his signature at that scene—a signature we should be able to read if we understand psychopathy." The BAU continues to study this fourfold model of psychopathy for use in profiling serial crimes; it is hoped that the unit can design a tool that will accurately distinguish this type of offender.

The violence in which psychopaths may engage is qualitatively different from that of nonpsychopathic offenders in that it is likely to be more predatory, motivated by identifiable goals, and carried out in a calculated manner without an emotional context. Psychopaths tend not to commit crimes of passion, such as during a domestic dispute. For the most part, their crimes are cold-blooded, and they feel excited rather than guilty. Psychopathic serial killers appear to have a strong tendency toward sadism.

So back to Kuklinski. Even as he murdered many people as a hit man for organized crime, on his own he lured men into business deals so he could kill them. He also murdered some of his closest associates, perfecting the use of cyanide as his weapon of choice. Their demise often amused him. Suspected in half a dozen murders in New Jersey and New York, Kuklinski attracted the attention of the FBI, who captured him in a sting operation in 1986. After he went to prison, Kuklinski became the subject of several books and documentaries, and he placed the number of his murders at just short of two hundred (although only the most gullible people believed his grandiose tales). He claimed he had placed some victims inside caves, leaving the rats to devour them alive, on camera. He'd then watch the films, he said, so he could "feel" something.

Kuklinski stated that he'd first killed when he was fourteen, and he had a brother who went to prison for murder as well. They had often witnessed their father beat up their mother; and Kuklinski once said that his father had even killed one of his own children. Following in his father's footsteps, Kuklinski developed a violent and explosive temper. In crime magazines he found ideas about how to take care of people who annoyed him, such as a gang of boys who'd bullied him. One ended up beaten to death.

As Kuklinski became more and more dangerous, he allegedly devised a number of different methods for killing, from a crossbow to poison to strangulation to shooting. He even described tying one man up in a way that slowly constricted his breathing. Kuklinksi also said he'd frozen a victim's corpse for two years to foil investigators' time of death estimate once he dumped the body where it could be found. In every instance, he'd had no feelings for his victims, no remorse for his acts, and no hesitation about killing someone under orders or for his own benefit.

Agents who must hunt down or come face to face with such killers are understandably nervous. Robert Ressler describes an experience he had with Edmund Kemper, a six-foot-nine killer of eleven people. Alone with Kemper in a room at Vacaville Prison, Ressler rang for the guard. Kemper joked that he could twist Ressler's head off before anyone came to save him. Because Kemper had nothing to lose, Ressler had a moment of panic, which Kemper found immensely entertaining. (Reid and Hotchner find themselves in a similar situation in "Damaged," when a death row serial killer with nothing to lose and an enhanced reputation to gain makes a similar threat during a prison interview.)

Some killers have said that to take a human life makes them feel like God, with power over life and death, while the occasional offender has identified himself with Christ. The driving force behind such murders is the need for outright control, and it's girded with the killer's belief that he is special in some superior way. Generally, these killers are narcissists or psychopaths.

The *Diagnostic and Statistical Manual of Mental Disorders*, fourth revised edition (DSM-IV-TR), used by most mental health professionals for standardized diagnoses, is divided into five sections or levels, called axes, which relate to different types of disorders or disabilities. In the second section, Axis II, three distinct clusters organize ten different personality disorders, which are persistent patterns of maladaptive behavior that cause interpersonal dysfunctions. Cluster A is for odd and eccentric disorders, B defines the dramatic and erratic disorders, and C groups the anxious and fearful personality patterns. Cluster B includes narcissistic personality disorder (NPD) with three other disorders that can manifest in extreme forms of egocentric behavior. (Reid mentions Cluster B in the episode "In Heat.") Although not all people with NPD are criminals, NPD is commonly found among sex offenders. They feel entitled to their victims, and their self-involved arrogance contributes to their sense of personal importance. Serial killer John Wayne Gacy, for example, seemed to truly believe that, although he was in custody with substantial evidence against him for a trial with the death penalty, he'd nevertheless beat the rap and even keep an impending dinner date.

The DSM lists a number of characteristics of NPD, most noticeably a pattern of grandiosity and excessive need for admiration. People with this disorder are compelled to be the center of attention; they possess a high level of self-regard, but they treat others as inferior beings. They obsess over power and success, they believe they're entitled to immediate compliance with their wishes, and they're certain that others envy them.

Narcissistic criminals, when captured, will attempt to make themselves into the most superior criminal ever seen. Often, they will defend themselves in court because they see no one else equal to the task.

In his book *Dark Dreams*, Hazelwood discusses how narcissistic criminals often keep records of their crimes as a way to relive them, reminding themselves of what they have done. "The crime scene," writes Hazelwood, "is a central feature of a sexual criminal's work product, his canvas, if you will. For many offenders, the work is so valuable that they devise elaborate and occasionally ingenious ways to preserve it for later delectation."

KILLER QUIRKS—

"In Heat" makes reference to conflicted gay men who kill boys or young men, and among such real-life killers we count Richard Rogers, a nurse from Staten Island. He cut his murder victims into seven parts before wrapping them in bags and dumping them along a highway. There was also Juan Corona, who killed and buried twenty-five migrant workers, and John Wayne Gacy, a married man who brought boys to his home when his wife was away, to have sex with them before killing them. He buried most in a crawl space in his basement. Then Herb Baumeister, a successful businessman and father of three in Indiana, committed suicide before he could be arrested for luring gay men to his estate for sex, torture, and murder. He was linked to sixteen murders, and the skeletal remains of several men were exhumed from his property.

Such killers seem to feel shame and anger over their predilections, and it may seem that killing the object of their desire would eliminate that thing about themselves that so disgusts them. However, they soon feel the desire again; hence they murder repeatedly. On "In Heat," Reid describes how the killer they're chasing might be taking on his victims' identities as he moves along. This episode might have been inspired by a unique spree-type serial killer who behaved in this manner. He wasn't gay (although he was sexually inadequate, according to a woman who knew him), but he did practice this invasive form of identity theft. He also demonstrated the traits of a narcissist.

In 1974, the FBI hunted down Paul John Knowles, released from prison in Florida thanks to the attorney of one of Knowles's female correspondents—now his fiancé. When he came to see her in San Francisco, she broke off the engagement. This apparently so enraged Knowles that he went out, selected three people at random, and slaughtered them. He then left California and went roaming across the country.

In quick succession, Knowles kept killing. He selected children, couples, older women, younger men, or older men . . . the victim type did not seem to matter to him. From Connecticut to Georgia, he continued to kill and rob.

One victim, Carswell Carr, was found dead on his bed, nude and with his hands bound behind his back. He had been stabbed superficially twenty-seven times with what appeared to be a pair of scissors, but the medical examiner found that he'd died from a heart attack, so the intent of the assault appeared to be torture. Down the hall, Carr's daughter, fifteen-year-old Mandy, had also been bound and left facedown, but she'd been strangled and asphyxiated with nylon stockings. Mrs. Carr, who was at work during the home invasion, identified things missing: most of her husband's clothing and his briefcase, identification, shaving kit, credit cards, and keys. What authorities did not yet know was that Knowles was now dressing and posing as Carswell Carr. Eventually, Knowles was captured but not before killing several more people.

For posterity, as if he was certain that people would care, Knowles had entrusted an attorney with a taped confession of all of his crimes. He'd also encountered a writer whom he believed would write a book to make him famous, and to her he identified himself with several savior figures. He fully expected to die young and during a prison transfer Knowles grabbed for a police officer's gun and was shot dead. At this time his tapes were reviewed and investigators learned that Knowles claimed to have killed thirty-five people, although only eighteen murders over a period of four months are officially attributed to him.

Conflicted killers with an agenda or an extreme degree of self-hatred can sustain a damaging spate of aggression, but just as intense—and sometimes more shocking—are the killers whose fatal aggression is melded into a paraphilia, a deviant form of sexual arousal.

Paraphilias are primarily male disorders that begin in childhood or adolescence and persist into adulthood. They become enduring patterns of behavior that focus on objects, unusual activities, or deviant situations for sexual gratification and are often driven by repetitive fantasies. The most common are listed in the DSM, and those we find most often among serial killers include the following:

- *Fetishism.* Sexual arousal from nonhuman objects, such as shoes, underwear, candles, or ropes.

- *Pedophilia.* Sexual attention involves children, either as pornography or as molestation or assault of actual victims; hebephilia is specifically about prepubescent girls.

- *Masochism.* Sexual pleasure from being hurt or humiliated via verbal abuse; bondage; and even being beaten, whipped, or cut.

- *Sadism.* Sexual pleasure from dominating, torturing, or abusing others via such activities as verbal abuse, whipping, burning, stabbing, raping, choking, and killing.

- *Necrophilia.* Sexual arousal from handling or having intercourse with corpses.

- *Vampirism and cannibalism.* Sexual excitement from drinking blood or eating human flesh.

Let's start with sadism and the shocking case of David Parker Ray. His MO was particularly fiendish—well beyond what even Kuklinski had dreamed up, because Ray was interested in pain.

His sadistic practices were discovered in 1999, when a hysterical woman, nude and chained, escaped from Ray's home in Truth or Consequences, New Mexico. She claimed to police that she'd been tortured and she was certain that Ray and his accomplices had meant to kill her. The police went there to investigate. Next to Ray's house they found a 15- by 25-foot trailer he called the "Toy Box," and inside it investigators discovered an enormous cache of fiendish surgical implements clearly devoted to sexual torture. Ray had used medical manuals on female anatomy and had a homemade electrical device that was clearly intended for inflicting pain. Then there were obvious sexual implements, such as large dildos, belts, breast stretchers, and whips. Among this disgusting collection police found a home video of Ray and his girlfriend using several nasty tools on a screaming woman.

Ray even had a closed-circuit TV monitor in a corner to display for his victims what he was doing to them. He would also show them drawings of other things he expected to do, as well as photographs of the torture he'd inflicted on women who'd been there previously. In addition, he had a series of dolls strung up in various states of bondage-torture and a page of handwritten directions for how to handle a sex slave. Verbal and other forms of psychological abuse were part of every move, including positioning the slave as he tormented her. "Keep her off balance," Ray wrote in his notebook as part of his list of sixteen techniques for brainwashing, which included isolation, terrorism, and abuse.

Ray described himself on an audiotape as a "dungeon master," claiming an affiliation with the Church of Satan. His sex slaves were not just for his own use, he told them, but for all members of his congregation. In other words, his victims were led to believe they would be repeatedly abused by people attuned to the most evil acts a human could devise.

In the recording, Ray claimed he'd killed at least one person a year for forty years. He was arrested and convicted of the abduction and sexual torture of three women. Although he died before being tried on murder charges, he'd confessed to one murder and he'd had several accomplices who admitted to others. Investigators suspect he had killed many more times.

Sadists seek traits that make a person appear vulnerable—youth, low self-esteem, inexperience, ambivalence, recent trauma, or naïveté. Once they have zeroed in on a target, they begin the seduction. They'll be friendly and will perhaps offer gifts or a place to stay. They'll seem harmless, genial, and even attractive. Some sadists draw out the courtship, but others take quick advantage and go right to the punishment stage. No matter how they chose to attract a victim, the goal is always to inflict pain, for as long as possible.

CONSUMPTION DELUSIONS—

Serial killers who drink blood or eat human body parts are not as rare as one might think. In fact, their particular paraphilias display a reliable pattern that makes linking their crimes, once victims are found, fairly obvious. Such killers have popped up throughout history and across cultures. (On *CM*, "Cold Comfort" dealt with necrophilia, while "Blood Hungry" offered cannibalism.)

Ironically, a Hungarian man was among the vampires. In 1916, officials learned about stores of petrol on the property of Bela Kiss, who'd gone off to war, so they confiscated seven seemingly full drums. When they opened the containers, they were shocked to find that each held the preserved body of a naked woman, drained of blood. Autopsies indicated that all had been strangled and all had wounds on their necks. Seventeen more barrels offered the same grisly contents, including Kiss's faithless wife and her boyfriend. During an investigation, officials learned that a "Professor Hoffman" in that town had lured these victims with matrimonial ads. Yet authorities believed Kiss was dead, so they closed the cases. However, the rumor persisted that he'd traded dog tags with a dead comrade and walked away from his crimes.

Among other infamous blood-drinking serial killers was Joseph Vacher in France, who, when caught in 1897, said he'd drunk blood from the necks of a dozen murder victims. Marcello de Andrade, twenty-five, sodomized and killed young boys because he thought he would gain their beauty if he drank their blood.

Among cannibals, besides the aforementioned Jeffrey Dahmer we have Karl Denke, the Mass Murderer of Münsterberg, who killed guests at his inn, pickling their remains. After his arrest in 1924, he claimed he'd eaten parts from as many as thirty-one people and for over three years human flesh had been his sole source of meat. He committed suicide in jail. Soon after, the police went through his rooms and found fingers, pickled flesh, suspenders made from skin, and other equally gruesome items.

At around the same time, Fritz Haarmann, the Hanover Vampire, had been arrested and convicted. His crimes seemed particularly deviant: He was a trained butcher with a psychiatric record. He would find wayward young men, invite them home, force sex on them, and then murder them. He teamed up with a male prostitute, Hans Graf, who could better lure the boys. Together over a period of five years, they trapped and killed around fifty young men. They were finally stopped, and Haarmann confessed.

He called his victims "game" and described how he grabbed them as they dozed after a large meal or intense sexual activity, and while sodomizing them, he would chew into their necks until they bled to death. As he tasted their blood, he achieved orgasm. He would then remove the internal organs and cut the flesh from their bodies, eat some or store it, and sell the rest as butchered meat. He was convicted of twenty-seven murders, and hanged.

Over the course of two decades in West Germany, Joachim Kroll, forty-three, managed to rape, kill, and mutilate more than a dozen people. On a whim, he'd tasted the flesh cut from the buttocks of a murdered woman and found that he liked it. Thereafter, he stalked females of various ages that he thought would yield tender meat. When police finally nabbed him in 1976, they found a kettle on his stove boiling carrots and potatoes, along with a tiny female hand. In the clogged toilet were the child's internal organs, while in Kroll's refrigerator on plates were more pieces of flesh, and larger parts had been wrapped and frozen. Kroll suggested that his perversion arose from being aroused as a teenager when he'd seen pigs being slaughtered.

COLLABORATIONS—

On "The Perfect Storm," "Identity," and "Open Season," the *CM* agents contemplate the crimes of two killers operating as a coordinated team. We know quite a bit about the dynamics of real-life team killers. Dr. Eric W. Hickey, a criminologist who did a study during the 1990s of more than four hundred serial killers said that for some such teams (making up an estimated 15 to 20 percent of serial killers), murder must be satisfying as both a "participation and a spectator endeavor." The pathology of the relationship operates symbiotically, because each participant contributes something to the other's excitement that the other might not achieve solo. There's a certain vile chemistry in these matches made in hell.

According to Hickey's study, 74 percent of team killers are white, female killers participate with males around one-third of the time, and the majority of cases involve only two offenders working together. Of victims of serial murder, some 15 percent were murdered by team killers, and in the majority of cases, the victims were strangers. Sometimes the team leader or dominant partner sends the others out to do what he wants, and sometimes he participates.

At times, teams are related or married, and other times they're strangers who happened to spark the right chemistry. When females get involved, it's generally the male who masterminds the homicides, unless the female is dominant or highly manipulative. One member always maintains psychological control.

James William Miller did whatever Christopher Robin Worrell told him to as they went on a fifty-one day spree in the late 1970s in Australia. Worrell would have Miller drive to pick up girls, and after he had sex with them and killed them, he'd make Miller help him dump the bodies. After his arrest Miller claimed complete innocence in the murders, although it was clear that in most instances, he knew what Worrell planned to do. Seven women died and one was buried alive before Worrell was killed in a car accident. Thanks to a tip from Worrell's girlfriend, the police caught Miller, and he led them to three of the bodies. He'd desperately loved Worrell, he claimed, so he could not turn him in.

Of teams based on kinship, a pair of cousins came to be known as the Hillside Stranglers. Their spate of murders began in Los Angeles on October 17, 1977, when they strangled nineteen-year-old Yolanda Washington and dumped her body near the entrance to

Forest Lawn Hollywood Hills Cemetery. Their next two victims were prostitutes, whom they picked up for sex and murder, dumping them afterward by the roadside, and then they killed a young dancer.

Soon thereafter two teenage girls were abducted from a mall, killed, and rolled down a fifty-foot embankment. The same night produced a seventh victim, an art student, whose bruises matched the others. Three days later, an actress, twenty-eight, was found near a freeway exit ramp, and a business student became the ninth victim. Another murdered prostitute was soon found naked on the side of a hill, posed in a spread-eagle fashion. This time, witnesses had seen two males with her. The murders stopped over the holidays, but then a woman was found stuffed inside the trunk of her abandoned car.

Almost a year later, in Bellingham, Washington, college roommates Diane Wilder and Karen Mandic were reported missing. A security officer said that one of them had indicated that they were going to do a house-sitting job at a private residence, assigned to them by Ken Bianchi, their team captain at the security firm where they all worked. Police found the address and located the girls' car. Their bodies were inside.

Detectives picked up Bianchi for questioning. He had a California drivers' license, so they called detectives in Los Angeles, learning about the string of unsolved homicides there. Bianchi was quickly linked with his cousin, Angelo Buono, who ran a car upholstery shop near many of the body dumpsites. Bianchi confessed and implicated his cousin. On Halloween 1983, a jury convicted Buono of nine of the eleven Los Angeles murders and gave him nine life sentences. Bianchi, who had pleaded guilty to five, was given five life sentences on top of the two he'd received in Washington. Together they had plotted these murders and carried them out, finding a thrill in sharing the experience.

A case of a father/daughter team occurred in Brussels, Belgium. Andras Pandy, a Hungarian-born priest, brutalized his daughter, Agnes, raping her repeatedly after she turned thirteen. She feared him, so she did what he told her, including participating in the murder of other family members. Finally, when she was in her forties, she went to the police and told them that Pandy had killed two wives and four of his children and stepchildren. Some had been shot and some bludgeoned to death with a sledgehammer. Agnes had helped him hack the corpses into pieces and wrap them in plastic. Some were dumped, others dissolved with an acidic drain cleaner. None was found, dead or alive.

A DNA analyses indicated that the body parts and sets of teeth pulled from the basement and refrigerators on Pandy's property actually belonged to people other than the victims Agnes had named, but authorities could not identify them. Pandy insisted that the relatives in question were still alive. None came forward, so the trial proceeded in 2002, based largely on Agnes's testimony. Pandy was convicted on five counts of first-degree murder, one count of attempted murder, and three counts of rape, getting life in prison, while Agnes received twenty-one years for her participation.

Yet just how genetics may affect the temperament for murder is not clear, especially because the familial manifestations are so varied. Such fatal teamwork, however, is not limited to people who are related. Among the most notorious husband/wife teams is Gerald and Charlene Gallego, who from 1978 into 1980 engaged in a series of sex crimes together in California and Nevada. Charlene (Gerald's seventh wife) would entice girls to get into their car so Gerald could rape, abuse, and shoot them. Often kidnapping two girls together, they killed ten people. Under arrest, Charlene turned on her husband and was the star witness in trials in both California and Nevada, where Gerald received the death penalty both times. Charlene got sixteen years.

Then there was the pair of occult practitioners in Mexico. Adolfo de Jesus Constanzo was the high priest and Sara Maria Aldrete his high priestess. Their deeds were revealed in 1987 when investigators went looking for a missing college student, Mark Kilroy, who'd gone with three classmates to Motamoros. A tip about a drug raid on a remote homestead, Rancho Santa Elena, led to the discovery of Kilroy's remains in a mass grave containing parts from fourteen other boys and men. A severed goat's head signaled that this cult was a form of Santeria that practiced human sacrifice. Constanzo and Aldrete had fled, and while Constanzo ordered his cult members to shoot him, Aldrete was arrested. She denied having any part in the human sacrifices, but was sentenced to sixty-two years in prison.

As mentioned in Chapter 2, Hazelwood and Warren undertook a study of twenty wives and girlfriends of sexually sadistic males. They hoped to learn more about the habits and sexual preferences of these men, as well as to understand how they persuade women to partner up with them and even get involved in killing. The researchers found that most of these women had physical and sexual abuse in their backgrounds, so they were used to such men. Once merged with their partners, they lost their prior identities because the male's sadistic fantasy became the organizing principle for their behavior as a couple. Thus they were considered compliant accomplices with weak self-esteem who believed they had to do whatever their partner wanted.

This idea of collaborations takes an even more perverse step in the episode "Bloodlines," when the *CM* agents realize they're tailing a nomadic family that kills over and over together. Their murders, spread wide apart around the country, span many years, although their motive was quite different from that in an actual case of a killing family. A gang of five, the McCrary Family, rampaged from Florida to California, grabbing young women from stores to rape and shoot, then dumping them from the car. The motive appeared to be a combination of profit and thrill. Family members included Carolyn and Sherman McCrary, the parents, and their grown daughter, her husband, and their son. The males generally did the kidnapping and killing, while the females offered support. The police ended their fatal spree during a shoot-out, and FBI evidence helped convict them of ten of the twenty-two suspected murders. Each family member served time.

Clearly, the more background in abnormal psychology an agent acquires, the more adept he or she will be in translating crime scene behavior into a workable profile.

FIVE

-Linkage Analysis-

For the imagination of man's heart is evil from his youth.
-GENESIS 8:21

In 1999, a series of home invasion homicides occurred near rail-road tracks in Texas. The victims were bludgeoned and sexually as-saulted, and items were taken from their homes. When three such incidents were reported to the Violent Criminal Apprehension Pro-gram (ViCAP), an analyst used the system to turn up a similar case from 1997 that had occurred near railroad tracks in Lexington, Ken-tucky: A male had been killed and his female companion assaulted. Linking the cases via MO allowed the respective task forces to find a DNA match common to all of the incidents, which indicated they should consider someone riding the boxcars. That he stayed near trains alerted investigators to his drifter mentality, and they soon focused on a Mexican immigrant, Angel Maturino Resendiz, who had often been in trouble with the law. His fingerprints matched those from various scenes, and his DNA matched the biological specimens removed from victims. Resendiz was linked to nine mur-ders in three states, all near railroad tracks (as in "Catching Out"). He was tried, convicted, and sentenced to death. Then Resendiz confessed to three more murders in two other states. In one case, when he had only a vague recollection of the incident, the victim was identified and her case resolved via the entry of an unsolved crime in the ViCAP database.

ViCAP, is a national computer network used to link serious crimes, from rape to arson to fatal product tampering to murder. Because there are many references on *CM* to ViCAP (for example, "Penelope"), let's take a look at its purpose and function. As mentioned earlier, ViCAP arose from the need for a central database for linking diverse cases to a single offender, especially when such offenders were highly mobile or crossed state lines.

The early BSU instructors trained local law enforcement to work with a profile, taught psychological analysis to hostage negotiators, and offered specialized crime analysis for other arms of law enforcement, such as the Bureau for Alcohol, Firearms and Tobacco (ATF). For instruction in linkage analysis, they used ViCAP data collected from police departments around the country, based on several criteria:

- Solved, unsolved, and attempted homicides (especially involving kidnapping or suspected to be part of a series).

- Unidentified bodies in which the manner of death is suspected to be homicide.

- Missing-persons cases in which foul play appears to have played a part.

The most obvious means of linking crimes is via the signature, or the psychological ritual that drives behavior in a manner that shows uniqueness and individuality. With physical evidence, this comes from a fingerprint or DNA, but for behavioral evidence, *signature* is the term that stuck. In a way, this is unfortunate, because it connotes artists signing their work with a triumphant flourish of ownership. However, the signature is more like an imprint left behind than the final touch of a master craftsperson, especially on botched incidents. If we view it like a fingerprint, then all criminals leave a signature of some type, as some criminologists contend; however, it's the truly deviant behavior that makes linkage analysis a viable tool. I mentioned several such cases in Chapter 4, but let's look at another that had a glaringly obvious signature.

Between 1990 and 1991, three prostitutes were murdered, and at autopsy it became clear that their eyes had been skillfully removed. On a tip from a woman who'd gotten away from a brutal john, Charles Albright was arrested. He was fifty-seven and married, but he apparently frequented prostitutes. A hair and fiber analysis on debris from his vacuum, a blanket, and the victims provided physical evidence that implicated him in the string of murders. Behaviorally, he had a fixation on eyes from his background in taxidermy, and a long history of deception and fraud, including an extensive criminal record he'd hidden from his wife. He was convicted of the murders, and while in prison, he could be found drawing pictures of wide, staring female eyes.

With serial crimes, the key lies in finding distinct commonalities among incidents, and enhanced informatics has made it possible for more jurisdictions to acquire such data at a faster rate. But it hasn't always been easy.

As noted, ViCAP grew from the vision of Pierce Brooks, after his painstaking investigations in California convinced him of its necessity for law enforcement everywhere. He'd described his ideas about such a system to Robert Ressler, hoping to set it up in California, but Ressler encouraged him to place it under the auspices of the FBI. It was a great idea, and the federal government had better resources for it. The National Institute of Justice and the Office of Juvenile Justice and Delinquency Prevention provided a grant to Sam Houston State University in Texas in 1983, and the National Center for the Analysis of Violent Crime (NCAVC) grew out of workshops conducted there.

ViCAP was envisioned as a national clearinghouse for law enforcement, with a vast database of cases from around the country, although it did not quite turn out that way. Investigators quickly learned they'd have to fill out forms that were long, time-consuming, and intrusive on busy schedules. An analysis performed a decade after ViCAP began indicated that only 3 to 7 percent of total cases had been submitted to the database annually, with very few from urban areas. Many investigators perceived ViCAP as just another part of the government bureaucracy, and when cases they sent in were not quickly addressed, they dismissed the notion that ViCAP would be a helpful resource.

Agents in charge knew they would have to change something, so they revamped the software to make it more accessible and affordable to state and local jurisdictions. State hubs were created and fifty desktop computers, loaded with the software, were given out to agencies in each state. In addition, the ViCAP form received a makeover, reducing its load of questions from 189 to 95. More analysts were hired to respond to cases and answer questions, and more applications for using ViCAP were offered to cold case squads. It became easier to query a case and learn if it was open or closed as well as to acquire information about an offender or victim. There was also a new ViCAP summary report that offered a quick glance at pertinent facts, a better data retrieval scheme, and the ability to import maps or images into case reports. Furthermore with the addition of sexual assault cases, ViCAP is quickly becoming a viable registry for sex offenders. Thus the database has grown and its value has become more evident. Even so, the offender who uses a range of methods or often changes location, defying linkage analysis, is still the bane of investigators at every level. *CM* refers to one such killer on "Scared to Death."

Gary Taylor, the "Phantom Sniper," changed his MO several times between 1957 and 1975. As an adolescent, he would wait at Florida bus stops to watch for women. When he found one alone one day, he bludgeoned her over the head with a wrench. He was arrested, but a jury acquitted him. He then went to Michigan, where he became a machinist. He also acquired a gun and one night in 1957, he shot at women through their bedroom windows after dark, wounding two. Since he seemed mentally unstable, he was detained at a psychiatric hospital, where he talked about a compulsion to hurt women, yet he was released in 1972 on a qualified leave. He ignored the rules and committed a rape. Released on another leave the following year, he began to kill. He invited two women home, strangling them and burying them in his backyard in Michigan before he went to Seattle and killed a woman there. Her body, too, ended up in a hole in his backyard. Then he headed to Texas, where he was picked up for several counts of sexual assault. He confessed to four murders, including a rape/murder in Houston.

Linkage blindness occurs when investigators fail to spot a connection among crimes or crime scenes, and this occurs from inexperience, tunnel vision (fixation on an idea that includes too few factors), communication problems, or the red herrings left by a savvy offender. Dennis Rader, who called himself BTK (for "Bind, Torture, Kill") and murdered ten people, was aware of the news reports about him. He knew what the FBI profilers would probably say about the unsub who had committed his crimes, so he purposely shifted his MO at times to deflect them and to amuse himself over confusing them. He murdered whole families as well as women alone, but he also once attacked a couple. Sometimes he sent notes afterward to take credit, other times he didn't. It was understandable that detectives weren't certain about connecting them all.

Another form of linkage blindness is tunnel vision: narrowing down a guiding hypothesis about a series of crimes before considering the facts from a number of angles. The danger of tunnel vision is that following only certain leads or deciding on only a certain type of offender means that significant clues might be overlooked. Sometimes, those clues are lost and cannot be recovered or reexamined. For example, most investigators will automatically decide that a serial killer is white, which occurred in Baton Rouge, Louisiana. Although a black male was seen loitering in the white neighborhood where a woman was murdered on that same day, police dismissed this report because they accepted the stereotypes about serial killers. In addition, many investigators believe the myths that serial killers always use the same method or always leave the same signature from one crime to another. However, a close study of cases indicates that, even with compulsive rituals, some offenders experiment, thus changing behavioral clues. It's also the case that most investigators believe that serial killers who commit overtly violent acts are male. Think again.

At eighty-seven, Norma Davis, lived quietly in a gated California community. It was just after nine o'clock in the morning on February 14, 1995, when a neighbor noticed that Norma was not yet stirring. In fact, Norma hadn't been seen for several days, so the neighbor decided to check on her. She went to the door and knocked, but no one came. The door was unlocked, which seemed uncharacteristic, so the neighbor entered and walked around the first floor, calling out, but again received no response. In the upstairs den, she found the elderly woman asleep in a chair, her feet covered by a brown afghan. But she seemed too still, so the neighbor went closer and saw that the woman was dead, with two wooden knife hilts visible in her body.

In the house, detectives found a severed phone cord and a Nike shoe print visible in the dust. Beneath the body was a bloody phone. To those who processed the crime scene, it seemed likely that the killer had known how to get into the secure community as well as into the house. There was no evidence of a break-in. The autopsy indicated that the victim had been stabbed eleven times and manually strangled.

Within a month, two more elderly women were fatally attacked in the same general area—one bludgeoned with an iron, the other stabbed multiple times—and an antiques dealer was attacked by a customer, strangled, and left for dead. But this victim survived and she surprised investigators when she provided a description: her attacker had been a middle-aged woman with a soothing voice. The use of one victim's credit cards led police to a former surgical nurse, Dana Sue Gray.

Gray, thirty-six, had known two of the victims and was related to a third one. She was currently living with a man who had a five-year-old son. When the police checked at the places where the stolen credit cards had been used, they learned that the card thief had a small boy in tow.

Officers arrested Gray where she resided and found items there that gave them reason to hold her for possession of stolen property: jewelry, a purse holding nearly $2,000, and many items of clothing purchased with the dead woman's credit cards. Gray had also withdrawn money from one victim's bank account.

During interrogation, she volunteered that she was depressed and had suffered many setbacks in life. She was cautioned about her rights, but she continued talking without an attorney present. After several hours of interrogation, she admitted to the use of the credit cards but said she'd found the bank book she'd used for the withdrawal (giving several different stories for this discovery). After more questioning, she said, "I got desperate to buy things. Shopping puts me at rest. I'm lost without it."

It turned out that on the same day as the third murder, Gray had gone right to lunch, had her hair permed at a salon, and purchased clothing and jewelry to the tune of $695. Those who encountered her that day described her as cheerful and happy. Her boyfriend's young son was with her, and she'd said to several people that she expected to go on a shopping spree that day. By the end of the day she had charged $1,700 on two cards. It was clear to police that she'd taken the boy along when she'd murdered the victim. Her approach struck them as brutal, cold, and calculated.

Gray tried a plea of not guilty by reason of insanity, but eventually pled guilty to two of the murders. As she received life in prison, her attorney claimed that her remorse was sincere. Gray remained a suspect in the stabbing and choking death of Norma Davis, her step-grandmother, but due to a lack of evidence, no charges were filed.

To help combat linkage blindness, in Washington State, Robert Keppel and Richard Walter devised the Homicide Investigation Tracking System (HITS). A unit of experienced homicide investigators operates this software to organize a statewide network of records. Created in 1987 with a grant from the Justice Department, the database holds thousands of case descriptions of solved and unsolved homicides, missing persons, and sexual assault cases. Each investigator was responsible for overseeing the cases in a specific region and providing consultation. Because HITS is made up of a team with a common goal and a system of communication, investigators can assist with linking cases from different jurisdictions.

ELUSIVE EVIDENCE—

It was the initial prison interviews that grounded the ViCAP database, although the resulting form dictated how incidents would be reported, effectively dividing the data into different types of analyses. Let's look first at the criminology angle.

Early data collection focused on solved crimes and the offenders who'd committed them, examining how such criminals think, what they look for in a victim, why they kill, how they minimize risk, how they behave before and after, and how they dispose of a body. No one knows his or her own fantasies like the rapist, arsonist, or killer. Firsthand, personal information about what and how the criminals were thinking, feeling, and acting before, during, and after an offense was considered invaluable for understanding not only the crimes but also offenders in general. In fact, killers have been known to study each other ("The Last Word"), and their stated inspiration can be helpful in unsolved or future cases.

When John Douglas and Corinne Munn wrote an article about signature aspects of crime, they made it clear that any serial crime could have a signature and stressed the importance of looking at the signature on a level equal with the MO. To prove their point, they described the case of Nathaniel Code in Louisiana. Between 1984 and 1987, on three separate occasions, he murdered eight people. However, there were many differences from one incident to another so that focusing on only the MO would have defied an effective linkage analysis. Code gagged some victims but not all; he stabbed some, strangled some, and shot others; their ages ranged from eight to seventy-four, and they were both male and female. Code took money in one incident but not the others. Yet, he always committed a bloody act with a lot of overkill: "Code slaughtered his victims, slashing their throats with a sawing motion, causing deep neck wounds," and further wounding them beyond what was needed to just kill them. He also positioned all victims facedown and bound them with some type of ligature material he'd found at the scene, using a handcuff style configuration on the wrists and ankles.

Some offenders record their crimes on tape or keep journals as part of the need to satisfy some inner demon, and one actually spelled it all out in a manuscript, giving investigators one of the most detailed descriptions on record, which helped to seal his conviction. It inspired the *CM* episode about serial arson, "Ashes and Dust."

On January 16, 1987, in Bakersfield, California, police responded to a call about a fire in a fabric store. Arson investigators found a time-delay incendiary device in the middle of the store, which consisted of three matches and a cigarette wrapped inside a piece of yellow paper that was bound with a rubber band. Then two nearby craft stores burned down in the same manner, and they knew they were looking for a serial arsonist. Plotting other recent fires along a map, they discovered that most had taken place near highways that offered a quick escape. Ironically, at the center of the most recent arson activity sat a building in which a conference had just been held for state fire investigators.

Considering the possibility that the arsonist was a firefighter, a check of the roster showed that fifty-five of the participants had traveled through the fire areas to get to the conference—too many people for a solid pool of suspects. A latent print was lifted off one incendiary device, but it was too faint to make a clear determination. With no other evidence, the investigation went cold.

Two years later, there were several more arsons, also near a firefighters' symposium. When this roster was cross-referenced against the 1987 list, ten names stood out—all of them among the top fire investigators in the state. Yet comparisons against the latent print again turned up no leads.

Two more years passed, and fires broke out in five department stores in Los Angeles. All had occurred close to a California free-way. Jerry Taylor, a criminal profiler for the ATF, examined the map and decided that a serial arsonist was definitely responsible for more than two dozen fires. The signature in serial arson involves the types of buildings selected, the avenues of escape, the use of certain accelerants or incendiary devices, and the place in a build-ing where the fire was set. One arsonist drew pictures on the walls, quite literally giving his signature.

Using advanced photography and colored filters in the Califor-nia incidents, technicians enlarged and enhanced the latent finger-print on file and ran it through California's fingerprint database. The search registered a hit: John Orr. He was an accomplished and respected arson investigator with the city of Glendale, California, and his skill for pinpointing the cause of a fire within minutes was legendary. Now it appeared that there was a more sinister reason for the fires.

Detectives constructed a timeline to establish Orr's whereabouts during each of the fires and they found that he'd been driving an unmarked law enforcement vehicle, which could cross any jurisdic-tional line without notice. In addition, there was no record of his whereabouts when each of the fires started, yet he seemed to have been at most of them. Because the chances that one person could be within an hour of thirty fires belied mere coincidence, Orr was arrested and charged.

Among his possessions was an extensive collection of home vid-eos of the very fires he was charged with setting. But soon investi-gators turned up something more: the draft of a novel written by Orr about a serial arsonist whom police learned was a firefighter. The manuscript paralleled many of the actual fires—which offered psychological evidence of Orr's involvement.

A federal jury found Orr guilty on three counts of arson. Orr then pled guilty to three additional counts and was sentenced to thirty years in a federal penitentiary. However, detectives believed Orr's manuscript solved more than just arson. In 1984, an Ole's Department Store had burned to the ground, fed by polyurethane foam inside the building. Four people had died, including a two-year-old boy and his grandmother. In the novel, Orr had described an identical fire in a store called Cal's, including the death of a fictional grandmother and her three-year-old grandson—who had the same name as the actual victim. With this evidence, Orr was convicted on four counts of murder.

COMFORT ZONES–

On "Lo-Fi," the third season finale of *CM*, several people fall victim to a shooter in Manhattan and a homicide detective recalls his experience with the Son of Sam spree—the case during which the real BSU began referring to these multiple murderers as serial killers.

New York came under siege in 1976 and 1977 from the ".44 caliber killer," who randomly shot couples in parked cars. Attacking thirteen people in just over a year, he killed six. He also wrote letters to the newspapers, calling himself the "Son of Sam" and he created an aura of terror throughout the city: it seemed that he could strike at any time after dark, anywhere in the city, and just melt away. A parking ticket led the police to David Berkowitz, twenty-four. He confessed, claiming a neighbor's demon-possessed dog had commanded him to kill, raising an insanity defense that failed. When he tried to sell his story, New York blocked him with the Son of Sam law that prohibited offenders from financially profiting from their crimes. Later Berkowitz admitted the dog-and-devil story was a hoax, but tried to claim that he'd been part of a large satanic ring still operating—"There are other Sons out there." He'd been only one of several, he insisted, responsible for only two of the eight shootings. He claimed that there were nearly two dozen core members of a killing cult at large in the city. The investigation was re-opened in 1996, without results.

When a video analysis on "Lo-Fi" makes it clear there is more than one shooter—possibly even three—the team recalls the Beltway Snipers of 2002. In fact, several signature items are similar to this case of outright terrorism.

For three weeks, from October 2, 2002 until they were caught in their car during the early morning on October 24, John Allen Muhammad, 41, and Lee Boyd Malvo, 17, randomly shot at people along the I-95 corridor from MD to VA, at least fourteen times. They hit thirteen, killing nine. There was no link among victims or a clear victim type, so Chief Charles Moose had a difficult time trying to stop them. Moose set up a tip hotline and requested the assistance of FBI profilers. Three BAU agents offered a profile, based on probabilities from past cases. Thus, they stated that there was 80% chance the unsub was a white male loner with no solid relationships, had military experience and a collection of guns, and was angry, egotistical, and familiar with the killing territory. He would be unstable and frustrated over inconvenience, feel underappreciated for his talents, be hypersensitive to criticism, and experience a lack of empathy. His victims were merely targets of opportunity, not people he knew. It was likely that his normal routine had noticeably changed, such as being more withdrawn than usual or suddenly hiding his vehicle. People who knew him would realize this.

Yet based on how fast the offender was able to shoot and flee, it seemed apparent that he had a partner—the driver. Given their mobility, the chances were slim they would be caught. But then they began to leave communications, which the profilers welcomed, because killers who communicated were often arrogant enough to make mistakes. "I am God" was written on a tarot card at the scene of the shooting of a thirteen-year-old boy at school. This confirmed the arrogance. Then at another shooting, a note was pinned inside a bag to a tree. It was a ransom note, demanding $10,000,000 to end the spree. Thus the shooters would have to offer police a way to contact them, another positive development.

Via ballistics and circumstantial analysis, the task force traced the snipers to an unsolved murder in Montgomery County, Alabama, on September 21. Two women had been shot and one died. The suspect had dropped a copy of a firearms magazine, with a readable fingerprint on it. The automated fingerprint database, AFIS, soon provided an identity: John Allen Williams. He had served in the National Guard and the army, earning a badge for outstanding marksmanship. Further investigation showed that he'd had a bitter custody dispute with his first wife and his second wife had filed a restraining order against him. One lived in Maryland and the other in Baton Rouge—another area where a sniper had shot someone. Williams, a.k.a., Muhammad, also had a companion, an adolescent named Lee Boyd Malvo, a Jamaican national. Even better, Williams had purchased a blue Chevrolet Caprice. He looked like a viable suspect, although he was African American. (The profile had cautioned that there was a 20 percent chance he was not white.)

On October 24, with the help of a long-haul trucker who spotted the car, the suspects were apprehended as they slept at a roadside rest area. Police found a Bushmaster XM-15 E2S assault rifle that proved to be the murder weapon in every case. In addition, the Caprice had been modified for long-distance shooting, with a porthole drilled into the trunk lid to accommodate the gun muzzle and scope. Both were convicted of multiple murders.

In this case, before the fingerprint was lifted, a method called geographical profiling was used as another means for assessing links among the crimes. No one doubted that the same person or team was responsible for all the shootings, but geographical profiling was a way to try to establish where the suspect lived or worked. Given the relatively tight geography of the shooting incidents, it seemed possible to analyze the geographic patterns to develop a suspect list (although in this case, it did not really help).

We see this technique used in "Normal," when the agents draw a tight circle on a map to encompass a series of geographically related murder sites. Geographical profiling focuses on where a victim was selected, where the crime was actually committed, the likely travel route for body disposal, where and how the bodies were dumped, and the relative isolation of the dumpsite. It reveals details about the suspect's mobility, method of transportation, and ability to traverse physical or psychological barriers. Their comfort zone is based on familiarity with an area, and most murderers begin a crime spree near where they live, with dumpsites they know and victims with whom they feel relatively safe. The killer has a "mental map," based on habits and centers of activity, which will influence—even dictate—behavior.

Vancouver Detective Inspector Kim Rossmo created the software Criminal Geographic Targeting (CGT) and tested it on a solved serial murder case. Using the scattered crime scenes, Rossmo generated a map, and his program pinpointed within four blocks where the perpetrator had actually lived. He thought this was a solid step toward proving the value of geographical profiling, so he looked for opportunities to utilize it.

Preferring to work with a psychological profile as part of the data, Rossmo has explained that a geographical analysis highlights the crime location, any physical boundaries present, and the types of roads and highways that come into both the abduction and body dumpsites. He also included the routine activity of the victims, because most people tend to stick with familiar territory. He likens his approach to a sprinkler system that spreads droplets in a circular pattern. If you started with the sprinkler, you couldn't predict where any single drop would fall (where an offender who lived in a specific place would kill), but if you saw the pattern of droplets (murders) without the sprinkler present, you could pinpoint with accuracy where it had been.

The most valuable crime sites for this kind of analysis, Rossmo says, reveal spatial intentionality—predatory acts and body disposal planning. Serial crimes provide multiple sources of data, and Rossmo applied his program to a case in which several dozen women—prostitutes and drug addicts—had gone missing from a ten-block area of Vancouver's Downtown Eastside. His analysis confirmed for him that a serial killer roamed that area, but he was unable to get his superiors to agree—until later, when they learned that body parts from at least seven of these women had been found on a local pig farm.

In a localized spree, investigators can tell nearly as much from the paths connecting incident sites as from the sites themselves. Geography is relevant in victim selection as well, in that for predators a place must feel right and offer a means for watching and evaluating potential targets (according to interviews with convicted offenders). When a killer travels in widening circles or along a linear path, much can be learned from the types of places in which he or she chooses to kill—and if it's an active spree, target populations can be alerted.

Like psychological profilers, agents who concentrate on geographical analysis are also trying to determine how sophisticated and organized an offender is, whether the crime was planned or merely opportune, and whether the offender approached a high- or low-risk victim. They then use objective measurements via computer analysis to pinpoint as precisely as possible the locus of criminal activity. Central to the approach is the idea that there is a difference between perceived distance and actual distance, and certain things influence how this disparity can affect the commission of a crime. Perceptions of distance vary from one person to another, and such factors as availability of transportation, number of barriers (bridges, state boundaries), types of roads, and familiarity with a specific region can influence it.

Another significant factor in geographical profiling is the concept of a mental map. This is a cognitive image of one's surroundings that is developed through experiences, travel routes, reference points, and centers of activity. The places where we feel safe and that we take for granted are within our mental maps, and the same holds for offenders. As they grow bolder, their maps can change and they may then increase their range of criminal activity. Some criminals are geographically stable (stay in a certain region) and some are transient (travel around). Whether they tend toward stability or mobility depends a lot on their experience with travel, means for getting places, sense of personal security, and predatory motivations. The mental map may also depend on whether the killer is a hunter, is a stalker, or has some other mode of attack because the type of approach used on a victim also has a relationship with the location of the killer's home base.

Rossmo lists the relevant offender styles as:

- *Hunter.* Searches for a specific victim in home territory.

- *Poacher.* Travels away from home for hunting.

- *Troller.* Opportunistic encounters while occupied in other activities.

- *Trapper.* Creates a situation to draw a victim to him.

Any of these types might attack the victim upon encounter, follow a victim before attacking, or entice the victim toward a more controlled area, and these, too, play a part in the calculations.

The construction of a geographical profile involves complete familiarity with the case file, examination of the crime scenes and area maps, interviews with investigators and witnesses, analysis of neighborhood demographics for both the abduction site and body dumpsite, and the overall computerized analysis of the data. Rossmo applied this successfully to a case in Louisiana.

For over a decade in Lafayette, a man had entered the homes of a dozen different women on the South Side to rape them. Despite thousands of tips and the descriptions from victims, police could not build solid leads. All they knew was that he was a white male, wore a knit hat and mask, held a flashlight up high to blind the victims, used a gun, and always wore wool gloves. When it was over, he made them urinate or take a shower, and he always claimed to be looking for money. He also told each woman he would *know* if she reported him, even as he offered fatherly advice about locking their doors and windows. One woman saw a brown Ford pick-up truck drive away. Investigators suspected it was someone in, or familiar with, law enforcement, but could identify no one who had a brown truck or matched the description. A profile, too, emphasized someone familiar with law enforcement procedures, as well as techniques to make the women less likely to report the rape. He made it seem as if it was their fault, not his.

In 1998, the Lafayette police invited Rossmo to apply his CGT algorithm to the crime scenes. With lead investigator Mc-Cullan Gallien, Rossmo walked the neighborhoods and did an aerial inspection, noting that most of the crime scenes did not have curtains. He thought the perp had watched for an opportunity and had noted that the women lived alone. Using specific measurements, Rossmo applied the program to produce a topographic map based on the locations of a series of similar crimes. Via color arrangements and graphs, the map revealed the "jeopardy surface," or likelihood that some area was the location of the killer's home or base of operation. It was then superimposed on a street map on which the crimes were pinpointed— "fingerprints" of the offender's cognitive map. The perpetrator's zone of familiarity was reduced to a half-mile square area, about two miles from each crime scene.

The police developed suspects, but DNA analysis cleared them all. Then a tip produced another suspect, a police officer named Randy Comeaux. Yet he didn't live anywhere near the area that Rossmo had pinpointed. Then Gallien learned that Comeaux had moved and that during the time of the rapes, he'd lived within the hot zone. In fact, he was engaged to a woman who volunteered at a local rape crisis center—so, just as he'd warned, he'd know if any rapes were reported. Detectives acquired a sample of Comeaux's DNA, which matched the samples from the crimes. He was arrested early in 1999 and received three consecutive and three concurrent life terms.

CGT uses movement patterns, comfort zones, and hunting patterns based on criminological studies. For example, right-handed criminals trying to escape will often run to the left, but toss weapons (if they get rid of them) to the right. Criminals tend to operate in areas close to home before they grow bolder or grow nervous and start fanning out. Rossmo prefers to have at least five crimes in a clearly linked series to analyze, or at least five crime activity sites. From that, and from records such as suspect lists, police reports, and motor vehicle information, he enters information into his program and builds from there. It can be added to or modified whenever new data come in. In another case of a serial rape, for example, Rossmo used facts from 79 percent of the crime scenes in the police files and was able to accurately provide the investigators with the spot where the man had taken his victims.

Another person who has focused on methods of geographical profiling is Dr. Grover M. Godwin, who uses a multivariate analysis he calls "Predator." It produces the same type of three-dimensional map as CGT and uses various colors to depict different results, with a light-colored area suggesting a high probability of the offender's residence.

Godwin did research with Dr. David Canter in England on fifty-four American serial killers, and they found that the abduction sites significantly affected the program's predictive power. The next step was to determine the geographical coordinates of both the location where a body was found and the physical address of where the victim was last seen.

Godwin's approach was affirmed in 1996 in a serial murder case in North Carolina. He read about the crimes in a Raleigh newspaper and added the facts into his database. The victims were all black women who were choked and beaten, and the geographical pattern indicated a relatively small area of operation, mostly around railroad tracks. Godwin believed the offender would turn out to be an explosive person between twenty-eight and thirty-five who committed his acts in an unplanned but stylized burst of violence. He also indicated where he believed the killer probably lived.

The day Godwin presented his profile to the police, John Williams Jr. was arrested for one of the crimes (unrelated to the profile). He soon became a suspect in the others as well as in five rapes. It turned out that Godwin was correct in his overall assessment, but most specifically in the geographic pattern as a clue to the offender's home. He managed to predict within one block where Williams lived.

Analyzing potential settings where a victim may have had contact with a killer helps narrow the focus of an investigation to promising areas for locating witnesses and for people who may have survived an attempt at grabbing them. The places where criminals shop, eat, and get involved in recreation play a significant role in defining their "crime awareness space."

In sum, linkage analysis relies on indicators from crime scenes and victim facts and habits to decide if several crimes are related to a single offender or criminal team. Geographical profiling is one tool that has provided valuable information on where suspects feel safe, although it hasn't always been accurate and it relies on criminals operating according to a limited set of psychological laws. Yet a good geographic profile can often prioritize suspects, develop strategies for linkage analysis of information, and even assist with devising an effective polygraph session. A series of crime scenes can certainly provide clues about an offender's spatial perception and mobility, but it's still true that insight into psychological motivation, degree of organization, and lifestyle make a more solid contribution to an investigation. The database is larger, more comprehensive, and more detailed, and that alone makes it the best bet for analysis based on probability.

With that in mind, let's look more closely at the types of crimes that supply information to *CM:* those truly suitable for behavioral profiling.

SIX

—Suitable for Profiling—

SERIAL CRIMES

[T]o the man who loves with fantasy and rapt attention, these suscepti-
bilities become a definite center of gravitation.

—HAVELOCK ELLIS

One of the original television shows that involved FBI profilers
was *Unsub*, a 1989 mid-season replacement, starring David Soul as
Westley Grayson. Then from 1996 to 2000, *Profiler* aired, featuring a forensic psychologist working with a Violent Crimes Task
Force. Howard Teten was one of the two FBI consultants for this
show, reading scripts and answering the writers' questions (and
"often being ignored"). On the DVD of the final season, the bonus
features include an interview with Teten. He describes his own
background as a crime scene investigator who got interested in
"psychological criminology" and who developed a theory about
linking a type of criminal to a type of crime scene. He then explains that, originally, profiling was considered a last resort. In the
early days, the unit that became the BSU realized that a behavioral
profile could actually throw an investigation off course by direct-

ing detectives to think along lines that might thwart a case from being solved.

Teten calculates that, of the fourteen thousand annual murders at the time, only about two hundred were the bizarre or extreme crimes suitable for the type of work the BSU agents offered. In the early days, they did not travel to distant jurisdictions, but instead brainstormed cases together in their FBI office. Teten dismissed a criminal like "Jack of all Trades," the nemesis for the fictional Dr. Samantha Waters, because a man that smart would avoid committing murder; instead, he'd apply his genius to illegally amassing wealth. Teten also bemoaned the way the writers stretched the truth to entertain.

The key idea on which he focuses in this interview is that the vast majority of criminal incidents did not require a profile, because they were related to issues involving people who knew one another or were the result of typical crimes fairly easy to solve, such as robberies, drug deals, and bar fights. Contrary to how the profiling shows focus on female victims, in reality, he says, about 75 percent of homicide victims are male.

Yet as the BSU (then the BAU) developed, behavioral profiling became tantamount to a discipline, and as a result the parameters for when a profile might be useful were expanded. There were other types of serial crimes besides murder, as well as many different types of murders and offenders. Sometimes, it's not clear that a profiler is even needed, but deeper digging can turn up surprises.

On "Limelight," the *CM* team is called to Philadelphia to sort through the contents of a storage area for which the owner had stopped paying rent. Inside are boxes of drawings and journals about bondage and torture involving adult women. Initially, there's no indication that the person had taken his paraphilic fantasies over the line into action, but then evidence indicates that he did (although it turns out to have been planted).

This episode recalls the convoluted case of James Mitchell "Mike" DeBardeleben II, whom the Secret Service investigated for counterfeiting and financial fraud but whose other activities drew both John Douglas and Roy Hazelwood into the mix. Hazelwood called DeBardeleben "the best documented sexual sadist since the Marquis de Sade."

The Secret Service had dubbed him the Mall Passer, because of his success in many malls at passing as real the counterfeit bills he'd printed himself. As he traveled through thirty-eight states, he managed to pass about $30,000 in fake bills. His MO was to go from store to store, buying low-priced items he didn't need, such as socks, dog collars, and greeting cards, to get real cash back from fake twenties. The agents tracked him and lost him on several occasions, but then caught up. They alerted the personnel in several potential malls to watch for money that didn't look right, and passed out a composite drawing of their man.

On April 25, 1983, the forty-three-year-old counterfeiter went into a mall that was under surveillance and purchased a $4 paperback at B. Dalton. He received $16 back. The clerk watched him go across to a toy store before alerting mall security, and they tracked De-Bardeleben through several stores and out to the parking lot, where they got his car make and license plate number. They also had him on videotape passing bad bills. DeBardeleben drove through several other states, dropping bills as he went.

On May 25, in Knoxville, Tennessee, the Mall Passer arrived in a car registered in two states, with license plates stolen in Virginia. He went into several stores in a local mall, where store clerks recognized and reported him. This time he was caught.

A search of his car turned up guns, counterfeit bills, numerous license plates, prescription drugs, a police badge, nine fake driver's licenses, and a substantial stash of pornography. That was important evidence, but they badly wanted to find DeBardeleben's printing press. Agents went to an apartment registered in his name and a search there led to a storage space at a mini-warehouse. Using a bolt cutter to remove the padlock, they opened the door. It was clear at once that the printing press was not there. Yet they decided to look inside the two oversize footlockers and soon realized they had potential evidence of other crimes.

DeBardeleben had collected an assortment of women's phone numbers and addresses. One bag contained handcuffs, a dildo, shoelaces, a chain, bloody panties, and lubricant. There were also hundreds of sexually explicit photos of females and several audiotapes.

Back at the Washington Field Office, agent Greg Mertz looked through the assortment of distasteful items and listened to one of the tapes. He was stunned by the intense torture sessions with women, who begged their tormenter to either stop or kill them. The tapes appeared to be somewhat scripted and revealed a sadist who had to experience pain in others to get aroused. He'd even put himself on an audiotape with a falsetto voice, playing the role of the victim. Among the notes, DeBardeleben had scribed a formula for making a woman into a sexual accomplice:

> Get his satisfaction early.
> Isolate her and keep her dependent.
> Make all decisions.
> Prevent her from acquiring any skills.
> Don't let her get educated or have any power.
> Be ready to cut her loose if necessary.
> Never show weakness.

The photos and tapes inspired a sweeping multistate investigation as the agents realized that DeBardeleben was possibly the elusive suspect in two cases of abduction and rape in 1979. His MO had involved posing as a law enforcement officer, gaining the trust of his victims or insisting they accompany him before forcing them to do his will. Those who'd survived his attacks reported that he had yelled a lot, sworn at them, forced them to perform degrading acts, and been unable to maintain an erection. One girl reported that he'd said he wanted to get back at women because he'd had a wife who'd given him a raw deal. Often, he took photos of his victims naked and engaging in forced sexual acts.

Back then, Special Agent Douglas had offered a description of this suspect's likely personality characteristics. Among those listed were that he'd had a weak father and domineering mother; a record of previous offenses, including voyeurism and burglary; adjustment problems in school and the military; a belief that his victims desire what he does to them; and sadomasochistic fantasies. He'd be a police buff, cagey and intelligent, and might be a regular stalker.

A court-martialed military man, DeBardeleben appeared to have had most of these traits, and whenever he grew anxious about his crimes, he devised a strategy to give himself more courage. He kept track of his acts and wrote down descriptions of what he could do next. Sometimes he wore women's clothing while he performed his fantasies. He would also take pictures, posing his victims in various ways. He recorded his feelings and plans, including the possibility that he might murder someone and had to be "ready."

DeBardeleben had married five times, getting divorced quickly, and had a prison record for auto theft. When he was thirty, he married his fourth wife, an eighteen-year-old girl. He subjected her and his next wife to complete degradation until they finally got away from him.

In 1982, as "Dr. Zack," DeBardeleben had asked Realtor Jean McPhaul in Bossier City, Louisiana, to show him some houses. After she failed to check in, they found her in one of the empty houses, lashed by the neck to a rafter in the attic. She had two puncture wounds to her heart, and no one could determine a motive.

After three trials, DeBardeleben directed his own defense, claiming that the seizure of the tapes and sexual paraphernalia were not within the limits of the search warrant for counterfeit equipment. He moved to have them suppressed, but the judge decided against him. Six trials all produced guilty verdicts, with many years of prison time. He remained a suspect in numerous other rapes and in four murders. The agents involved in the investigation believe that he'd done far more than they could uncover, both in number and degree of evil.

Because he'd written so extensively and had kept so many tapes and photos of his victims, DeBardeleben proved to be a fascinating subject for experts who studied this kind of perversion. One was Hazelwood from the FBI's BSU. His specialty was sexual crimes and he had transformed the investigation of aberrant sexual offenses into an integral part of the FBI training program.

Hazelwood used the four categories of rapists first discussed by Dr. A. Nicholas Groth in *Men Who Rape*.

- Power-reassurance, or the "gentleman rapist," involves a belief that the act is consensual.

- Power-assertive involves a belief in entitlement, with minimal fantasy content.

- Anger-retaliatory is motivated by anger and the need to get even with women for real or imagined wrongs.

- Anger-excitation involves sexual sadism and gaining power over women and is driven by complex fantasies.

Hazelwood believed Debardeleben was in the anger-retaliatory category, the most dangerous one. In his journals, Debardeleben had defined sadism for himself as "the central impulse to have complete mastery over another person, to make him/her a helpless object of our will, to become her god." Moreover, he wanted to enslave women.

The anger-excitation rapist forms a plan that he knows how to execute and will do it over and over for as long as he can get away with it. He rehearses every detail and has all the equipment necessary. He will also recidivate. Hazelwood knew that sexual sadism counted for no more than 7 to 10 percent of sexual crimes committed; the sexual sadist was the premier predator. Such men, Hazelwood discovered in his study of thirty sexual sadists, viciously despise women. With forensic psychiatrist Park Dietz, Hazelwood wrote a forty-page report to help the Secret Service agents understand DeBardeleben's behavior.

They saw behavioral evidence of narcissism, which meant that DeBardeleben had to build an illusion of omnipotence around himself that protected him from insult or humiliation. He had to reign supreme, and anyone close to him, such as a wife, had to fully support his self-perception. The slightest dent in this psychological armor would provoke rage and potential annihilation for the person who crossed him. In fact, it seemed that one of DeBardeleben's four wives had undermined him in a way that fueled his rage and motivated him to keep hurting other women.

In this case, the profile came not from the crime scenes but from a suspect's own records. That happens as well with serial killers who decide to communicate with authorities.

MENTAL MAPS—

On "The Fisher King," a killer sends cryptic clues to each member of the team, challenging them to save a targeted victim. He weaves his puzzle through references to John Fowles's book *The Collector* (see Chapter 4). Killers like this who send letters, codes, or maps in real life often overlook something that eventually reveals their identity. This was true for BTK (Dennis Rader), the DC Snipers, Peter Kürten, and Theodore Kaczynski, but one rather notorious killer was either lucky or unusually clever.

According to former FBI profiler John Douglas, many serial killers are motivated by a "desire to create and sustain their own mythology." One of the most complicated cases along those lines was the Zodiac killer, a fan of the short story "The Most Dangerous Game" (see Chapter 4). He operated in and north of San Francisco during the late 1960s. Exactly which murders are to be credited to him is controversial, due in part to inconsistencies in his communications. Only after someone made a tentative connection to the 1966 killing of Cheri Jo Bates in Riverside, for example, did Zodiac claim credit. That vicious murder did seem to bear his signature, and letters had been sent to the police, the press, and to the girl's father in a way that echoed the Zodiac's later communiqués.

The next incident was the murder of a couple, David Faraday and Betty Lou Jenson, on December 20, 1968, near the northern California town of Vallejo. In the same general area, in July 1969, another couple, Darlene Ferrin and Michael Mageau, were assaulted with a semiautomatic gun. Michael survived to provide a description; however, no one was arrested.

Then letters arrived at the *San Francisco Chronicle*, *San Francisco Examiner*, and *Vallejo Times-Herald*, each containing specific references to the murders along with what turned out to be one-third of a cryptogram. The three pieces had to be published and put together to give someone a chance to crack it. A letter emerged from the symbols that seemed to have been written by a man skilled at ciphers, and it attested to how much he loved to kill—especially people. A week later another letter came to the Vallejo paper specifically from "the Zodiac."

All leads went nowhere until there was another attempted double murder at Lake Berryessa of a couple (the young woman was killed), and the near-public slaughter in San Francisco of a cab driver. These deaths were followed by a letter that contained a piece of the driver's bloody shirt, which alerted police to the possibility of an arrogant madman in their midst—especially when he sent another letter that warned of a bomb. The communications kept coming as taunting postcards, drawings, and letters until 1984.

At one point, Zodiac sent a map of Mount Diablo, a Bay Area landmark. Something interesting would be found, he said, if the police placed a radian—a specific unit of measure—on Mount Diablo. When investigators drew the angle on a map, placing the apex on Mount Diablo and drawing one leg of the angle across the Vallejo murder sites, they found that the other leg went through Presidio Heights in San Francisco, where the cabbie was killed.

This clue shifted the investigation, because prior letters had seemed primitive and clumsy, but now it was clear they were dealing with a perpetrator with a high IQ. The misspelled words and poor grammar from the letters now appeared to be a clever manipulation. However, despite developing a list of suspects, they were unable to arrest anyone. The case remains unsolved to this day.

The motives behind communications with authorities vary from one offender to another, and while many seek notoriety and the thrill of being undiscovered while their exploits are printed in the newspaper, a few get annoyed at the police for not finding the bodies and linking them. Robert Ressler was invited into such a case.

As a juvenile and young adult, Colin Ireland committed a series of petty crimes. Once he felt bold enough for something stronger, he prepared a murder kit containing handcuffs, extra clothing, rope, gloves, and plastic bags. Then between March and June 1993 he went to gay clubs in London to select "easy" victims: men who would willingly allow themselves to be bound for kinky sexual escapades. The first victim was West End theater director Peter Walker, forty-five. Ireland bound and tortured him in his South London flat and then suffocated him with a plastic bag. He spent time with the corpse, placing condoms in his mouth and nostrils, and posing two Teddy bears in an obscene position.

Then Ireland waited for the news reports. To his disappointment, nothing about the crime was printed, so he telephoned a newspaper, the *Sun*, to leak the story himself. Not giving his name, he mentioned that the murder was the result of a New Year's resolution.

Two months later, Ireland suffocated Christopher Dunn and left him in a sexually provocative position, handcuffed and wearing a black leather harness, with evidence of burning in his pubic area. When investigators failed to link the two crimes, Ireland made another anonymous call to push them along. The police investigated, but found no leads.

After strangling a third man in June, Ireland anonymously told the police there were two important clues at the scene. However, they were unable to figure out what these clues were. With three unsolved murders, they contacted Robert Ressler for a profiling assessment. He noted that the victims had all frequented the Coleherne Pub, where a few years earlier gay serial killer Michael Lupo had picked up some of his own victims. Ressler also speculated that the unsub was seeking a thrill from media attention. The crimes were nearly identical, and all had been followed with phone calls, so it was clear to him that this killer wanted to be identified.

Then a fourth victim quickly turned up, murdered in his apartment, with his dead cat placed against his exposed genitals. This time, a fingerprint from an unknown source was preserved. Ireland made several anonymous phone calls to police, claiming he was losing control. He warned them he would kill one victim per week if they did not stop him and expressed frustration over their inability to link the four murders. It seemed clear to Ressler that he would make a mistake.

On June 15, Ireland managed to handcuff and strangle a fifth victim, and again he sent police to the scene. Ireland stated he now qualified as a serial killer, so he could stop. Scotland Yard learned that the victim had traveled home that night by train so detectives checked surveillance cameras that had recorded activity on the relevant transit platforms. The one at Charing Cross Station showed a blurred image of the victim, in the company of another man. That person's image was sharpened and made public. Right away, several other men came forward to say they had met him. Ireland saw the image, too, so he went to his lawyer to admit he was on the tape, but he denied being a killer. However, the police had his fingerprint, and when they arrested Ireland, he confessed in detail. In the end he received five life sentences.

Ressler was not surprised to learn that Ireland was a loner in his thirties, unemployed, and with a history of mental instability and violence. Despite Ireland's protest to the contrary, Ressler viewed him as a self-loathing gay man punishing others for his own predilections. Ressler was convinced that pressure from long-building fantasies, not a New Year's resolution about becoming a serial killer, had motivated the crimes.

DRIVEN BY A MISSION—

Some signatures indicate that a set of murders has a common theme. In the *CM* episode "A Real Rain," a mission-oriented killer goes on a rampage because he can no longer deal with seeing cases get as far as the courtroom but remain unresolved. The killer becomes a vigilante against criminals he thinks should be punished. In real life, it's most often prostitutes who take the brunt of a mission killer's need to punish or wipe out a specific population.

Over a period of two years, from 1982 to 1984, numerous female victims were found strangled or stabbed and discarded around the Green River in Washington State. In 1983 alone, twenty-seven women had disappeared, nine of whom were found dead. Many were prostitutes or runaways. They were often dumped in one of four areas, and sometimes more than one was found in a single day. A few had stones pushed into their vaginas and one victim was posed with a wine bottle and a dead fish. The *Seattle Post Intelligencer* received a letter in 1984 with the heading, "whatyouneedtoknowabout-thegreenriverman," and the author claimed to be the killer, signing the letter with "callmefred." John Douglas, a member of the task force, examined the letter and decided it was unconnected to the murders, although it cited facts not released to the press.

DNA samples were taken from many suspects. A few were eliminated via polygraphs while others failed to pan out with evidence. The task force eventually was disbanded, but several detectives kept the case alive. Finally in 2001, the thrice-married Gary Leon Ridgway was linked via DNA analysis to several victims and arrested. As his trial approached in 2003, he admitted to his crimes and showed authorities more graves until his final toll reached forty-eight. (Some people believe it is probably higher, and Ridgway himself estimated the number to be around sixty.)

Ridgway said he'd written the "callmefred" letter, but despite becoming a suspect much earlier in the investigation, he'd managed to beat a polygraph examination in 1984 and was released. While he would not say upon his 2001 arrest when he last had killed, he hinted that it might have been in 1998. He'd killed some of the victims in his home and had then changed the rugs to eliminate evidence.

Ridgway often watched for his victims, sometimes sleeping only a few hours so he could use the night hours to troll for them. He thought of the ones he killed as his possessions, to do with as he pleased, and he enjoyed the feeling of control. Once he even killed a woman while his young son waited for him in the truck. (Ridgway was said to have used photos of the boy to make women feel more comfortable around him.) He did not like it when victims were found, because he then "lost" them. He told the police that he saw himself as a helper to law enforcement, because he was ridding the world of prostitutes.

Another mission killer turned up in a hospital. Seven intensive care patients died unexpectedly between May and September 2006 in Havlickuv Brod Hospital in the Czech Republic. On December 1, Czech authorities arrested thirty-year-old male nurse Petr Zelenka. A doctor had noticed as early as May that the facility had an unusually high number of cases of internal bleeding, and some patients died before the condition could be reversed. Zelenka was often part of the healthcare team, and when he went on vacation in August, the epidemic ceased. Then Zelenka returned, and there were more such patient deaths.

It was found that Zelenka had been administering heparin, a blood-thinning drug, which in high doses can cause internal bleeding. Apparently, he'd inject it and then complete his shift, aware that the patient was dying. Gambling on whether a doctor would step in to save the patient had become a game. Sometimes they did, sometimes they didn't. When he confessed to seven murders and ten attempted murders, his attorney let it slip to reporters that Zelenka might have been injecting patients to "test" the doctors. He'd believed that the doctors at the hospital were incompetent, so he'd set about to prove it. Thus his mission did not target victims per se but exploited them to undermine the doctors and make the hospital notice the supposed problem.

Some mission killers are psychotic when they commit multiple murder and their purpose derives from their delusion. From October 1972 until February 1973, a series of murders occurred around Santa Cruz, California. The victims were four campers (killed in a mass slaughter), a priest, a man digging in his garden, a young girl hitchhiking, a couple, and a mother and her two children. The police caught the offender minutes after he'd killed his thirteenth victim; he was Herbert Mullin (spelled Mullen in some sources), age twenty-five.

It was soon learned that Mullin had been institutionalized in 1969 for shaving his hair and burning himself after hearing voices but had been released. Hospitalized and released again, he became a drifter. According to his account, he'd stopped taking his anti-psychotic medication and had then heard a voice that urged him to kill. He believed that the earth "understood" its death rate and for a while the Vietnam War had appeased it. But that was over, and the lower number of deaths could trigger natural disasters to rectify the situation. Thus it became Mullin's mission to save the people of California from a super earthquake that was going to break up the state and send it into the ocean. (Sometimes he referred to California as "my continent.") He thought he could accomplish his mission by creating "small disasters." He decided he had to "sing the die song" to persuade thirteen people to either kill themselves or allow themselves to become human sacrifices (which he said they conveyed to him telepathically). With a knife, rifle, revolver, and baseball bat, he attacked his victims at random until police picked him up. Diagnosed with paranoid schizophrenia, he pleaded not guilty by reason of insanity. Nevertheless, a jury found him to be legally sane, and they convicted him on two counts of first-degree and eight counts of second-degree murder (with another one added later).

Then there are racist mission killers, as depicted in "Fear and Loathing." In 1980, Douglas was drawn to offer a profile of a New York killer. A slim white man was seen shooting a black youth in Buffalo, and the murder was linked to four more in the space of a day and a half. Buffalo Bill, as he was called, waited two more weeks before apparently killing two black cabbies and removing their hearts; he then attempted to murder a patient in a hospital. Douglas surmised that the organized killer was a right-wing member of a hate group. He'd be around age twenty-eight, have a sizable gun collection, and might have joined the military. However, he'd be a discipline problem to his superiors. Douglas thought the cabbies were the victims of someone else, because the MO and signatures were too different from the other crimes. Soon thereafter, in less than a day, five black men and a Hispanic man were stabbed in Manhattan; four died, but one of the survivors fingered a white male as the culprit. Then a man was killed in Rochester, and three more were attacked in Buffalo.

At Fort Benning in Georgia a few weeks later private Joseph Christopher was placed under arrest and restraint for attempting to kill another soldier, and he claimed he'd killed black men in Buffalo and Manhattan. Ballistics tests on a weapon found in his home confirmed this. He was twenty-five, hated African Americans with a vengeance, and had inherited a collection of guns from his father. He'd recently joined the army, and had gone on his killing sprees while on separate leaves. Confessing to thirteen murders, he did not admit to involvement in the two cabby incidents, but he also did not deny it. Found competent to stand trial, he received life in prison.

Besides murder, the BAU might tackle other types of serial crimes.

PRODUCT TAMPERING—

In "Poison," we have an example of product tampering, and the BSU was involved in one of the most sensational examples of this crime in America. In 1982, Douglas was called in after seven people mysteriously died in the Chicago area. One had lingered in agony for two days before finally succumbing. Detectives discovered that the victims had all purchased a bottle of Extra-Strength Tylenol and had consumed capsules laced with cyanide.

The Tylenol manufacturer, Johnson & Johnson, immediately

recalled all packages of the product. The country was witnessing a unique new form of terrorism—someone, somewhere, could contaminate almost anything that people innocently purchased and consumed. In the FBI code language, the case became known as "Tymurs."

The problem that faced them was the random nature of the product tampering. No specific person had been targeted or any specific store, and there appeared to be no motive. No one was using it to blackmail a company into paying a ransom.

Douglas interpreted the poisoning as an act of anger, without a need to see a victim or to be present at a murder. This crime involved psychological distance. He also believed the person would have periods of depression and hopelessness. He was like an assassin, a white loner who hated society and sought some expression of power and punishment.

Douglas's profile indicated that this unsub would probably have a record of complaints of injustices against him (he did not consider that the person might be female), and that he'd have a psychiatric record. He'd probably experienced some stressful event around the time when the first deaths had occurred late in September. He would also be talkative about the news to anyone who'd listen. Douglas suggested that newspapers print articles that humanized the victims and urged graveside vigils for at least a week, in case the perpetrator wanted to venture close to relive his sense of power.

Yet despite all efforts, no one was ever identified. Then, as suddenly as they had begun, the cyanide poisonings stopped (although other cases of product tampering occurred in other places). This case forever changed the manner in which over-the-counter drugs were sold in this country. Now all such products have tamper-proof seals and warnings not to use the contents if the seals have been broken.

MIXED MULTIPLES—

In "Charm and Harm," the *CM* team was drawn into an investigation in which the identity of the offender, a combination of serial and spree killer, was known. He was on the run, having been associated with a series of murders, and he was known to be a charmer. This episode seems to be based on the "Beauty Queen Killer," Christopher Wilder (as is the MO for the killer on "Plain Sight"). Wilder began as a serial killer, but once he realized he was a suspect, he took off across the country, killing several women as he ran.

It was the disappearance on March 4, 1984, of Elizabeth ("Beth") Kenyon, a teacher in Miami, Florida, that started things rolling. Her parents told the police about a former boyfriend whom Beth had declined to marry: Christopher Wilder, thirty-nine. He was an entrepreneur with a construction business as well as an amateur photographer, but he also had a record for sexual deviance. Further, he'd been associated with another missing woman, Rosario Gonzales, who'd disappeared on February 26 after being with Wilder at a race track.

Wilder had moved to Florida fifteen years earlier to elude a criminal investigation in Australia in which he was a suspect. Then in Florida, he'd been arrested for forcing oral sex on a girl, and a doctor who'd examined him then had declared him unsafe in an unstructured environment. Psychiatrists had recommended supervised treatment, but then the jury acquitted him. Three years later he'd raped a girl, but got only probation.

When Wilder realized the police wanted to question him about Elizabeth Kenyon, he withdrew money, took his business partner's credit card, and fled. Yet along the way, Wilder stopped to pick up pretty girls. He met one at a shopping mall and lured her with the promise of a modeling career. She ended up dead. By the time they found her body, Wilder had grabbed and imprisoned another girl in a hotel room. There he tortured her by shocking her with electricity and applying Super Glue to her eyes. The girl managed to lock herself into a bathroom and yell, so Wilder fled.

He sometimes killed women just to take their cars, so he could change quickly to allude the police, but he continued to kidnap attractive girls. On April 3, the FBI placed Wilder on its Ten Most Wanted list and issued a nationwide alert. He abducted and killed more women, racing to California and then going to New England before a New Hampshire state trooper recognized him. In a struggle over a gun, Wilder was killed. Another abductee had just managed to escape by jumping from his car.

Found in his possession were handcuffs, rolls of duct tape, rope, a sleeping bag, a specially designed electrical cord, and John Fowles's novel *The Collector*. (Therapists who'd treated Wilder over a period of time knew that he'd practically memorized it.) He's credited with eight victims, but he's tentatively linked to so many others it's impossible to know just how many women he raped and murdered.

SERIAL BOMBER—

In the first season of *CM*, "Won't Get Fooled Again" uses quite a few aspects of the real-life story of serial bomber Mark Hofmann from Utah. He was among the convicted offenders interviewed for the FBI's database, and in some ways the episode follows his story closely because it focuses on the signature of a bomber as well as the categories of motives for setting bombs. The *CM* agents quickly dismiss the notion that the bombs were set for political reasons, and because the victims seem targeted rather than random, they believe the unsub was using bombs to cover up another crime. When the unsub becomes a victim, the agents mention that with bombing incidents, victims are among the initial suspects, due to the dangerous nature of handling bombs.

This is exactly what occurred in the Hofmann case, but what he was covering up was unique in the annals of crime. His case began on October 15, 1985, when the police in Salt Lake City, Utah, were called to the Judge Building in the business district to investigate an explosion with an apparent fatality. The man's right thigh was torn open through his pants, which had been ripped clean away; pipe shrapnel had hollowed out his chest; and a sturdy nail flying off the bomb had gone into his eye and pierced his brain. His name was Steve Christensen, one of the partners of a law firm.

Not many hours later, a bomb in another area claimed a second victim. Kathleen Sheets had picked up a package left at her home, detonating it. When police arrived, they found a scrap of brown paper that showed the bomb's intended recipient: Kathy's husband, Gary. Detectives now knew that the victims had been targeted, so they began to look for links between them.

Investigators learned that Christensen was a bishop in the Church of Jesus Christ of the Latter-Day Saints and was considered to be an honest businessman with an interest in Mormon history. On his schedule that morning had been a meeting with church officials over a rare collection of religious documents. He'd also intended to meet with his business partner, Randy Rigby, who thought the bomb was associated with the Mormon document deal on which Christensen had been working.

One document that Christensen had purchased for the church was quite controversial: the "Salamander Letter," which proposed an alternate version of how founder Joseph Smith had discovered the golden plates that became the basis for the Book of Mormon. Smith's version was that when he was fourteen, an angel revealed their location to him, but the Salamander Letter from 1830 told a different story. Supposedly written by Martin Harris, a close friend of Smith's and the man who'd funded the Book of Mormon's initial printing, it confirmed that Smith had found the golden plates.

However, when he reached for them a white salamander guarding the plates transformed into an "old spirit" and struck Smith three times. This creature did not want Smith to take the plates, but the boy did anyway. This rendition of events undermined Smith's testimony about what had occurred and thus threatened the foundation of Mormonism.

Document dealer Mark Hofmann had located the Salamander Letter and brought it to the church's attention. He proved its authenticity by comparing it with the farmer's handwriting, found in the back of an old prayer book. Christensen had purchased the controversial letter to donate to the church, to keep in its vaults. So Christensen was a viable target for Mormon fanatics.

But it was important to find the link with Gary Sheets. It turned out that his company was faltering, and he was the beneficiary of an insurance policy taken out on Christensen for half a million dollars. While he had no clear part in the document deal, he needed money to stay afloat. Yet he did not have much insurance on his wife, and he'd have known, if he was the bomber, that she'd pick up the package.

The next afternoon, a florist saw a man open the door of a blue Toyota sports car. As he leaned inside as if to grab something, the car had exploded. But the man had been only injured, not killed, so an ambulance whisked him to the ER.

It was Mark Hofmann, the documents dealer, also a viable target for fanatics. When he was able to talk, he said he had been about to meet with an attorney representing a customer to whom he was selling documents. He'd gone to his car and seen a package on the seat, but when he'd opened the door, the package had fallen to the floor and exploded.

The detectives were aware he was a business associate of Steve Christensen's. He had a family, had just purchased a nice home, appeared to have a good marriage, and was in good standing with the

Mormon Church. In fact, he'd been collecting controversial documents for the church to keep them out of the hands of anti-Mormon dissidents. He had no criminal record. But Hofmann was supposed to have met with Steve Christensen the day before to close a deal on some rare Mormon documents known as the "McLellin Collection." That made his movements of some concern.

The car was now a crime scene, and the bomb had been made with the same smokeless gunpowder as the other two and had a model rocket igniter and a mercury switch. The bomb investigators determined from this signature, or unique construction, that the same person had designed all three bombs and that they were different from any other bombs in the country. Yet in some ways, they were also different from one another. The first one had nails, the other two did not. The one in the car had been a different size from the other two, slightly larger. But they all shared the same type of pipe for a casing and the same type of gunpowder, switches, battery packs, igniters, wiring components, and brown paper packages.

Then bomb experts discovered from evidence in the car that Hofmann had lied about his movements. The scenario that made the most sense was that Hofmann had picked up and dropped the bomb by mistake and then fabricated the story he was now telling. The evidence said that Hofmann was the bomber. They soon learned that Hofmann was in debt. He'd bought an expensive house, had run up bills, and owed a lot of people money.

Church officials denied knowing Hofmann, but upon learning that the Library of Congress was to pay him for a document called the "Oath of a Freeman"—supposedly the first document printed on an American press—they had approved a thirty-day loan for the McLellin Collection, which had historical value for the church. Steve Christensen had been brokering the deal when he was killed. The parties involved had discovered that the loan had expired without payment and that no collection had been forthcoming. They'd all been duped. The church agreed to send the Salamander Letter to the FBI for analysis.

In the meantime, investigators seized Hofmann's van to search for possible traces of the bombs. Inside was a $25 receipt for a facsimile copy of the Oath of a Freeman from Argosy Bookstore and a grain of smokeless gunpowder consistent with that used in the bombs. They also located a man, Shannon Flynn, who admitted that Hofmann had asked him to purchase blasting caps and *The Anarchist's Cookbook*, which detailed the construction of bombs. Yet document dealers across the country who heard about the investigation defended Hofmann, who'd been selling documents all over the country over the past five years. If he'd been cheating everyone, they all had a lot to lose.

While Hofmann took and passed a polygraph, another team of detectives pieced together Hofmann's complex document dealing business because they believed it was associated with the murders. Special Agent George Throckmorton, in charge of the authentication process for the Salamander Letter, located other documents that had come through Hofmann. He scanned three letters alleged to be from Joseph Smith and decided that something was amiss. Throckmorton knew that a man writing three letters on the same day from the Carthage, Illinois, jail in 1844 would not have used different paper, a different writing instrument, and different ink for each one and would not have had reason to change the style of his handwriting. Yet that's what these letters revealed. It seemed that Hofmann's forgeries had passed into many different hands.

Among Hofmann's effects taken during a search, Throckmorton and Flynn found a copy of *Great Forgers and Famous Fakes*. Using it, Throckmorton figured out the recipe and method Hofmann had used for making the iron gall ink that had thus far defied authentication tests for determining its age. Using a control group of non-Hofmann documents, he also noticed that unique to all

Hofmann-handled documents, and to no others, were two characteristics: ink that ran in a single direction and that cracked like alligator skin. That, he knew, resulted from artificial aging processes.

Throckmorton realized that many experts and documents dealers had been fooled. All of Hofmann's documents—hundreds of them—had been forged. This included the Salamander Letter. Hofmann was emerging as one of the cleverest forgers in the world.

In February 1986, Hofmann was charged with twenty-seven felonies, including multiple counts of fraud and forgery and two counts of homicide. At his hearing, he claimed he was innocent, but within months, discussions were under way for a plea deal. On January 7, 1987, Mark Hofmann agreed to plead guilty to two counts of second-degree murder, second-degree theft by deception in the sale of the Salamander Letter, and second-degree fraud for other documents.

Part of the deal was to explain himself, so Hofmann described how he'd removed blank pages from nineteenth-century books, learned how to age ink, and then developed a way to forge someone's handwriting from other extant samples. So many documents had come from him that when the FBI later used seventeen samples to authenticate one of his "historical signatures," it turned out that Hofmann had faked fourteen of them.

The bombings had occurred for complex reasons. Hofmann had claimed to have discovered a cache of historic papers and diaries potentially embarrassing to the church known as the McLellin Collection (although there really was no such cache). Christensen was going to help authenticate the collection for the church. The elders had sanctioned an unsecured loan to Hofmann of $185,000, and Christensen was going to purchase the McLellin Collection. But things had quickly unraveled: Hofmann could not deliver, Christensen had pressured him, and the loan had come due.

So Hofmann had panicked. When Christensen set up a meeting

in his office for the morning of October 15, Hofmann had left the fatal bomb. But later that day, church leaders assured Hofmann that Christensen could be replaced. They assumed, as Hofmann hoped they would, that because the second bomb killed Kathy Sheets the violence was related to some business transaction unassociated with the church. That had been Hofmann's sole motive for leaving a bomb at the Sheets home—to buy himself some time. But it was not enough, so he'd made a third bomb, but this one went off in his car, ending his lucrative forgery career. Hofmann pled guilty to several counts of murder and fraud in exchange for a life sentence.

Retrospective profiling, whether for serial bombings, product tampering, or serial murder, is the typical approach to criminal behavioral analysis. However, in a limited context, which *CM* has included, it's actually possible to use specific behaviors to predict potential criminal acts—including serial murder.

SEVEN

–Proactive Profile–

RISK ASSESSMENT

Under the conditions of an all important moment, even an average man
will be driven to commit an act, which he will regret for the rest of his life.
In such moments, involving his deepest passions, he tends to lose sight
of everything except the desired end.

—JAMES MELVIN REINHARDT

I've already made a case that profiling is done retrospectively—after
a crime is committed—avoiding the practice of racial profiling or
similar forms of a priori prejudice. Now, I'll reverse that within a
qualified domain, because for certain types of crimes, the behavioral patterns from one perpetrator to another are so similar that
it's possible to do *prospective* profiling in the presence of certain red
flags. It's a form of threat assessment, in which a collection of behaviors that are consistent across such cases can guide the analysis
of whether a certain person might be dangerous or repeat a violent crime. For this purpose, we'll look at two types of offenders for
which the *CM* agents have conducted this type of threat assessment:
stalkers and healthcare serial killers.

DEATH THREAT—

First, a note about threat assessment, also called the analysis of dangerousness or risk assessment: It's not an exact science. Not even close. Nevertheless, in recent years, as it has grown less subjective, has become more statistically precise, and can be quite helpful when someone is questioning what to do in a potentially threatening situation. Relying on the latest best practices tool can also cover someone who might be sued over a mistaken prediction. Briefly, threat assessment involves making educated predictions from a variety of factors about whether a given offender might repeat his or her offense. The assessment of dangerousness must be segregated into component parts: risk factors, harm, and likelihood of occurrence. Then the array of risk factors must be assessed from multiple domains, such as past history, support systems, medical history, and the presence of certain types of personality disorders. The potential for harm must be assessed with several instruments and scaled for degree of seriousness. The database from which threat is predicted must be large and broadly representative, and the ultimate goal should be ongoing management.

The Research Network on Mental Health and the Law of the MacArthur Foundation examined the relationship between mental disorder and violent behavior directed against others and associated with both risk assessment and risk management. They devised a comprehensive list of risk factors that have been associated with violence in prior research, and that are consistent with existing theories of violence or mental disorder. This list included factors not previously studied, such as social support, impulsiveness, anger control, psychopathy, and delusions. Experts in these fields developed risk assessment instruments, such as revising Hare's Psychopathy Checklist (PCL-R), to assist with measurement and prediction. Only changeable factors were deemed relevant to risk management. These factors were field tested and submitted to a full-scale study, using official arrest and hospital records, regular self-reports over a one-year period, and collateral reports from knowledgeable informants. It was a significant step in standardizing threat assessment.

The MacArthur study found that the propensity for violence is the result of an accumulation of risk factors, no single one of which is either sufficient or necessary for a person to behave aggressively toward others. There are several standardized risk assessment devices to help gather the right type of information to make the best predictions. Notably, a high score on the PCL-R has been significantly correlated with repeat offenses. That is, someone with callous disregard about others and who uses crime for entertainment or self-enrichment, as psychopaths often do, will probably continue to commit crimes—especially violent crimes—until he or she is caught. This is especially true with highly impulsive offenders and those who fail to learn from punishment. Profilers who have experience with the best tools and the latest research on threat assessment have an edge for offering recommendations for an offender's future behavior.

Another solid instrument is the Violence Risk Assessment Guide (VRAG), which was developed in a maximum security psychiatric hospital in Ontario, Canada. The researchers tested predictor variables in relationship to an outcome variable (any new criminal charge for a violent offense) using records of institutionalized offenders, including any violent conduct in the institution for which a patient would have been criminally charged had it been done in the community. The VRAG includes twelve key variables, including elementary school maladjustment, victim injury, *DSM-IV* categories, and the PCL-R score. Individuals at the upper end were almost certain to recidivate their violent crimes.

But threat assessment doesn't involve only the potential offender.

With stalker evaluations, the target person must be evaluated in terms of vulnerability to attack, fear of the threatening person, personal lifestyle, and degree of sophistication about self-protection. Interviews with this person are part of the assessment, albeit taking care to avoid further stimulating a stalker's interest.

Threat assessment is of interest to all mental health personnel who might become the confidante of a potentially dangerous person, largely due to repercussions from a California-based case.

During the late 1960s, Prosenjit Poddar, a native of India, attended the University of California at Berkeley and met a female student, Tatiana Tarasoff. They became friends and he developed a strong romantic interest in her. When they shared a quick New Year's Eve kiss, he developed a belief that her feelings for him were stronger than they actually were. Tatiana set him straight, but he developed an obsession that became increasingly more intrusive. He believed he would have to kill Tatiana to be free of it.

Poddar sought outpatient psychiatric services at a hospital in Berkeley. The treating psychiatrist diagnosed paranoid schizophrenia and prescribed medication. He then referred Poddar to a psychologist, Dr. Lawrence Moore, for counseling. Despite their sessions, Poddar persisted in his delusion that he must prove himself to win Tatiana's love. He told the doctor he'd purchased a handgun to orchestrate a life-threatening situation from which he could "rescue" her and win back his honor. Moore said that he might have to have Poddar restrained, which sent Poddar from the office in a rage. As per protocol, Moore discussed the danger with colleagues and notified the campus police, but officers who questioned Poddar thought he seemed rational and in control.

In October 1969, Poddar went to Tatiana's house, armed

with a knife and pellet gun. He shot her, then stabbed her fourteen times, killing her. Poddar turned himself in and at his trial pleaded not guilty by reason of insanity. He was convicted of second-degree murder and served only a short sentence before he won an appeal for a new trial, which never occurred. Instead, Poddar was allowed to return to his home country.

The Tarasoffs, Tatiana's family, instigated a civil case of negligence against the Regents of the University of California. In 1974, the California Supreme Court found that, despite patient-psychotherapist confidentiality, a duty to warn exists when the therapist determines a warning is essential to avert a danger rising from a patient's condition.

Tarasoff v. Regents of the University of CA imposed a duty on other mental health professionals to take protective measures when it appears that a patient may harm another person in the near future. Most jurisdictions across the country now recognize a Tarasoff-type duty, but limit it to situations in which the patient communicates a serious threat of physical violence against an identifiable victim. Therapists are legally obligated because they are supposedly in a special relationship—assuming care and custody of a patient, which encompasses the potential victims of that patient: The therapist should possess expertise in predicting who may be violent.

However, this does not constitute an automatic duty to warn a potential victim. In fact, issuing a warning can be not only ineffective but a catalyst to violence. In any event, there are alternatives to an outright warning, such as notifying law enforcement or involuntarily committing the patient. Disclosure need occur only where there are sufficient indicators of threat to lead a competent physician to reasonably conclude that an individual will act out violently toward a specific person. The predictive value is good for only a brief period. The critical factor in whether or not to hold a professional responsible is that there be a comprehensive assessment and a treatment plan that logically arises from the results of the assessment, such as increasing sessions, prescribing or referring for medication, or doing a neurological workup. To hold therapists negligent for any possible future act of a patient would be to hold them to an impossible standard of care.

Hedlund v. Orange County Superior Court extended the therapist's civil liability not only to an intended victim but to anyone within a "zone of danger." The American Psychological Association (APA) protested this concept as unworkable, and Justice Mosque, the dissenting voice, said that the majority opinion in this case perpetuates the myth that mental health professionals have a clairvoyant ability to predict dangerousness. To have to extrapolate from a specified third party to anyone who fits a similar profile demands too much of the "special relationship."

Within the range of assessing for violent threats, profilers know that some types of crimes are compulsive, triggered by a certain set of circumstances. A convicted pedophile, for example, who has shown no sign of aberrant behavior in prison may recidivate immediately once he gets around children again, as occurred on *CM* in episode "P911." Many factors must be calculated, and the profiler's database on the type of crime in question can be a valuable asset for making decisions.

Kansas v. Hendricks: Legislation for sexually violent predators involves involuntary civil commitment after an offender has served the stipulated sentence. Kansas implemented such a statute in 1994, which was immediately challenged as a form of double jeopardy, and thus unconstitutional. Under the Sexually Violent Predator Act, if an offender has a "mental abnormality" that makes him or her likely to repeat predatory acts of sexual violence, that person can be confined indefinitely. In 1997, the

U. S. Supreme Court upheld the involuntary commitment of Leroy Hendricks, a repeat pedophile who'd been unable to complete any treatment programs. He admitted he could not control his urges to molest children, so he was deemed too dangerous to release. The confinement was not considered to be punishment, so it did not involve double jeopardy. If a person's harmful behavior cannot be prevented, due to a mental disease, they can be held. However, this raises issues with other disorders, such as psychopathy. It also raises questions about the criteria used for prediction of dangerous behavior.

In many ways, all profiling involves some form of threat assessment. When Special Agents Gregg McCrary and John Douglas went to Scarborough, a neighborhood of Toronto, in the 1990s, they evaluated a series of rapes that had escalated in brutality. At the time, they told the task force that if they didn't identify the rapist soon, he would start killing, because the violent nature of his words and acts revealed that he would need more than sexual assault to satisfy him. They were right. It wasn't long before that offender committed three murders.

However, that's not the same as prospective profiling. As mentioned before, retrospective profiling uses behavioral patterns at crime scenes to assess personality and possibly predict a specific unsub's future behavior. Prospective profiling relies on a set of characteristics and behaviors against which to compare suspects to decide if they might be dangerous now and in the near future. The analysis is appropriate for certain types of stalkers.

STALKERS—

In "The Crossing," the *CM* agents follow a potentially violent stalker. Although this sort of case is not really what profilers do, because the perpetrator had traveled six hundred miles to follow his inamorata and appeared to have an obsessive form of erotomania that would probably escalate, they decide to get involved. From what the agents know about persistent stalkers who travel, they believe it's likely he will become violent.

Erotomania is a disorder in which a person develops a delusional belief that another person—usually a celebrity or someone of higher social status—loves him or her. Also referred to as de Clérambault's syndrome, it has a long history. The symptoms include a perception of "secret gestures" from the target person that confirm the delusion and a persistent need to contact the supposed inamorata. Such stalkers may send letters or packages, make numerous phone calls, or take up a determined pursuit. Sometimes there are fatal consequences.

Ricardo Lopez, twenty-one, developed an obsession with Icelandic pop singer, Bjork. He was driven to become a significant figure in her life, no matter what it took, and finally it seemed to him that violence was his only option. First, he penned a 803-page journal and made twenty-two hours of videotape about his plan to harm her. Finally, he put it into action.

Lopez sent a bomb infused with sulfuric acid to Bjork's London address, concealed in a hollowed-out book. He'd envisioned that when she opened the book, the bomb would detonate and spray acid in her face, killing or disfiguring her for life. He even demonstrated for himself how it would work by exploding a trial bomb against a photo of her. Once Lopez mailed it, he committed suicide while filming himself listening to Bjork's song, "I

Miss You." Decomposition odors eventually alerted a neighbor, who notified police. Thanks to the videotapes, they learned how Lopez had assembled and mailed the bomb, so they contacted Scotland Yard's anti-terrorist branch. These officers intercepted it before it came into Bjork's hands.

Apparently, Lopez believed that, in death, he would achieve his longed-for union with the singer. His detailed accounts provide a vivid picture of a hermetically sealed world, ruled by his delusion.

In legislation, a stalker is defined as "someone who willfully, maliciously, and repeatedly follows or harasses another person and who makes a credible threat with the intent to place the victim or victim's immediate family in fear of their safety." There must be at least two incidents to constitute the crime, and the stalker must show a "continuity of purpose" or credible threat.

In 2008, the Department of Justice's Bureau of Justice Statistics relied on the largest survey undertaken to date to update information about victims of stalking. In a twelve-month period from 2005 to 2006, an estimated 3.4 million Americans reportedly experienced such disturbing contact. The most common forms are phone calls, letters, e-mails, or starting rumors. More than one third reported being followed or monitored in some manner. Over 75 percent knew their stalker, usually from a romantic association. The most vulnerable age range was eighteen to twenty-four, especially if divorced or separated. Nearly 10 percent believed they might be murdered. Many had to give up their current job—even their residence—to escape the unwanted attention. It's estimated that one in twelve women has been or will be stalked, and one out of every forty-five men.

Many stalkers threaten harm, and the latest study indicates that nearly 25 percent carry out their threats—including damage against property or harm to pets. The targeted people most likely to be murdered have been in a relationship with their stalkers.

One method of categorizing stalkers comes from the team who wrote the FBI's *Crime Classification Manual:*

1. Nondomestic stalker, who has no personal relationship with the victim
    a) Organized (based in a calculated, controlled aggression)
    b) Delusional (based in a fixation like erotomania)

2. Domestic stalker, who has had a prior relationship with the victim and feels motivated to continue the relationship; this constitutes around 60–70% of stalkers and the aggression often culminates in violence

In terms of risk assessment, certain items stand out that are common to stalkers who have been violent:

1. an unhealthy level of obsession

2. delusional expectations

3. anger about something the person did

4. access to or knowledge about a means of punishing the target person

Growing tension in the stalker signals internal conflict that could erupt in homicidal violence, and what these people often lack is insight about themselves and the explosive nature of their personal issues.

Stalkers tend to be unemployed or underemployed, but are smarter than other criminals. They often have a history of failed intimate relationships and tend to devalue their victims. They also idealize certain people, minimize their resistance, imagine motives and actions that have no basis in truth, and rationalize that the target person deserves to be harassed and violated. Many stalkers view their actions within a delusional framework and therefore see no need to get help. (Although some have fixated on their therapists.) The case that brought national attention to the problem helped instigate the first anti-stalking laws in America.

Twenty-one-year-old Rebecca Schaeffer had played a wholesome and innocent character on the 1980s television sitcom *My Sister Sam*, and she'd recently starred in her first movie. As her popularity grew, she received fan mail. A nineteen-year-old man from Tucson, Arizona, named Robert John Bardo wrote to her, and in return she sent him a signed photograph. He thought this meant she cared about him. He built a shrine to Schaeffer with media photos and videotapes. In 1987, he went to Warner Brothers Studios to try to meet her, once with a teddy bear and once with a knife, but was denied entrance. In his diary he wrote, "I don't lose. Period."

Then Bardo saw a movie in which Schaeffer was in bed with someone. He decided that she'd violated her image of purity and had to be punished. He got her home address through the Department of Motor Vehicles and formed a plan.

On the morning of July 18, 1989, Bardo went to Schaeffer's Hollywood apartment. Taking with him a copy of J. D. Salinger's novel *The Catcher in the Rye*, Bardo decided on a bold approach. After a courier delivered scripts to someone in the building, he surmised she was the recipient, so he rang the buzzer.

As Schaeffer opened it, Bardo pulled out the photo she'd sent him and told her he was her biggest fan. She asked him to leave. Bardo did, but then returned and buzzed again. He stepped into a hiding spot, which brought Schaeffer across the threshold. At that moment, he burst out with a gun and shot her. She screamed, "Why? Why?"

Bardo had told his sister of his intent to visit the actress, penning the note, "I have an obsession with the unattainable. I have to eliminate what I cannot attain." When she heard about the murder, she turned her brother in. He was extradited to California where he was convicted of first-degree murder and sentenced to life in prison without parole.

Schaeffer's murder, along with a near-fatal assault on another actress, Teresa Saldana, provoked California Governor George Deukmejian to sign a law that prohibited the DMV from releasing addresses and inspired the Los Angeles Police Department to create the first Threat Management Team. Countrywide, stalking was taken more seriously. California's law was passed in 1990, effective on January 1, 1991, the first of its kind, and other states soon followed this example.

In fact, celebrity stalkers are a breed apart, creating rather complex scenarios that motivate them to pursue or harm the person who has caught their attention. It's not always about love or possession, sometimes it's about over-identification with the person they're stalking. They want to *be* that person, or be associated with that person, and when he or she does something they dislike they feel an extreme need to exercise control.

Mark David Chapman had long been a fan of John Lennon, the iconic musician and founder of the rock group the Beatles. In fact, Chapman reportedly married a Japanese-American woman because she reminded him of Lennon's wife, Yoko Ono. Chapman had a history of drug addiction and mental illness and had been hospitalized in the past for suicide attempts. He claimed to have had thoughts of killing several different celebrities, but he fixated on Lennon after he came to believe that the former Beatle was "selling out." From a book he'd read about Lennon's life, he considered Lennon to be a phony in the way he called for love and peace while enjoying the privileged lifestyle of a millionaire. Chapman was also upset by a remark Lennon had made to the effect that the Beatles were "more popular than Jesus," which he considered blasphemy. Reading *The Catcher in the Rye*, he grew obsessed with taking a stand against hypocrisy, and he thought Lennon fully embodied it.

Chapman, a former maintenance man, went to New York City in October 1980 to find his target, but did not follow through. He returned two months later, in December, determined to carry it out. He had purchased a gun in Hawaii and, on the fateful day, the forty-nine-year-old bought a new copy of *The Catcher in the Rye*, then spent fourteen hours outside the Dakota, Lennon's apartment building. Lennon even autographed a record album for Chapman that day, but hours later Chapman shot Lennon four times with hollow point bullets. Afterward, he waited for authorities to arrive, offering *The Catcher in the Rye* as his statement. Confined, he underwent hundreds of hours of psychiatric and psychological exams, claiming that "little voices" had commanded him to shoot and that he'd experienced "urges" he could not control. He eventually pled guilty to murder, insisting God had told him to do so. He received a sentence of 20 years to life.

Chapman would later blame the fact that before the shooting, he "just had too much time to think." He also said, "I felt like nothing, and I felt if I shot him, I would become something." While he claimed to have been angry, he also admitted to jealousy over Lennon's glamour. He saw only the image and not the person. "I saw him as a cardboard cutout on an album cover . . . you get caught up with the media and the records and the music."

Chapman was easily influenced. After seeing *Around the World in 80 Days*, he took an extended trip around the world. Upon reading *The Catcher in the Rye*, he viewed himself as the protagonist, Holden Caulfield. He even acted out some scenes from the book prior to the shooting. It was after viewing *Ordinary People* that he initially changed his mind about killing Lennon, but *The Catcher in the Rye* had a more sustained influence. Reportedly he believed that committing the murder would transform him into Holden Caulfied. He was also seeking a way to make himself famous.

This is the type of impressionable and marginally adjusted person who can easily turn dangerous, and while Chapman's act was an isolated incident in 1980, others like him would start coming out of society's cracks to take aim.

In 1983, Michael Perry developed an obsession with singer Olivia Newton-John after seeing her in *Xanadu*, because he thought she was responsible for dead bodies he claimed to see rising from beneath the floorboards in his home. He escaped from a mental hospital to "rescue" Newton-John, camping out in the hills behind her property. But he was caught and returned to his family. He then shot five relatives.

Ralph Nau also stalked this actress, following her for a decade. Nau believed that he and Newton-John were involved in a romantic relationship. He wrote Newton-John hundreds of letters, some of them threatening, and collected pictures and posters of her before returning to his family in the U.S. Subsequently, Nau beat his younger brother to death with an ax.

Although most stalkers do not commit violence, those who do share certain traits in common, notably lonerism, obsessiveness, feelings of being a loser, the need for notoriety, fixations that provoke delusional fantasies, and an interest in acts of violence. They often telegraph their intentions to someone, and they're usually mentally unstable. However, they do not have a history of violence, so people who know them tend not to believe they'll actually do what they say they'll do. The agents on *Criminal Minds* were correct to take seriously a stalker who would follow his "love object" six hundred miles and persist in making her realize he was literally right behind her.

Another type of prospective profile can be done for a different category of offender: the healthcare serial killer.

HEATHCARE SERIAL KILLERS—

In "Scared to Death," the profilers notice the absence of sexual activity in the murders of four young adults and surmise that the killer is acting out in a way to acquire power and ease his low self-esteem. They track down a psychiatrist who has lost his practice but poses as a phobia expert to troll for victims among his clientele. He would be among the subcategory of murderers known as the healthcare serial killer (HCSK).

This type of person usually goes into a healthcare career to gain some degree of personal power, control, attention, or gain. Victims are readily available—especially among the very old and very young or comatose—and in the past it hasn't been difficult to cover up certain types of murders in a major hospital. (Computer systems have helped track the misuse of medications.)

While most HCSKs initially claim, when caught, that they killed out of mercy, few were telling the truth. They exploit the atmosphere of trust and the belief that someone would enter this profession only to help. The HCSK might be a physician, nurse, psychiatrist, or any of the key support staff. A study published in the *Journal of Forensic Sciences* in November 2006 examined ninety cases from twenty countries of criminal prosecution of HCSKs that occurred between 1970 and 2006. Fifty-four of the defendants had been convicted. Most had used one or more of the following methods: the injection of lethal substances, suffocation, poisoning, and/ or equipment tampering. Nurses made up 86 percent, and the number of suspicious deaths among the fifty-plus confirmed cases was over two thousand.

Understandably, co-workers, hospital administrators, and potential patients want to know how to spot and stop dangerous healthcare workers. So do investigators who might be called in, because these deaths are notoriously difficult to document as murders. Knowledge about what HCSKs share in common contributes a lot to the totality of circumstances that help make a case. HCSKs tend to show the same types of behaviors, from one to another, even if operating from different motives. Thus we can offer a list of red flags that will assist in identifying the behavioral and personality signals.

Among the few known physicians who became serial killers, former Marine Michael Swango is a shocking case. Given how he was forced out of his job more than once, and how he took a particular thrill in experimenting with patients, he is probably closest in pathology to the killer on the episode, "Scared to Death."

Swango entered medical school in 1980 at Southern Illinois University. His colleagues quickly realized he was lazy, ill-mannered, and untrustworthy. More to the point, he paid a lot of attention to dying patients. In 1983 Swango obtained an internship at the Ohio State University Medical Center, and that's when the trouble really started.

Among his patients was a woman named Ruth Barrick, who'd hit her head and nearly died. Swango mentioned to a nurse that he was going to check on her. The nurse who later checked on Barrick found the woman barely breathing. Calling a code, she and the medical team stabilized Barrick's vital signs, and she recovered. A few days later, another nurse saw Swango again enter Barrick's room. He spent half an hour with the patient, who was soon having difficulty. Although the nurse tried to revive her, she died. The nurses on that floor suspected that Swango had injected her with something. Before he left this hospital for other employment, five patients had died in a similar manner and several more had grown seriously ill. Yet a brief investigation cleared Swango of any wrongdoing.

Throughout his medical career, administrators covered for Swango, but his fellow students dubbed him "Double-O Swango" for his supposed "black thumb" when it came to administering medical care. People kept getting worse or dying. Despite the concerns of those who worked closely with him, this athletic, blue-eyed blond always managed to charm people to look past his poor performance. He had a reassuring air and the ability to convince people he'd learn from his errors and improve.

Swango returned to Illinois and joined a team of paramedics at the Adams County Ambulance Service. To them he supposedly described his ultimate fantasy: They're called to an accident—a school bus hit head-on by a tractor trailer filled with gasoline. Simultaneous with their arrival, another bus plows into the wreckage, causing a massive explosion. The force throws the children's burning bodies onto nearby barbed-wire fences and telephone poles. Swango also described to colleagues how he'd love to go on a cross-country killing spree and wished he'd been on the scene of a mass murder in 1984 at a McDonald's restaurant in San Ysidro, California. He'd told a female paramedic he'd like to plunge a hatchet into the back of her head.

But eventually Swango crossed a line. One day, he brought a box of doughnuts for his fellow paramedics, who grew severely ill. Another time, he offered soft drinks to two colleagues, who also got sick. They found poison in his locker and turned him in to the police. On August 23, 1985, Swango was convicted of six counts of aggravated battery and he received a five-year sentence.

Despite this, Swango bounced back. After serving his time, he was accepted into several more positions in West Virginia, South Dakota, and New York. He simply lied, faked his credentials, falsified his criminal record, used aliases, and made sure no one learned his past history. He even forged a letter from the governor of Virginia, stating that his civil rights were restored, based on exemplary reports from colleagues. Then whenever too many people got sick or died, he'd leave before authorities could fully investigate. The one snag was his attempt to join the American Medical Association. The association's officials checked his records thoroughly. What they discovered made them warn Swango's employer, who fired him.

But Swango simply shifted his plan: He found a psychiatric residency at the Northport Veteran's Administration Medical Center in New York. Once again, some of his patients died for no apparent reason. But his employer from South Dakota tracked him down and called the center. The dean fired Swango and alerted other teaching hospitals.

Not to be dissuaded, Swango looked for opportunities abroad, landing in Zimbabwe, where he acquired employment at Mnene Hospital. For a year, he experimented on patients until an investigation revealed him as a killer. He was arrested and charged with five murders, but fled the country. In his usual style, Swango found various short-term positions in Europe and Africa. But in 1997, he decided to come home to see relatives, and the FBI was waiting for him as he landed in Chicago.

It took three years, but Swango was finally tried for murder. By this time, he'd served at seven different hospitals, overdosing patients with prescription medicine or using arsenic on co-workers. In many cases, someone had seen him with a syringe, and several patients who recovered indicated that it was "the blond doctor" who'd injected them before they lost the ability to feel and move.

Arraigned on July 17, 2000, Swango pled guilty to fatally poisoning three patients in 1993 at a New York hospital. In addition, he was convicted of another murder in Ohio. In a plea deal, he was sentenced to life in prison without the possibility of parole. In his diary, Swango said he killed for pleasure, and many colleagues recounted his fascination with serial killers. Swango had stated in a diary that murder was his "way of reminding himself that he was alive."

Healthcare providers such as Swango know how to use subtle means of murder, and they have access to drugs that can poison without being detected. Unless some behavior inspires suspicion, they may effectively hide their crimes. A common thought is that older people are expected to die, so they're not as likely to have their deaths investigated. Infants and children cannot communicate that someone has done something to them, and thus they can become easy targets. Even when patients complain that someone has injected them, it is often overlooked. Institutions protect their reputations, so "accidental" medication may get ignored or covered up.

It's not possible to provide a generic profile of a HCSK because each case, while exhibiting common behaviors and contexts with other cases, is unique. Some experts believe that attempting a profile based on a psychological and behavioral blueprint is risky as it could inspire selective attention to stereotypical details and neglect of distinctive indicators, but others believe there is sufficient overlap in these cases to devise a reasonable risk assessment.

The available cases indicate that doctors often kill from the desire to feel a godlike sense of power over patients or from experimental curiosity. They view themselves as superior, and their decision to kill is often narcissistic. Many nurses feel undervalued or ignored. Their killing sprees appear to have other types of motives, such as gaining attention, finding a small realm of power in an otherwise powerless world, assuaging depression, paying back an unfair system, and acting out to relieve frustration or workload.

Male nurses are disproportionately represented among caretakers who harm patients. The 146,000 male registered nurses represent 5 to 7 percent of nurses, yet this group makes up about 33 percent of nurses who have killed patients in the United States since 1975.

Nurse Donald Harvey was caught when an autopsy revealed a toxin in the body of a male patient, John Powell. Harvey then confessed to more murders to his public defender, who then urged the DA to look for more evidence. Harvey had actually lost count of how many people he'd killed (including people outside the hospital), and at one point he took credit for eighty-seven. He was convicted in 1987 of thirty-six murders and one charge of manslaughter, spanning cases in Kentucky, Indiana, and Ohio.

Harvey insisted he was a mercy-killer, but over the course of eighteen years in several different institutions, he'd killed for petty reasons. One man he just didn't like; another he killed out of revenge. And then there were the acquaintances he poisoned with arsenic who'd annoyed him. There seems little doubt that he was engaged in occult practices when he chose some of his victims; he liked to light candles that represented specific people, deciding from a candle's flicker whether the person should die. He supposedly believed he was receiving commands from some spirit named Duncan. A psychiatrist who examined him said that he was a compulsive killer, murdering to relieve tension, although his attorney thought it was to relieve depression.

While there are many overlapping methods and motives between male and female HCSKs, there are also some key differences. Females, too, rely on injecting drugs, but they often have some form of mental illness. Genene Jones, convicted in Texas of killing a child and attempting to kill another (and suspected in many more assaults on infants) seemed to suffer from Münchhausen syndrome by proxy, in which people injure other people to get attention. On Jones's shift, the pediatric intensive care unit (ICU) death rate rose 178 percent; a child under her care was ten times more likely to die and twenty-three times more likely to suffer a seizure. Jones seemed thrilled at the excitement surrounding cardiac arrests, and her colleagues thought she particularly enjoyed holding the corpse of a deceased infant, often sitting in the morgue with it in her arms. In England, Beverly Allitt attacked nine children and murdered four in a British hospital. Seriously disturbed since adolescence, Allitt had reported many illnesses over the years and even mutilated herself on so many occasions that she had become a notorious patient for area doctors. Once Allitt was arrested, the only motive the police could determine was that she had been seeking attention.

Often, these killers have been allowed to drift from one hospital to another, fired under a cloud of suspicion but rarely brought to justice until after their murder toll has reached shocking levels. Thanks to the number of cases successfully identified, officials now understand how to use statistical analysis to determine the comparative death rate on the shifts of suspects versus their colleagues. If a suspicious number is documented, they examine whether a high percentage had been unexpected, or if the death symptoms failed to match the patients' conditions. They can also look at the suspect's record to see how many institutions have employed him or her, as well as whether there have been complaints from patients or colleagues. In particular, it's important to investigate whether a suspect has a history of mental instability, depression, or odd behavior— especially aggression toward patients who annoy them.

Several professionals have collected these cases worldwide. Former Dutch nurse Paula Lampe has identified the way nurses who kill become compulsive and secretive. British physician and toxicologist Robert Forrest has examined the most common substances HCSKs use as well as noting common victim characteristics, and Dr. Vincent Marks, professor emeritus of clinical biochemistry in Britain, has focused specifically on killers who've injected insulin. D. Lucy and C. Aitken from Scotland have shown how statistical evidence can document a killer at work, while in Germany Karl Beine undertook a study in 2003. Three years later, Beatrice Yorker, collected the details of known cases since 1970. Thus it's possible to make a comprehensive list of traits and behaviors that show up in these serial killers.

Certain signals pointing to a specific suspect are common to a number of these cases, and those on the following list (from *Inside the Minds of Healthcare Serial Killers*) should be taken quite seriously. While none is in itself sufficient to place someone under suspicion, a number of them together should raise an alarm. Accordingly, the suspected professional:

- Has been given macabre nicknames by patients or others on staff, such as "Death angel," "The Terminator," "and "Dr. Death."

- Was seen entering rooms where unexpected deaths occurred.

- Has moved a lot from one facility to another.

- Is secretive or has a difficult time with personal relationships.

- Likes to predict when someone will die.

- Makes odd comments or jokes about killing patients or being jinxed.

- Likes to talk about death with colleagues or shows odd behaviors related to the death (excitement, ownership, undue curiosity, strange fantasies).

- Seems inordinately enthused about his or her skills and likes to arrive early or stay late.

- Makes inconsistent statements when asked about the incidences.

- Prefers shifts on which fewer colleagues and supervisors are around (generally the night shift).

- Is associated with several incidents at different institutions.

- Craves attention.

- Tries to prevent others from checking on patients.

- Hangs around during the immediate death investigation.

- Possesses the suspect substance in his or her home, locker, or personal effects.

- Has lied about personal information or credentials or falsified reports.

- Has been involved in other criminal activities.

- Has books about poison or serial murder or talks about serial killers.

- Has had disciplinary problems.

- Appears to have a personality disorder.

- Has a substance abuse problem.

Identifying such people as soon as possible requires documenting patterns of behavior and items of physical evidence that link the suspected individual to the crimes. Unfortunately, healthcare-based killers have the perfect arena in which to get away with murder for extended periods of time because the means to kill patients are readily available. In addition, for a number of reasons, medical murders are not easily detected. Stopping them requires a sharp eye, knowledge about their typical traits and behaviors, and a desire to ensure that suspicious people be taken seriously.

In the event that such a person is identified and cornered, the next series of psychological skills will come in handy.

EIGHT

−Negotiations−

The world breaks everyone and afterward many are strong at the broken places.

−ERNEST HEMINGWAY, *A FAREWELL TO ARMS*

An important psychological skill is the ability to talk with people in different types of crisis situations. This could involve an eyewitness, a crime survivor, a suicidal jumper, or a deranged man holding hostages, and agents might have to induce a trance, spot a liar, or even save themselves. Understanding the art of negotiation for a variety of circumstances requires both knowledge and experience. We'll look at victim issues, interrogations, and negotiating with hostage-takers.

VICTIMS−

In "Bloodlines," Prentiss tells a crime survivor that she's going to assist her to recall details by using a "cognitive interview." This forensic technique focuses on the retrieval of information from memory. Its aim is to mentally reinstate the context of the incident in order to assist a witness to recall every possible detail in the right order. To start such an interview, the interviewer invites free recall with an open-ended question. When the witness is finished, the interviewer returns to specific aspects of the account to ask more questions. Finally, the interviewer summarizes for the witness what was said. Prentiss takes an additional step, which is not necessarily part of a typical cognitive interview, by inducing a light trance that will link the girl's memory holistically to its original context, including both sensory and cognitive components. This raises the issue of forensic hypnosis and the Encoding Specificity Principle.

The accuracy of eyewitness reports relies on the quality of three different perceptual processes: encoding (processing information), storage (retaining information for short-term use of long-term recall), and retrieval (locating the stored information). The quality of each of these processes depends on how many interfering factors are present.

Factors that can affect memory encoding include how often an item is rehearsed, whether the encoding is mentally arranged into meaningful units or patterns, whether the person was traumatized during the incident, or if the person felt pressured to recall the incident in a certain way. These factors can influence the retrieval cues, or associations. The Encoding Specificity Principle indicates that retrieval is more successful when cues match the situation in which the experience occurred.

Memory is a process of construction, organized via a cluster of related facts and experiences. Our memories can be distorted and made consistent with our schemas (prejudices, expectations, internalized plots), and we may ignore memories that contradict them. Exposure to new information between storage and retrieval can also affect what is recalled, even if that information is wrong.

When we encode an experience, we tend to select certain aspects and ignore others. We accept those things that make sense and reconstruct memory to work for us. Leading or suggestive comments tend to influence this process, as do preexisting expectations. We all have internal "scripts," or widely held beliefs about sequences of actions that typically occur in a certain way.

Take the results of this research, for example: Subjects were exposed to a film of a murder in a crowd. They then received written information about it, but half were misled about certain key details, such as describing a car that's actually green as white. Those who had been exposed to the wrong information tended to report the errors rather than what they'd actually seen, with a rate of mistakes as high as 40 percent. In similar studies, people have reported nonexistent broken glass, a clean-shaven man having a mustache or nonexistent hat, stop signs as yield or mileage signs, or a building where none existed. Our experience and our cultural "plots" train us to anticipate certain traits and behaviors, and we fill in gaps in recall to make a story work the way we think it should.

In an experiment about scripts and juries, researchers questioned subjects to determine popular beliefs about a common scenario: a convenience store robbery. The "scripts" were widely shared among the subjects about how a criminal cases a store, uses a gun to demand money, and leaves in a getaway vehicle. The second stage of the research was to expose the same subjects to a mock trial of a robbery. Many aspects of a typical script occurred, but some key elements were missing: The robber did not case the store, use a gun, or take money. Nevertheless, when researchers asked the subjects to describe the trial afterward, most "remembered" these elements. The implication is that prior ideas and beliefs influence recall of actual events when a person is making sense of familiar situations.

Human memory can be contaminated, distorted, and reformed. The more plausible or anticipated the added details are—especially if they fill in gaps—the more likely that they will be integrated as part of the actual memory. Thus investigators who interview eyewitnesses or crime victims should be careful in how they handle the person to get the story. This is especially true with guided interviews or trance induction. Forensically speaking, such techniques can make a memory inadmissible in court.

Due to the foibles of human memory, hypnosis has been used to try to fill in gaps, add detail, and ensure accuracy in eye witness testimony. The most popular techniques involve past-memory regression and memory enhancement. A hypnotist exploits the subject's suggestibility to induce a trance that produces a relaxed mental state. The subject becomes attentive, focused, and less prone to critical judgment that can block memory. Going into a trance purportedly allows the heightening of imagination, with the hope that some detail might be recalled that would otherwise remain inaccessible. Hypnosis appears to bypass an individual's psychological defenses and allow repressed or forgotten material to crystallize, allowing access to thought, feelings, and memories that are not available during normal consciousness.

The first use of hypnosis to solve a crime was in 1845, strangely enough when a clairvoyant went into a trance to help identify a fourteen-year-old boy as a thief. Some cases that involved hypnosis got into court over the next several decades, but by the end of the nineteenth century, the California Supreme Court had ruled that evidence discovered through hypnosis was inadmissible. Other states followed the example, but in some this blanket dismissal would eventually change.

There are problems with the technique, which include the possibility that a recovered memory is incomplete, inaccurate, or influenced by a leading suggestion. In fact, erroneous information can be implanted through hypnosis, and the "memory" feels just the same as if the person had actually experienced an incident. This is hypnotic recall, which can produce "memory hardening," in which a subject feels supremely confident of a false memory. There also might be hypermnesia or confabulation—filling in the gaps with false material, which our brains can do, especially when it supports self-interest. Also, personal beliefs and prejudices may influence how an event was initially encoded and thus how it's interpreted during recall. Each of these problems has been documented in experiments, along with the realization that a false memory, once articulated, can be difficult to erase.

Some situations made the courts reconsider, setting precedents. In the 1968 case of *Harding v. State*, the victim of a shooting and attempted rape identified her assailant only after she was hypnotized. The Maryland Supreme Court decided that hypnosis was like any other memory aid device and allowed it. A more restrictive approach arose from cases that went to an appeals courts during the early 1980s, notably *State v. Hurd*.

In 1978 in New Jersey, Jane Sell was attacked with a knife while sleeping in her bedroom. She escaped, but afterward, could not recall the details. Under hypnosis by psychiatrist Herbert Spiegel—who did not interview her before the procedure—she identified her attacker as Paul Hurd, her former husband and the father of her two children. The evening before the assault, Jane's current husband, David Sell, had engaged in a heated phone conversation with Hurd regarding visitation rights. While Jane identified Hurd during a trance, in her posthypnotic state she expressed doubts, but the investigating detective encouraged her to accept her identification to protect her children. Thus she gave a statement identifying Paul Hurd as her attacker, and he was indicted and charged with numerous offenses, including assault with intent to kill. Defense counsel argued on the basis of *Frye v. United States* (a 1923 decision that had set the earliest standards for the admissibility of scientific evidence) that hypnotically refreshed testimony should not be admitted. More specifically, the attorney argued that Jane Sell's testimony had been tainted by both suggestion and coercion. The case went to the New Jersey Supreme Court in 1981, which resulted in a set of guidelines for the use of hypnosis.

Among the guidelines were that witnesses must use a psychiatrist or psychologist trained and experienced in the use of hypnosis, and this professional had to be independent of the prosecution, police, or defense. Information given by any party to the hypnotist should be written or recorded, and the session(s) had to be videotaped or audiotaped, including preinterviews and postinterviews. Only the expert and the witness should be present during the hypnosis, recording the subject's prehypnosis memories for the events in question before any procedures are used.

In the case before them, the New Jersey Supreme Court determined that Sell's trance-induced testimony had failed to follow these safeguards. Thus Paul Hurd's appeal succeeded. However, with clear guidelines in place, hypnosis had a better chance of being allowed in court. Still, while hypnosis can generate information helpful for an investigation, the memories it produces might be tenuous. Given the potential difficulties of hypnotic recall, courts that don't ban it outright usually adopt conservative measures, evaluating the probative value on a case-by-case basis. A guided interview seems to be a better bet, as long as there are witnesses or a videotape setup that will allow court personnel to evaluate it.

Witnesses usually want to tell what they remember, unless they have something to hide. In that case, interrogation techniques might work better.

INTERROGATION—

On *CM*, the agents who interview or interrogate people must understand different types of personalities and mental conditions to successfully get the responses they need. In "Soul Mates," Rossi and Morgan bring in a man once suspected in two rapes to question him for a series of abduction/murders of young girls in the local area, some black, some white. As they struggle to get him to admit his involvement, they look for leverage, but he's an attorney, so he's cagey enough to spot what they're doing and deftly sidestep them. They face one of the most difficult types of interrogation situations: a suspect who knows his rights, knows the techniques that police use, feels no remorse, and has no fear of repercussions.

More difficult is the interview that Gideon did in "Lessons Learned" with a terror suspect at Guantanamo Bay. He had to step carefully because the lives of people were at stake, watch the detainee's body language, and determine when he might be lying.

There is a difference between interviewing a person of interest and the outright interrogation of a suspect. Interviewing is used to acquire information to confirm or further develop leads, which requires establishing rapport, while interrogation aims toward extracting a confession. Torturing a suspect is illegal, and all suspects are made aware that they have the right to say nothing at all. However, psychological pressure and deception are allowed, and sometimes this involves moderate sleep deprivation or solitary confinement. Some countries employ truth-producing drugs.

One of the most used, albeit controversial, approaches for interrogation is the Reid technique, which develops via a series of calculated manipulations. Prohibited in some countries on vulnerable populations, the technique has three components: factual, interviewing, and interrogation. Relying on what the investigation has turned up from a crime or crime scene (factual), investigators begin with a nonaccusatory interview to elicit more information and observe a suspect's behavior. They might ask questions designed to provoke certain behaviors as a baseline for detective deception. Typically, the questioner's demeanor is compassionate and understanding, designed to seem sympathetic. However, leading questions are embedded in the interview to try to get a guilty person to start the process of confession.

The interrogation stage, relying on moral justification, involves nine distinct steps. Interrogators directly confront suspects with an assertion of guilt, keeping up a monologue as they develop a theme that excuses the crime. At all times, they interrupt the suspect's effort to deny guilt and use whatever they can to overcome objections to what the interrogator is doing or saying. They try to prevent a passive suspect from withdrawing into silence or refusal, and this might involve a false show of sympathy and understanding, or even a face-saving alternative ("We know you didn't mean to do it"). It might also involve intimidation or outright lies ("We have a witness who places you at the scene"), as well as an appeal to their best interest. However, interrogators are not allowed to threaten harm, promise leniency, use brutality, or continue with the questioning after the suspect has exercised the right to remain silent or see an attorney. (Healthcare serial killer Harold Shipman actually turned his chair around to demonstrate his refusal to participate in the process, and although the investigator continued to ask him questions, the interview went nowhere.)

Any admissions the subject makes are used to set up a choice between two incriminating alternatives, or a set of alternatives that would likely pressure the suspect into accepting his or her guilt: "Either your grandmother killed your sister, or you did." Essentially, the guilty person is steadily backed into a corner wherein the only way out is to give interrogators what they want. If there is more than one suspect, interrogators might try to play them off each other, scaring or enticing each into taking the deal first by turning on the other. The thrust of this technique is to get the suspect to admit to details of the crime and then to convert the oral statement into a written and signed confession.

Psychopaths are insensitive to altruistic interview themes, such as sympathy for their victims or guilt over their crimes, so interrogating them calls for different measures. Instead of guilt, their inherent narcissism, selfishness, and vanity can often be exploited by praising their intelligence or assuring them of attention and even fame.

Problems do arise from the firm presumption of guilt that grounds each session, because it can create tunnel vision about other options or suspects and make the sessions so unrelenting that an innocent person could capitulate to the pressure.

Thus a negative result of interrogation techniques is a false confession, or admitting to a crime that one did not commit. Some false confessions are voluntary, others coerced. A coerced confession is usually offered when the person is exhausted, naive, frightened, or mentally impaired. On rare occasions, a suspect might even internalize the incident and come to believe that he or she committed a crime. That occurs when an interrogator seems confident of the suspect's guilt and uses several forms of manipulation over a period of time. The characteristics of those most likely to falsely confess include youth, low IQ, mental instability, a high degree of suggestibility, a trusting nature, low self-esteem, or high anxiety.

Twelve-year-old Stephanie Crowe was murdered on January 21, 1998, and prior to conducting a responsible investigation, the lead detectives quickly decided that the crime had been an inside job. Thus, they honed in on Stephanie's older brother, Michael, only fourteen, and subjected the stunned and frightened boy to rigorous and deceptive interrogation until he finally surrendered and admitted he'd killed his sister. He even came to believe it, providing a motive and implicating two friends. One of them offered a lengthy false confession. Yet just before the trial, Stephanie's blood was found on the clothing of a mentally ill transient, Richard Tuite, who had been in the area that evening, last seen next door to the Crowe residence near Stephanie's estimated time of death. He was eventually convicted, but the bungled investigation had devastated the lives of three young men and their families.

Psychologist Saul Kassim is among those who have studied the phenomenon of false confession, and he has described the "compulsive type—attention seeker," or the person who uses confessions to gain notoriety, impress others, or get attention. Given the prominence of the BAU, the agents must be wary of such motives when they interview a suspect, especially an incarcerated felon with things to gain and nothing to lose.

The most infamous of these false confessors was Henry Lee Lucas, a one-eyed drifter arrested in 1983 in Texas. Picked up on an illegal weapons charge, he shocked the courtroom by confessing to two murders and then said that he'd killed more than 100 around the country. He included Ottis Toole as his partner in crime, and together they confessed to numerous murders in many states—around 360. However, when an enterprising reporter caught Lucas in several lies in 1985, instigating better investigations, Lucas recanted everything. It became clear that many law enforcement professionals had actually fed him details as a way to close their open cases. Yet for a time, Lucas had enjoyed his status as the world's worst serial killer, especially because it got him better food, frequent outings, and plenty of notoriety. He had figured out how to milk details from eager investigators and offer them back as a "confession."

"I set out to break and corrupt any law enforcement officer I could get," Lucas said. "I think I did a pretty good job." In the end, he was convicted of eleven murders. The one for which he received the death penalty turned out to be impossible for him to have committed, so his sentence was commuted to life. He died in prison of natural causes.

An alternative to the Reid technique, which is gaining ground among law enforcement in several countries, is the PEACE model

(PEACE = planning and preparation, engage and explain, account, closure, evaluation). Although it appears to minimize false confessions, all interrogators are faced with one of the trickiest aspects of any type of negotiation: spotting a liar.

DECEPTION DETECTION—

From fraud to fabrication, deception can take many forms, and an important skill in forensic contexts is the ability to spot it. An offender might stage a crime scene, falsely accuse others, lie outright, or fake an illness. Despite some claims on TV, there is no simple formula for catching a liar. Even many people with repeated exposure to deception perform no better than chance, but they can improve their skills with solid observation and sophisticated techniques. Let's review some currently in use:

BODY LANGUAGE—

A popular notion is that lying requires more effort than truth telling, so it produces such physiological signals as a heightened pulse rate, dilated pupils, twitches, and certain facial expressions— especially when the stakes are high. However, truthful but anxious people may also display such symptoms, while lying psychopaths may not. In fact, watching the face can be highly unreliable.

The trick to accuracy is to question people of interest long enough to observe their default behaviors. People who feel anxious usually either freeze or defend themselves, thus displaying behaviors of discomfort. Although there are no hard-and-fast rules, the types of behaviors that can signal discomfort, and thus potential deception, include these:

- Language with more negative than positive statements, overgeneralizations, deflections, and increased vocal pitch.

- Speech hesitations and pauses, a lack of spontaneity, taking longer to respond to questions, appearing to plan what they will say, responses that seem too long or are irrelevant.

- An increase in number of shrugs, blinking, and nervous habits like stroking.

- Changes in the eye pupil.

- Increased leg and foot movements in response to specific themes.

- Venting the body, like pulling a shirt or collar away.

- Feet pointed toward an exit.

- Blanching, flushing, breath holding, sighing.

- Reduced use of hand gestures; lack of head movement.

None is definitive, but these behaviors occur more often in those with motivation to deceive—possibly because they are trying to plan and control what they say. Sometimes their deception will have a rehearsed quality, with the timing slightly off.

STATEMENT ANALYSIS–

Statement analysis is a common tool for interrogations and witness statements. An investigator asks an open-ended question, "What happened?" and leaves the person to fill in all the blanks in the form of a recorded oral or written statement. The subject picks the starting and ending point. Statement analysis focuses on several things: what's said about events leading up to a crime, the crime itself, and the aftermath. Investigators watch for the distribution of detail in each area and note whether subjects provide more information than requested or skip something crucial. Also, a change in tone or speed of delivery can reveal their comfort (or not) with what they're saying. Another clue is a change in language regarding another person or sensitivity about some item, which might be apparent in a shift from first to third person. Information that is left out, about which investigators know the individual has some knowledge, is a good source for follow-up questions.

A similar method called *criteria-based content analysis* closely examines how an incident is retold, comparing it against the typical method of recall in a truthful session versus fabricating a supposed recollection. Psychologist Aldert Vrij, of the University of Portsmouth in England, is among the leading figures in developing this method. Accordingly, analysts look for specific features of a narrative: coherent and consistent but not strictly chronological; detailed, with superfluous elements; reiterating dialogue and personal interactions, including feelings and theories about a perpetrator; and spontaneous corrections. In truth telling, people easily admit to memory gaps and wonder if they're recalling it correctly. Although useful, with an error rate of up to 30 percent, this method alone is unlikely to reveal a skillful liar, especially a pathological one who can easily add details.

Computer software known as *Linguistic Inquiry and Word Count* (LIWC) analyzes written content derived from the statement analysis approach and looks for three markers: fewer first-person pronouns, more words that convey negative emotion, and fewer exclusionary words (except, but). The software has been more effective than human judges, but the accuracy rate is still only about 67 percent.

PHYSIOLOGICAL MEASUREMENT DEVICES—

The polygraph in use today is a compact portable device that measures three or four key involuntary physiological responses to questioning: skin conductivity, abdominal and chest respiration, blood pressure, and heart rate. Some questions are designed to establish baseline responses, some are neutral, and others attempt to register "guilty knowledge," or at least a sense that the person knows something that confirms him or her as a suspect. While practitioners vouch for its accuracy and investigators rely on it to at least spook people into giving up information, research indicates that it falls short as a sure thing. In research, skin conductivity increases when subjects see or think about information they're trying to conceal, but in such experiments, the stakes are low because there are no real consequences.

Even less accurate is the Psychological Stress Evaluator (PSE), sometimes referred to as a voice stress evaluator. (It goes by other names as well, but relies on the same principle.) Advocates claim that the voice itself reveals deception, even if the subject is unaware of being evaluated. Supposedly, during a lie, the voice reaches a higher pitch than when someone is telling the truth. While the PSE does measure variations in emotional stress, that's not the same as detecting deception.

BRAIN ASSESSMENTS—

When a serial killer hits his head and wakes up four years later with amnesia on "Tabula Rosa," Reid proposes the use of "brain fingerprinting" to access the part of the killer's brain in which the memories are stored. Even if he's faking amnesia, supposedly he cannot "cheat" this test.

Psychiatrist Lawrence Farwell developed the brain fingerprinting process, based on the notion that all experiences, including a crime, are stored in the brain. The electrical activity of a suspect's brain is monitored via a headband equipped with sensors that are hooked up to a computer while the subject is exposed to words or images that are both relevant ("probes") and irrelevant to the crime. Certain information would be meaningful only to the actual perpetrator and would include such items as what was done to a victim, where the victim was taken, items that were removed from the victim, and items that might have been left at a scene. The subject would not see this list until the test itself was performed. Irrelevant stimuli might include a different type of weapon, the wrong landscape, a different MO, or acts not performed during the commission of the crime.

Probes are known only to the investigators, the test maker, and the perpetrator. If the brain activity shows recognition of relevant stimuli—a distinct spike called a MERMER (for memory and encoding-related multifacted electroencephalographic response)— then the subject has a record of the crime stored in his or her brain. Innocent people will display no such response to crime-relevant stimuli. To strengthen the results, Farwell might test the suspect's alibi for the time of the crime, by devising a scenario to test to see if the brain has a record.

This procedure is not about monitoring the truth; it's about neurological recognition. Suppose a crime scene occurred in a garage that contained a blue Honda Civic, a series of shelves, and an oil stain on the floor and the body was left on the floor near the rear of the car; all of this information can be used to set up the test. While the *CM* agents would not have been able to use it in court as they did on the show, brain fingerprinting has been successfully used to get a confession.

Sheriff Robert Dawson engaged Dr. Farwell to conduct a Brain Fingerprinting test on Missouri murder suspect James B. Grinder, in the hope of solving the murder of a young woman, Julie Helton. The test proved that the record stored in Grinder's brain matched the scene where the body was found. Faced with a conviction and probable death sentence, Grinder pled guilty in exchange for life in prison. He also confessed to the unsolved murders in Arkansas of three other young women.

Whether this technique is as accurate as Farwell claims has yet to be established by independent researchers. In fact, on "Tabula Rasa," it doesn't work, despite the killer's memories eventually returning. However, brain scans appear to be in our near future for use in court.

At the University of Texas Southwestern Medical Center, functional magnetic resonance imaging (fMRI) scans are used to detect differences in neural activity between lying and truth telling. In the experiments, subjects were paid to perform a "theft" of one of two items (either a ring or a watch) and conceal information from the researchers. First, each was asked neutral questions while being scanned as well as questions about minor wrongful deeds commonly committed. This way, the researchers could identify typical neurological patterns during truthful responses. Then each subject responded to questions in a way that was truthful about an object he or she did not steal, but was deceptive about the stolen object. The rate of accuracy for the fMRI was around 90 percent. Apparently, the trick lies in scanning brain regions that activate to suppress information and resolve internal conflicts; these regions are quiet when the person is telling the truth. (Other researchers using similar techniques achieved less impressive results.)

Similarly, researchers at the Max Planck Institute for Human Cognitive and Brain Sciences in Leipzig, Germany had subjects make decisions about adding or subtracting numbers before the numbers were shown on a computer screen. Bursts of activity in the prefrontal cortex (thought signatures) signaled what the results would be. While the setup is simplistic, more disturbing possibilities are on the horizon. Scientists might one day be able to tell, without consent, what a person is thinking or feeling, including the intent to deceive.

It's clear that the frontal lobe activates when someone wishes to conceal information, as if additional brain resources were needed. However, whether these responses are exclusive to deception is not yet known. There is as yet no one size fits all signal in the neurocircuitry to indicate a person is lying, but it does appear that brain scans are better at revealing tells than is watching someone fidget and sweat under questioning. Identifying the right combination of brain signals for a high rate of accuracy when a person lies or hides the truth is still in the future, but possibly not far away.

OBJECTIVE ASSESSMENTS—

Certain psychological tests can pick up a specific type of deception: feigning a mental illness, or malingering. The Minnesota Multiphasic Personality Inventory (MMPI-2), which picks up "faking bad" and "faking good," and the Structured Interview of Reported Symptoms (SIRS) specifically detect malingering. However, these sessions require a clinical psychologist for administration and interpretation. We'll revisit this topic later.

Some researchers believe that certain people with high levels of emotional intelligence have a knack for spotting a liar; in fact, they can see certain signals that others cannot. Paul Ekman from the University of California San Francisco and Maureen O'Sullivan at the University of San Francisco float the notion that a few rare people are "naturals"—that is, they are highly accurate at knowing when someone is trying to deceive them. (In fact, these researchers and their colleagues have become consultants for another television series that focuses on such elite lie detectors, and they train interviewers in many types of security positions.) Often, these lie detectors have jobs for which it's an important skill, such as law enforcement or psychotherapy. When the stakes are high, such as with a violent crime or a threat assessment, they're even better at it because they're more vigilant.

Decades ago, Ekman pioneered a technique called the Facial Action Coding System (FACS), which he is in the process of automating for law enforcement. He claims an accuracy rate of 90 percent when combined with measurements for voice stress and speech factors. He believes the best cues are found in the voice and face for deception about feelings and locates the best "hot spots" in gestures and words when a person lies about beliefs and actions. Extremely slight gestures can leak emotional states that a person is trying to hide, providing a "tell" to a skilled and observant detector.

However, other research contradicts the notion that certain select people are human diving rods. Psychologists Charles Bond Jr. and Bella DePaulo ran a large-scale study and found that lie detection is not about the observer but the observee. A person's perceived credibility plays a strong role in whether someone judges him or her to be deceptive. That's not necessarily because a person is honest; it's because they comport themselves in a credible manner. These people appear to be honest right from the start, affecting gut instinct, while others appear to be dishonest. Averting one's gaze or having a long or wide face, as opposed to a more innocent-looking baby face or charming smile, can count against someone's general presentation. (A girl who escaped a serial killer in South Korea claimed he was good-looking and seemed like a trustworthy man, so she got into his car.) Participants in the study more often believed liars with high credibility ratings than truth tellers who were perceived as low in credibility. When Bond and DePaul evaluated numerous other studies about deception, they realized that individual differences among judges of deception hovered near the same rate as chance (50 percent). No one appeared to have an innate advantage. No "naturals" stood out.

Some researchers think that liars take slightly longer to start answering questions or show a rehearsed quality, as if they'd already thought about what they might say when questioned. If they've planned well, they might actually jump in more quickly than a truth teller, because they have their act in a nice package. Yet they're generally more negative and say less than truth tellers. They'll also repeat phrases more often and appear to be trying to manage the interviewer's perception of them.

In the real world, lies are often identified in context, when compared over a period of time to other behaviors or narratives. The judgment generally involves a number of factors, not just a response to some questions at the time a lie is told.

Lies are one thing, but faking a mental disorder is another, and when negotiators must deal with someone who appears emotionally unstable or to have a serious disorder, they must know how to spot malingering. In that case, they must be versed in psychological disorders and possess the skills necessary for dealing with both the real and the faked presentations.

WHOM DO WE TRUST?–

Among the most often malingered disorders is dissociative identity disorder (DID)—once called multiple personality disorder—and paranoid schizophrenia. Both are diagnosed in genuinely ill offenders, but many normal offenders with something to gain have learned how to act out the symptoms.

While DID is not considered a psychotic condition, it has been confused with schizophrenia as a split identity. With DID, two or more subpersonalities reportedly develop within a single human being (a host body), each with its own identity, and each takes turns controlling the personality and behavior. The "core" person generally experiences periods of memory loss (amnesic barrier) and might even "wake up" in a foreign place with no idea how he or she got there. One "person" may have full access to the memory bank, while others have only partial access.

Experts believe that people with genuine DID develop it from an early childhood trauma, such as sexual abuse or violent, erratic beatings. They learned to dissociate—to mentally remove themselves from the situation—and this psychological flight then becomes their survival mechanism, disturbing the normal integrative functions of identity. Some cases of polyfragmented DID have involved several hundred different identities.

A repressed memory may have sufficient energy to emerge in such symptoms as depression, sleep disorders, hypersensitivity, and reactions to certain environmental triggers. There may also be vague flashbacks, or the memory might return years after the incident. These people may "trance out," feel out of touch with reality, ignore genuine pain, and experience sudden panic attacks. They may also act out with eating disorders, abuse of others, self-abuse, or addictions. Generally, they have trouble with intimacy.

To confirm an alter personality, it's important to collect data from a variety of people who have seen evidence of it—friends, relatives, and co-workers. While alter personalities can be elicited through hypnosis, it's also possible to suggest them into existence. Malingerers tend to believe that this disorder involves a mere split personality. However, that's a mistaken notion. As popular as the idea is, DID is not about a good person and an evil person living in the same body. Even so, one notorious serial killer managed to fool a number of mental health professionals.

Kenneth Bianchi was arrested in the late 1970s, one of the "Hillside Stranglers" who had murdered nearly a dozen young women, but he quickly convinced his lawyer that he was suffering from amnesia. He'd seen the classic movies about multiple personalities, *The Three Faces of Eve* and *Sybil*, so he was ready for launching an insanity defense. He allowed a psychologist versed in multiple personality to believe he was under hypnosis and then "emerged" as his evil persona, "Steve Walker." It was Steve, he said, not Kenneth, who had killed those girls.

Yet sometimes when Bianchi was supposed to be "Steve," he referred to Steve in the third-person. The expert apparently didn't notice, but enraged detectives watching the procedure did. When several more psychologists bought the act, one detective decided to look into this "Steve Walker." He thought the alter's name sounded familiar, so he went through Bianchi's papers and found it: Steve Walker was a pseudonym that Bianchi had used to apply for a diploma—in fact, it was the name of another student from a college Bianchi had attended. The investigators gave this information to the prosecutor, who invited another mental health expert into the case. Dr. Martin Orne set a trap, telling Bianchi that it was rare to have only two personalities for MPD. He figured that now a third one would show up. Orne was right: Bianchi introduced him to "Billy." He also presented symptoms that were inconsistent with the diagnosis when he pretended to have visual hallucinations. So Bianchi overplayed it and was caught. Armed with this, the DA offered him a deal: roll on his cousin and escape the death sentence for himself. He admitted his ruse and took the deal.

Even the experts can be fooled, especially with conditions like dissociative identity disorder that are easy to fake and difficult to diagnose with certainty ("The Big Game"). To detect the malingering of psychiatric symptoms, one may look for an exaggerated presentation, inconsistent information, a strangely deliberate manner, an attempt to display obvious (and stereotypical) symptoms, and an inconsistency with the person's past psychiatric diagnoses. Clinicians might check the defendant's past history of psychiatric confinement (if any) and any statements from witnesses (friends, family, prison guards, hospital staff) as to a person's condition, current and past. They might also observe the subject in various settings over a period of time.

Malingerers make a point of getting people to pay attention to their illness, while most truly mentally ill people would rather not be so visible. (There are always exceptions.) If the person says the delusions or hallucinations were sudden, this is inconsistent with the clinical picture of mental illness, except for drug-induced psychosis. Defendants who have a hard time retaining the voice and personality of the alter they blame for their crime are also suspect, as are defendants who appear not to be confused by their criminal behavior.

Similar issues occur when offenders malinger schizophrenia, and many of the same techniques are used to detect a fraudulent presentation. Yet there are times when investigators have to deal with a real case, and this calls on a different set of skills—especially if there are hostages.

HOSTAGE NEGOTIATION—

On "Derailed," a psychotic man takes the passengers on a train hostage, a special agent from the BAU among them. This man demands that an imaginary microchip be removed from his arm and insists on talking to God. To perform a safe rescue, the team must learn about all of the hostages, including the patient's therapist, who believed the man was cured.

This raises the issue of dealing with psychotic individuals who may not be able to listen to reason, because their sense of reality is warped, and their fear or anger can be intense. Extreme mental illness involves bizarre and disturbed emotions, behaviors, thoughts, and beliefs that may interfere with a person's ability to function in work and relationships. In severe forms, it can make people dangerous to others and/or themselves. Psychiatry has categorized the types of mental illnesses in various texts, notably the *International Classification of Diseases* and the *Diagnostic and Statistical Manual of Mental Disorders* (DSM-IV).

Psychotic individuals are generally classified according to the first axis of the DSM-IV, in categories such as schizophrenia, bipolar disorder, extreme anxiety, and other conditions that involve transient or substance-related psychoses. The most prevalent of the psychotic disorders, schizophrenia, is marked by a confusion of thinking and speech that is at times chronic. It occurs equally in men and women, and generally appears between the ages of fifteen and thirty-five. There appears to be a significant genetic component, in that a person may inherit a tendency toward it that can be triggered by an outside stressor.

Schizophrenia often causes sufferers to retreat into delusions and fantasies that disturb their relationship with reality. Research evidence suggests that the cause of schizophrenia is either a chemical or structural abnormality of the brain. The most common form in violent individuals, which involves command hallucinations and the sense of bodily invasion, is paranoid schizophrenia.

A profile of a disorganized offender may include suggested procedures for how to interrogate such suspects once arrested, and information on how the individual may respond to certain types of questions is included. If confrontation seems merited, then the recommendation is made. If not, then another approach is suggested. If the offender's identity is known, but he or she has not been arrested or is holding hostages, a negotiator is used.

On December 14, 1994, in Albany, New York, twenty-six-year-old Ralph Totorici responded to the "voice of God" commanding him to take a college classroom hostage at the State University of New York. He put a hunting knife and high-powered rifle under his coat before he tied the doors to the classroom shut and announced to the students in a history class that he was taking them hostage. He ordered them to gather against the wall on the other side of the classroom. He then instructed the professor to go get congressional representatives and reporters, because he had a microchip planted inside his penis by government agents. He wanted to see the President about getting it removed. Negotiators arrived and used the PA system to try to talk with Tortorici, but they failed to persuade him to let anyone go. He was determined to see the President. Although he insisted no one would get hurt, one student rushed him and got wounded in the process. Tortorici was arrested, tried, and convicted in a controversial proceeding that seemed to ignore the extent of his psychosis. He later hanged himself in his cell to get relief from the voices that tormented him. He'd repeatedly said about the hostage situation, "I did what I had to do."

When a desperate person uses innocent people as bargaining chips with law enforcement, it becomes a hostage situation that requires a specific set of skills. The first concern is to ensure everyone's safety, so it's important to keep people calm and keep the hostage-taker talking. The negotiator is responsible for freeing the hostages without loss of life, while making an arrest falls to police officers.

If possible, communications with the hostage-taker begin with a set of parameters on which both parties agree. The negotiator listens to the demands and assures the hostage-taker that he (or she) is being taken seriously. At the same time, the negotiator must stay in touch with any efforts from law enforcement to disarm the hostage-taker, and must be in position to gather all pertinent information.

The negotiator must find out the number of hostages and their current condition as well as the name of the hostage-taker. They must also try to discern what the person might really want, apart from the articulated demands, and to determine his emotional state as well as the possibility of substance abuse. In addition, they're aware that hostage-takers will exercise care to avoid being deceived or baited, so negotiators must work to gain his trust.

The operative thing is to listen and refrain from arguing or dissuading the hostage-taker from whatever position he holds or beliefs he espouses. It's important that negotiators be convincing and appear to genuinely care and understand. Once trust is gained, they can begin to assert authority, which might help to free one or more of the hostages. While managing stress, negotiators will try to bring the situation to a conclusion. If hostages need food or medical help, this has to be done with urgency. It's possible to wear down the hostage-taker by keeping him talking as well as to appeal to his human side by asking for a gesture of goodwill—release of hostages in exchange for things like food and water.

However, sometimes situations get far more dangerous than anyone wished.

Reid and Prentiss are taken hostage on "Minimal Loss," when they go undercover to investigate allegations of child abuse in a cult. This episode was clearly based on an infamous incident in American history.

On February 28, 1993, agents from the Bureau of Alcohol, Tobacco, and Firearms (ATF) moved on the Mount Carmel Center outside the Texas town of Waco. The place was occupied by members of an apocalyptic religious group led by David Koresh, who was being investigated for the sexual abuse of minors. Rumored to be stockpiled inside the compound were explosives and illegal weapons, so the ATF took over. The agency first sent in undercover operatives to check it out, and then deployed a "secret" attack, but the Davidians had spotted the operatives, guessed what was about to occur, and were thus armed and ready. Someone fired a shot, and the gun battle commenced.

The skirmish continued for two hours before a truce was called, allowing the ATF to remove their dead and wounded. Twenty agents had been hit, and four of them died. Agents then arranged to communicate with Koresh, but he refused to give himself up. This was the day for which he and his apocalyptic group had been preparing—the government's "inevitable" attack. Former members advised the ATF that a siege could trigger a mass murder/suicide of the 100-plus people inside.

The ATF was soon reinforced with local police officers, Texas Rangers, members of the FBI's Hostage Rescue Team (HRT), the FBI's Special Agent in Charge from the San Antonio office, a bomb squad, and several U.S. Marshals. Throughout the standoff, FBI negotiators insisted that tactical behavior only fulfilled Koresh's prophecy, while HRT personnel believed that encroaching on his territory weakened him in the eyes of his followers. A psychological consultant was convinced that Koresh himself would never surrender.

Koresh released fourteen children, and claimed he'd been wounded. Negotiations went back and forth for days, with nothing resolved. A few more people emerged.

The siege lasted fifty-one days, as the negotiators tried to resolve things peacefully and save the largest number of people possible. Promises and threats were exchanged, and Koresh practiced several delaying tactics. Just after dawn on Monday morning, April 19, the FBI warned that they were going to use tear gas. Three minutes later, two Combat Engineering Vehicles sprayed gas into the compound.

Abruptly, the Davidians opened fire. Several hours went by as the standoff continued, but just after noon the buildings erupted in flames. Agents heard gunfire and they assumed that the people inside had decided on mass suicide. By the end of that day, more than eighty people were found dead, twenty-three of them children under seventeen. Koresh's body was later identified by dental records. He'd been shot in the head. Many of the victims had died from gunshot wounds. Over one hundred firearms were eventually recovered from the scene.

It's not always possible to deal with someone who believes that any and all officials are corrupt and who sees a confrontation as the beginning of the end. Yet negotiations don't just include a hostage-taker. Sometimes they include a hostage who's been deeply affected by the captivity.

In "Bloodlines," the agents must deal with an unsub who has Stockholm syndrome in order to get her to give up the location of her son and an abducted girl. She herself was abducted as a child but is now married to her abductor and has been brainwashed into thinking she wants to commit criminal acts with him.

Stockholm syndrome occurs under the unusual conditions of extreme stress in captivity, where there may be torture and unrelenting uncertainty. Kidnapping victims, abused spouses, and tortured prisoners are most prone to developing it. After a while, the captive appears to become involved to some degree with his or her captor, and even to consent to abuse and captivity. That person may express feelings of affection in a way that surprises outsiders and makes them wonder just how captive and abused the person really is.

What appears to occur, according to those experts who have studied the phenomenon, is that the person "freezes" as a way to avoid further torture and then yields to try to appease the captor. If the captor then takes care of basic needs, the captive may feel gratitude bordering on affection and even the propensity to hear the captor's tale. Such victims become susceptible to suggestion, and having their own world shrink to that shared with the captor may make them sympathetic. Identifying with the captor and seeing no way to escape, victims find it easier to acquiesce, even to the point of acting as if they love their captors. They are trying to arrange their otherwise unsafe and difficult world for maximum comfort and safety.

It doesn't help negotiators that so many people are now exposed to what's known as "serial killer culture," which involves media renditions of investigations and a lot of attention to serial killers. Superficial notions, erroneous claims, hoaxes, and simplistic stereotypes abound, and inevitably, the agents on *CM* must confront the issue. Some even contribute to it. Let's see how.

NINE

The Mass Market
—and the Culture of Serial Murder—

We have to appreciate that the famous serial killer effectively and economically satisfies a double need . . . the need for representations of death and the need for celebrities.

—DAVID SCHMID, *NATURAL BORN CELEBRITIES*

Near the Duomo in Florence, Italy, the Museo Criminale displays wax replicas of offenders such as Ted Bundy, Andrei Chikatilo, and Elizabeth Bathory. Their taped stories are recounted to museum-goers via headphones, and in some cases their former residences are on display. The living room where John Wayne Gacy had hand-cuffed his victims before raping and strangling them is re-created, and his replica is wearing the clown suit he'd donned to entertain sick children. The victim toll for each killer is listed and compared to others, as is the MO. Profiling is on display as well, among the diverse methods used to catch these killers. One reviewer called this place both "disgusting" and "the most entertaining venue in the city."

Criminal Minds sometimes refers to items from the culture at large that encourage fascination with serial killers. In "The Angel-Maker," the agents discuss copycats and serial killer groupies—

people who become so obsessed with these offenders, they want to marry them or emulate them in some manner. To get close, they collect items the killer touched or artwork depicting the killer, known as "murderabilia." Anyone who investigates serial killers must know about this subculture because some unsubs got their start as fans of serial killers, and some killers have actually communicated with their incarcerated hero figures. One man falsely posted information on the Internet claiming responsibility for sixteen murders and naming a specific missing woman as one of them. He called himself the "catchmekiller" and offered people who came to his website a game that would reveal clues for locating the bodies. The police were not amused. In addition, some victims have been serial killer groupies.

The episode "Zoe's Reprise" addresses this cultural phenomenon in several ways. Rossi is out promoting his profiler books when a fan accosts him with her ideas about linking a suspicious series of deaths in Cleveland. The killer copies famous serial killers from the past (like killer Jimmy Rode using Ted Bundy's advice), and after he's caught, he says he's a fan of Rossi's work and hopes to be included in a future book. Rossi wonders aloud whether his books are doing more harm than good.

COLLECTORS–

Relatives of victims are horrified that some people think it's "fun" to own a Jeffrey Dahmer doll with dismembered human parts in its belly, Jack the Ripper trading cards, or Ed Gein aprons for cooking, but there's no end in sight for such grisly commercial ventures. In addition, in states with no prohibitive Son of Sam law, the killers themselves can launch commercial ventures. One could argue that some convicted offenders can look forward to a life of notoriety, even profit.

Massachusetts grappled with this issue in November 2005 when four-time sex-killer Alfred Gaynor's pencil sketch of Jesus Christ kneeling by a rock showed up on an online auction. The public demanded it be removed, but entrepreneurs have spotted the market value in America's fascination with murder, which has been a cultural pastime for well over a century. In Chicago in 1892, after the public learned about the "murder castle" that H. H. Holmes, a.k.a., Herman Mudgett, had built to house and murder young women, an enterprising police officer named Clark acquired the lease and sold entrance fees (15¢). But the place soon burned to the ground. Shrewd entrepreneurs have always sold grizzly souvenirs because as disgusted as people might be by depravity and murder, they're also fascinated. And they'll pay money for associated items, from a killer's clipped toenails to books and films.

Imprisoned killers have time on their hands. Whether or not they have talent, they acquire eager agents and collectors. Julian P. Hobbes made the documentary *Collectors* to depict people obsessed with the many elements of serial killer culture. He focused on Louisiana mortician Rick Staton and his business partner, Tobias Allen. These two went around the country together to various famous murder sites to collect items for sale. Staton also encourages incarcerated serial killers to give him their artwork to sell in his "Death Row Art Shows," acquiring pieces from the likes of Richard Speck, Ottis Toole, Henry Lee Lucas, John Wayne Gacy, Charles Manson, and Elmer Wayne Henley. (Gacy even gave Staton a painting of Staton's young son.) Allen created a serial killer board game that comes in a miniature body bag. The object in this game is to kill the most babies (game pieces) to become the "best" serial killer. Banned in Canada, it turned out not to be such a hot commodity. More interesting, perhaps, is a board game called Ripperopoly, although it's now difficult to locate.

Speaking of games, Reality Television decided to introduce a game modeled on movies like *Saw* and *Friday the 13th*. First broadcast early in 2009, *13: Fear Is Real* featured thirteen people who compete to stay alive "as they face down their worst fears." They must endure terror and horror, designed by a mastermind "killer," who is one of them. Each week, a "victim" is "killed" until one "survivor" is left to claim the prize—$66,666. A CBS series *Harper's Island* offered a similar venue, with each character representing a type: the good girl, the flirt, the outsider. Live online chats and other multimedia features accompanied the show and episode titles, such as "Sploosh" and "Seep," referred to the way each victim would die.

Back to the art shows. John Wayne Gacy reportedly made over $100,000 from his paintings, which featured anything from Disney's seven dwarves to other killers to himself in a clown outfit. After he was executed in 1994, his death enhanced the value of his art to collectors. (However, one collector, proud to own Gacy's self-portrait in a clown outfit, eventually sold it at a loss because he believed it was causing him bad luck.)

It's not difficult for the most violent offenders to find buyers, because, after all, they've become celebrities. They receive plenty of publicity. Gerard Schaefer, convicted of two 1970s murders and suspected in thirty-four others, published a collection of gruesomely illustrated short stories before he died. Charles Ng, formerly partnered with Leonard Lake to torture numerous people to death, has sold his hand-crafted origami. Lawrence Bittaker once offered greeting cards, and Charles Manson used string from his socks to make finger puppets. Infamous celebrity killers like Richard Ramirez, the Los Angeles Night Stalker, have maintained their reputations by drawing devils, dismemberments, and gory stabbings. Even back in the 1960s, Albert DeSalvo, the supposed Boston Strangler, made and sold choker necklaces for profit.

It's possible that the profilers are somewhat responsible for this fan-demonium. During the late 1970s, Thomas Harris watched the BSU at work before he penned *Red Dragon* (1981) and *The Silence of the Lambs* (1988). As mentioned earlier, both were made into movies. BSU chief Roger Depue was supposedly the model for Jack Crawford in *The Silence of the Lambs*, although some sources indicate that it was Robert Ressler, while others say it was John Douglas. Harris spent time with all of them, as did the movie crew. Douglas describes in *Mind Hunter* how he showed Scott Glenn, the actor playing Crawford, some crime scene photos as a way for him to understand what the life of an FBI profiler was really like.

The book and film of *The Silence of the Lambs* gave the erroneous impression that young recruits can become profilers and that female agents might be left alone with dangerous killers. The edginess in this story won a lot of interest for the unit, and plenty of kids now wanted to be "mind hunters," tracking notorious serial killers.

In the midst of all of this, several of the first-generation profilers had retired from the FBI and began to publish books. They became stars, and thanks to the media's rush to cover the unit's work, profiling gained a more magical aura than it deserved. So did serial killers.

During the 1980s and 1990s, a number of repeat offenders made claims of outrageously high victim counts, agreeing to interviews and writing books to enhance their status. Larry Eyler, Donald Leroy Evans, Richard Bigenwald, Glen Rogers, Pee Wee Gaskins, and Paul John Knowles all said they'd killed many more people than police were able to link to them, while Joseph Fischer's numbers increased with each talk show appearance. The public was so fascinated with serial killers that people would believe anything they said. Yet in many cases, the numbers were exaggerated or entirely falsified.

When Internet auctions gained momentum, it wasn't long before there was a community of sellers and buyers for serial-killer items. Even Ed Gein's gravestone was stolen for profit. Prominent in this arena was eBay, until protesters forced it to revise its standards. Members of victims' rights groups signed a petition to the effect that the Internet's function as a network for millions of people could have a detrimental effect on society if no limitations were imposed on certain practices. The glorification of killers and the frenzy to purchase and own things that they'd touched, created, or grew (hair and fingernails) glamorized killers, thus rewarding them for what they'd done and possibly encouraging others toward violent ambitions.

In May 2001, eBay banned the sale of certain types of murderabilia. Most items found up for auction on this site that are associated with killers are manufactured trinkets and T-shirts. Some killers attempted to sell their wares via accomplices, and a few have been unmasked and punished. But there will always be a dark underground.

Among other items for sale on various websites are John Wayne Gacy's Bible, Doug Clark's driver's license and death certificate, bricks from Jeffrey Dahmer's now-defunct apartment building, a hatchet supposedly from Ed Gein's farm, Bobby Joe Long's sunglasses, recipes from self-professed cannibal Arthur Shawcross, and the refrigerator said to have stored parts of Dahmer's victims. At a serial killer traveling exhibition, you can supposedly see the truck that Gein once owned. (Many of these items are fake, but who's checking?)

There's no end of possibilities for killer kitsch. Interested parties can purchase paintings of Dorothy Puente or David Berkowitz, drink coffee from a mug featuring Ed Gein or Charles Manson, or enjoy a Night Stalker snow globe. Jack the Ripper has a whole line of accessories that feature bloody knives, T-shirts, action figures, throw pillows, baseball jerseys, caps, camisoles, thongs, aprons, tote bags, and even a teddy bear. Necropreneurs have made calendars with dates indicating murders or killers' birthdays and death days.

Then there are serial killer coloring books, with cartoonish drawings and games, such as a maze through which you can assist Gacy to find space in his dirt floor basement for another victim. There was also a 1992 comic book that depicted his sexual habits with victims. Online quizzes test trivia knowledge and determine what kind of serial killer a participant might be. In addition, Persona 4, a game for adolescents, offers players the chance to check into the Midnight Channel to investigate a serial killer who likes hanging kids upside down from telephone poles.

The Internet Movie Database (IMDb) lists everything from serial killer comedies, such as *Arsenic and Old Lace*, about a pair of elderly females, to various renditions of *Helter Skelter*. Several films are closely based on actual killers, such as John Christie, Keith Jesperson, Karla Homolka, Ted Bundy, Albert DeSalvo, and Andrei Chikatilo. Others simply play off the public's fascination with killers. In fact, the intelligent, clever serial killer is so overplayed now that critics complain when they see it in movies like *Saw* and its seemingly unending sequels.

Among the more intriguing films is *Kalifornia*, which features Brad Pitt and David Duchovny. It's about a journalist who drives cross-country with his girlfriend, a photographer, to document famous crime scenes. The "Kali" part of the title refers to the Indian goddess who demanded blood sacrifices. Pitt, as the killer, is convincing. A more gruesome depiction of people taking a violent jaunt is *Natural Born Killers*, which is a disguised commentary on the public's consummate and oblivious fascination with serial killers, and this movie has inspired several young couples to plot similar killing sprees.

Television shows, too, have serial killers showing up on everything from daytime soaps to HBO. The various crime series, such as the *C.S.I.*s and *Law and Order*, are natural venues for plots about such investigations. So are the hospital shows, and *Grey's Anatomy* jumped right in with a killer on death row requiring surgery. Usually, the killers are the bad guys—the foils against which detectives (and other types of investigators) can hone their skills. But one show has led the way into making them the good guys: *Dexter*. To make a serial killer into a likable hero suggests that this icon has lost (or may lose) its edge. Perhaps we may yet see a serial killer plush toy that talks when you pull a string.

Actor John Malkovich was so caught up with the Austrian serial killer Jack Unterweger (see Chapter 11), that he produced and starred in a stage play that debuted in Los Angeles before heading to Europe for a road show. Bill Connington scripted a one-man monologue for the stage based on Joyce Carol Oates's novel, *Zombie*, which was inspired by Jeffrey Dahmer.

Many novels about serial killers climb to the top of the best-seller charts, and some stay there a while. Notable are Erik Larsen's *The Devil in the White City*, about H. H. Holmes. In addition, *The Silence of the Lambs*, *American Psycho*, and *The Alienist* captured an enormous number of readers, with two becoming popular films.

But, while disturbing at times, it's often mundane fare. Collecting such items might even be a throwback to superstitious times when it was believed that owning something associated with a killer was a talisman that offered protection.

One reason serial killers prove to be so fascinating might be that evil-doers support our cultural myths and complete parts of ourselves while offering the illusion that they are separate from us. We then exploit that illusion to create frames in which we can act out a scenario of conquering the monster, without having to admit to our own capacity for evil.

Psychologist Michael Apter suggests that once something is labeled "dangerous," it exerts a magical attraction and that makes us feel alive. However, it may also make us anxious, so we develop "protective frames." That is, we develop narratives about the evildoer in which we mentally create a buffer of safety: The monster rises up, and we have the weapons to cage him or bring him down. Thus we experience the arousal of excitement without being overwhelmed by anxiety. Within the frame, we welcome risk, and we'll go to the edge to experience the exhilaration. We can actually enjoy danger and allow ourselves close.

More complex are the people who clamor to get close to serial killers, even marry them.

GROUPIES—

Ted Bundy came to represent the epitome of the handsome and charming serial killer. Caught in 1978 after a quick succession of murders in Florida, he admitted to a number of other vicious crimes dating back to 1974 in the Pacific Northwest—to the tune of more than thirty.

Bundy would use his charm to pretend to be in need, asking attractive young women for help to get them close to his Volkswagen Beetle. Then he would overcome them and kill them, often returning to their bodies later for necrophilic acts. He moved on to Utah and Colorado, where he was caught and identified by a woman who got away. It turned out that Ted Bundy was a former law student who had worked in a crisis center.

While awaiting trial for these crimes, Bundy escaped and made his way across the country to Tallahassee, Florida. On January 15, 1978, he attacked and killed Lisa Levy and Martha Bowman in their sorority house at Florida State University. Less than a month later, he abducted twelve-year-old Kimberly Leach from her school and killed her in the woods. Then he was caught for good.

Bundy received a great deal of media attention and, with it, plenty of fan mail from adoring women. In *The Stranger Beside Me*, author Ann Rule (a former friend of Bundy's) noted that some of these women were frightened of Bundy even as they viewed him in the most romantic light. A few firmly believed that he was innocent of the charges, and during his trial they crowded the front rows of the courtroom to show their support. Many of them looked like his victim type—girls with long brown hair, parted in the middle. Some even dyed their hair brown to get his attention. From among these women, Carol Ann Boone became his steady girlfriend.

Boone believed in Bundy's innocence and took every opportunity to describe how he was being unfairly railroaded. She moved to Florida to be near him and offer her complete support. Even after he was convicted, she maintained her stance, and during the penalty phase of his 1980 trial, she testified on his behalf. Bundy took advantage of an old law in that state that allowed a declaration in court to constitute a legal marriage. He stood up and proposed. Boone accepted, and Bundy pronounced them married. She also had a child with him but eventually came to believe he was guilty, and she took her child and moved away.

Some people define serial killer groupies in narrow terms, such as women who fall in love with killers who've been caught and are awaiting trial or who are in prison. Other definitions include anyone, male or female, who shows some obsession with serial killers, to the point of extreme emotional attachment. It's not always clear whether the phrase *serial killer groupie* refers to people who just love the idea of a serial killer and would be aroused by any sort of contact or more strictly to those who have become attached to a specific killer in a romantic relationship.

In any event, serial killers prove to be magnets for some people, mostly (but not always) females. Experts who have taken the time to learn about them rather than just dismissing them as needy losers, have offered a variety of reasons for loving men who kill.

Some groupies have "rescue fantasies," in which they want to believe they have the ability to change someone as cruel and powerful as a serial killer, or they might find their need to nurture met, as they "see" the little boy the killer once was. More understandable, perhaps, at least for women who've been abused, is the notion of the "perfect boyfriend": She knows where he is at all times, and while she can now claim that someone loves her, she does not have to endure the day-to-day issues of most relationships; she can keep the fantasy charged up for a long time but not cook or clean for someone or have to report in. She's free to do as she pleases, but she's got someone to love.

The association with notoriety cannot be downplayed. Some women want celebrity status, and their attachment to a killer gains them media exposure—even if there is some dubious quality to it. They go on talk shows to proclaim their love, or they like being interviewed and allowed the chance to insist that the convicted murderer got a raw deal, was not capable of those crimes, or is different now. They may even take credit for reforming him, as if their love were all he needed, the magical ingredient. They also get to participate in the drama of a trial and the appeals process—and perhaps even the execution.

When police questioned Michael Ross in connection with a murder in Connecticut, he confessed. Later Ross added other murders he'd committed, telling police about attacking young women in several states, since 1983.

Ross presents an unusual background for a serial killer. Born in 1959, he grew up to become an Ivy League graduate with substantial ambitions. He excelled in school and went on to study agricultural economics at Cornell University. With an IQ of 122, he planned one day to own his own farm. No loner, he was socially active, joining clubs and having several girlfriends. He even got engaged, but in secret, he was spinning violent sexual fantasies that resulted in stalking and then rape, especially after the engagement ended. Just before he graduated he committed his first fatal sexual assault. Thereafter he continued to rape and murder, sometimes two girls at once.

In July 1987, Ross went on trial for the murders of Deborah Taylor and Tammy Williams. He pled guilty and received a sentence of 120 years. Then he was found guilty in four other murders and received two life sentences and six death sentences. He decided to give closure to the families and himself by volunteering to skip the appeals and be executed. It was a controversial decision that necessitated a competency evaluation. The process took about four years, with Ross changing his mind several times, but in 2004 he stopped all appeals and accepted the sentence. Then a female correspondent begged Ross to reconsider, promising to marry him if he would elect to live. The newspapers were full of their romantic exchanges, and many people wondered if Ross would reconsider. It was the first time that news accounts of a serial killer's last days took on a soap opera quality. But Ross opted for death. On May 13, 2005, Michael Ross was executed.

Some women are sexually excited by violence—known as hybristophilia—or become enamored of the exclusivity of their position: There's a real sense of ownership of the facts about the killers among those who feel intimately associated with them.

In addition, low self-esteem can be a factor: Some women believe they cannot find a man and because men in prison are desperately lonely, it's an easy way to get romantically involved. In fact, if the killer gets a lot of press, these women evolve from nobodies into somebodies. They align themselves against the world in a heated defense of their beloved, which conveys a sense of purpose.

And, finally, we have the Beauty and the Beast syndrome. Some groupies like the idea of getting close to a dangerous alpha-male who will probably not hurt them, but there's always the slight chance. Ironically, in their minds, he appears to be a good protector. That is, they may equate this sort of violence with masculine strength and then seek it as a way to bring such a male into their lives, for protection and for producing hardy offspring. Thus they're responding to a biological drive of which they may not even be aware.

"In a twisted kind of way," says Elliott Leyton in *Hunting Humans*, "the male who is the most strong and dominant—the most violent—will appear to be the most male." The fascination among females with multiple murders that Leyton had witnessed struck him as the most excessive he'd ever seen.

Many serial killer groupies are educated and attractive. Some have money and some are already married. Quite a few are mothers, and it's often been the case that many have worked in some field related to law enforcement or rehabilitation, such as psychology or criminology. Such women devote themselves entirely to the man and make significant sacrifices, sometimes sitting for hours every week to await the brief face-to-face visit in prison. They may give up jobs or families to be near their true love, and they will most certainly be spending money on him—perhaps all they have. A few even go into debt. When the men are merely using them, which happens often, they fail to recognize it. (In some cases, a groupie has used money or influence to free her soul mate, only to be murdered, exploited, or abused by him.)

And the man doesn't have to be attractive to attract groupies. Henry Lee Lucas, a one-eyed serial killer who'd confessed to over three hundred murders, recanted, and confessed again, has had his share of female admirers. Despite his apparent sexual relationship with Ottis Toole, he was still compelling as a potential mate. (One woman even came up with a plot to free him by posing as his supposedly murdered former girlfriend—a girl that Lucas had strangled and cut into pieces.) Overweight, narcissistic and whiney, John

Wayne Gacy, killer of thirty-three young men during homosexual encounters, married in prison as well.

One of the most astounding stories about groupies began in the summer of 1984, when a seventy-nine-year-old woman was slain in her home near Los Angeles, California. Her throat was slashed, and she was stabbed several times. She was the first of a long line of victims; within eight months two more murders bore similarities, and then two young girls were abducted, raped, and dropped off in another location. More fatal assaults ensued, and police got the description of a smelly young man dressed in black with longish hair and bad teeth. In one incident, this killer removed a victim's eyes and took them with him. In another, he beat two elderly sisters and left satanic symbols on the thigh of one. Called the Night Stalker for his penchant for climbing into unlocked windows, by August 1985 the unsub was credited with some fourteen murders.

Then he killed a man, raped his fiancé, and escaped in a stolen car. When he later abandoned the car, police got a fingerprint. Thus they learned who he was: Richard Ramirez, a drug user and Satanist, whose favorite song was "Night Prowler." His picture was widely publicized, and when he tried to steal a car on August 30, a group of citizens in East Los Angeles recognized and grabbed him. He was ultimately charged with thirteen murders and thirty other criminal counts, including attempted murder, rape, and burglary.

It wasn't long before he attracted a collection of supporters, mostly female. As he awaited his trial, he received letters and visits from admirers, including the daughter of Anton LaVey, founder of the Church of Satan. A great many women wanted Ramirez's attention. Never before had he had so many female admirers, and lines soon formed to visit with him. While some claimed to believe in his innocence, others just thought he was cute or sexy.

Among them was Doreen Lioy, a freelance magazine editor with a BA in English literature. She'd seen Ramirez's picture and indicated in later interviews that she'd fallen madly in love. Sensing that he needed a friend, she wrote to him. He responded, and she soon became his primary advocate, insisting to anyone who listened that Ramirez could not have done the things he was accused of. She reportedly wrote seventy-five letters to him before she ever met him, and once they were face to face, Lioy felt the firm confirmation of their bond. For his part, Ramirez was pleased to have such a devoted spokesperson.

She sat through every day of the trial, decrying its unfairness to the press. She purchased clothing for Ramirez to wear and jealously watched other women who showed up. In the meantime, another woman was cutting in on her action, and this one had Ramirez's full attention. Cindy Haden was an alternate juror, and she, too, appeared to have fallen in love. She'd told others that she had an important destiny in Los Angeles, and her role on this jury was definitely pivotal. She had the power to hang the jury or derail the death penalty, especially when Ramirez's attorney had a primary juror dismissed. She accepted her new role with visible excitement, and Ramirez kept his eye on her. He hadn't failed to notice how she watched him and he may have believed he could manipulate that fascination toward his advantage. On Valentine's Day, Haden sent Ramirez a cupcake with a message, "I love you," on it. He took this as a sign that she'd vote in his favor.

However, not only was he convicted but he was also given the death penalty. When the verdict was read, Haden made a gesture to Ramirez that indicated she'd had no choice but felt badly. When he returned to his cell, Haden requested to see him, so he invited her to do so. There, she told him she loved him. Then she brought her parents to meet him. She became his new advocate, going on talk shows to insist that the Night Stalker had been poorly represented. She sometimes expressed the wish that she'd resisted the other jurors longer and caused a hung jury. In her opinion, Satan had possessed Ramirez and his lawyers were remiss in not raising this issue.

But despite Haden's devotion, Lioy remained in the picture. Finally, she persuaded Ramirez to marry her, and on October 3, 1996, Lioy became Mrs. Richard Ramirez. She accepted that she'd be a virgin for life, and never a mother, but she had Ramirez, and that's what mattered to her. She still believed in his innocence and continued to give interviews about how funny and kind he was. "I just believe in him completely," she insisted.

It's rare that any notorious serial killer will fail to attract a dedicated groupie, but Ken Bianchi (see Chapters 4 and 8) did much more; he inspired a rather extraordinary act on his behalf. When the trial commenced in 1982 for his partner-in-crime, Angelo Buono, a female prisoner took the stand for the defense. The story she told was stunning. Bianchi had already tried faking out the court with a case of multiple personality disorder, but failing that, he'd persuaded someone to stage a murder to make him appear innocent of the murder charges he faced.

Recall that in Bellingham, Washington, college roommates Diane Wilder and Karen Mandic were found murdered. Bianchi's idea was to send his devoted groupie Veronica Lynn Compton back there to commit a murder so similar to the double homicide that detectives would have to admit they'd locked up the wrong man. At the very least, there'd be reasonable doubt in his case, and he could then throw all the blame for the LA murders on Buono.

Compton, a playwright who'd contacted Bianchi to learn more about the mind of a serial killer, had given him an idea. He exploited her attraction to him and persuaded her to carry out the plan. She smuggled out semen to plant on the body, and then traveled to Washington to select a victim. If she succeeded, she'd select another victim in another place.

Compton checked in to the Shangri-la Motel. She went to a bar nearby and looked around. The bartender was female, so Compton chatted with her and invited her back to the room. There, she attacked her prey, but the woman was stronger than Compton had anticipated. They struggled, the woman fled, and the police returned to arrest Compton for attempted murder.

Her hope to get Bianchi out of prison and unite with him had separated them permanently. He wanted nothing more to do with her (and probably would have felt the same even if she'd succeeded). Even more damaging was her testimony on Buono's behalf, revealing the sinister plan. However, all three eventually found love in prison.

In 1986, Buono married Christina Kizuka, a mother of three. Bianchi married Shirlee Book three years later after a long correspondence. Reportedly, Book bought her wedding gown and invitations before she had even met Bianchi.

Compton, too, got involved, but it was with another serial killer. In addition to revealing the bizarre plot she'd dreamed up with Bianchi during Buono's trial, she also admitted that she and Douglas Clark, a convicted killer of prostitutes, were corresponding heavily. (He wanted her to frame his killing partner, and when she failed to offer the incriminating testimony, he broke off with her and ended up with another groupie.)

Victoria Redstall also stood out, although she has insisted, "I'm nothing like those lunatics who want to seek out serial killers." In the summer of 2006 she made headlines for her multiple meetings with serial killer Wayne Adam Ford. What set the one-time weather girl apart was this: She was a former spokesperson for a breast enhancement supplement, Herbal Grobust, and he was renowned for delivering to police a severed female breast in a plastic bag. Tabloid reporters made much of this match.

Ford, a former long-haul trucker, was convicted in June 2006 on four counts of murder. In 1997 and 1998, he'd bound, strangled, and stabbed four women, three of them prostitutes and the other a hitchhiker. He'd dismembered two, keeping parts in his freezer. He stabbed his first victim, twenty-seven times, removing her head, arms, legs, and breasts to "make her smaller." Ford tossed her torso into a waterway, as he would do with the next three. After he confessed to his last assault, turning himself in so he would "stop hurting people," he claimed to be a different man.

Redstall befriended Ford while on a tour of the West Valley Detention Center in Rancho Cucamonga. During the spring, she visited Ford regularly. She romanticized him, believing that who he was during his killing spree was not the man she knew. During Ford's trial, Redstall entered as part of the press, claiming she was making a documentary. The judge allowed her to take photographs and bring in a camera. She and Ford had worked out a series of hand signals, so he could assure her he'd received her notes. She took pictures so freely, in fact, that the court reprimanded her. After closing arguments, she drove alongside the van in which Ford rode back to the prison, so he could see her in her red convertible. Once he was convicted, however, his own defense team blocked all such visitors.

Besides groupies, convicted killers also receive visits from profilers. The prison interview program continues, as seen on "Damaged," when Reid and Hotchner interview a killer willing to talk. The database has expanded, with greater statistical sophistication, and the method of profiling has been included in several courts. Yet, on appeal, it's been more thoroughly scrutinized. That issue is next.

TEN

−Profiling on Trial−

Truth is the trial of itself, and needs no other torch.

−BEN JOHNSON, *ON TRUTH*

BTK. The Baton Rouge serial killer. The Olympic Park bomber. All are pet cases for critics of profiling, especially defense attorneys who put FBI profilers on a witness stand. In the *CM* episode "Tabula Rasa," a defense attorney grills Hotchner over mistakes made by profilers so he can tarnish the credibility of the profiling process, along with diminishing Hotchner's positive impact on the jury. The prosecutor already has a weak case, so any erosion of public trust in the FBI official is useful for him.

During the 1990s, attorneys had only a slim chance against the aura a profiler brought to the courtroom. While profiling is not a science, some professionals have acted as if a profiler's judgment were unerring. In addition, pseudo-profilers have taken the stage to comment on cases without anyone checking their credentials, bringing to the method an air of confidence that makes the public feel safe. Yet it's also a setup for highly visible failure, and as a result, the odds have improved for defense attorneys.

This decline in confidence began when journalists sought people for commentary who would provide a priori profiles of types of killers during active investigations or offer instant profiles without knowing the facts. Responsible investigators resisted the demand, but that left a hole into which noncredentialed people could—and did—step. Some people even offered seminars that fraudulently certified eager young novices as profilers.

As with all things that go up, coming down was inevitable. Because profiling is not a miracle technique and because its success relies on both the information available and the skill and experience of the person interpreting it, there were bound to be mistakes.

"You have to be careful that the information you're using is accurate and complete," says Gregg McCrary. "If there's information out there that hasn't been collected, that can affect the profile's accuracy." He wrote a piece for the *Congressional Quarterly* in 2003 to make this point, saying that "if either the profiler or data are compromised, so is the potential for a successful outcome."

Where once those mistakes might have been absorbed and forgotten during the course of an investigation, the media glitz was too intense for that to occur. Between charlatans, overeager professionals seeking the limelight or selling a book, and simple human error, the love affair the media had with profiling had reached the honeymoon's end. Now they scrutinized the warts. Psychologists who disliked how profiling had been touted by people with no psychological training supplied reasons why it was a poor method, and even best-selling novelists were featured on television programs as having more insight into a crime than FBI agents. In 2002, the attack on profiling gained its best leverage to date with the Beltway snipers case (see Chapter 5).

Over a three-week period, people living along the I-95 corridor from Maryland to Virginia were getting shot and killed as they performed mundane tasks such as shopping or filling their cars with gas. With no behavior to assess, except accurate marksmanship, commentators shot from the hip and offered all sorts of ideas about the "white loner with military background driving a white box truck or van." One media favorite with no profiling background even said that the box truck was now ditched in a lake. (Of course, that it would never be found made it a safe bet for the profile.)

It soon became clear that the offender was listening to what the commentators and police were predicting, because whatever was concluded about "him" was soon undermined. "He doesn't shoot children"—then he did. "He doesn't shoot on weekends"—then he did. So that was a bit of additional behavior, as were the quick getaways that suggested a team working together.

McCrary pointed out to reporters that when there are few clues in a case, people can develop tunnel vision, such as believing that the sniper drove a white van or truck, which was based on only a single witness report. No one really knew if a white van was involved, yet the media and the investigators were clinging to it. They also embraced the notion from a profile offered on television that the shooter was white (because most lone snipers up to this point have been white). But it turned out, once the perpetrators were arrested, that they had all been wrong about the van, the offender's race, and the idea that they could publicly say whatever they wanted without inflaming this unsub to keep killing. The shooter turned out to be a team: an African American man and his adolescent protégé. One of them later admitted that he'd shot certain people after watching the police chief on news programs trying to anticipate their behavior.

Because it was such an unusual spate of crimes, data from past cases that bore no relationship to it fueled erroneous conclusions. Yet all behavioral scientists know that human behavior is full of anomalies. While it was reasonable to say this shooter was white, that did not eliminate the possibility that he was of another race— or gender. In truth, the FBI did not actually make the statement that the shooter was white, the media profilers did. When Chief Moose later published a book about his experience, he affirmed this, but the media continued to convey the impression that all profilers had collectively held the same erroneous opinion.

Similarly, profiling took a hit in 2004 in the case of the Baton Rouge serial killer, a man who'd murdered five women in Louisiana. Contrary to the FBI's predictions of an unskilled loner who was awkward around women, the killer, Derrick Todd Lee, turned out to be personable and able to hold a job. He even had a family. A profile was posted online, purportedly done by the FBI and with the appearance of authenticity, which stated that this killer would be white, but the BAU issued several statements that the unsub's race had never been stated in the profile. Although the actual profile was mistaken on a couple of points, it was correct on many more: the killer's approximate age, controlling behavior, physical strength, tight finances, and nonthreatening manner. However, most media outlets focused on the errors.

What got lost was the fact that profiles are merely tools, only as good as the local jurisdiction's information. Profiles are also based on probability from the analysis of past cases that are similar to the one under investigation. If most past serial killers have been white males, it's reasonable to suggest that a current unsub will be a white male. Collecting more data on female, black, Asian, and Hispanic serial killers in the future, the range of possibilities will become more flexible. Until that time, as long as most serial killers remain white males, the probability analysis is still going to favor a white male. Probability always has a margin of error.

Not long after that, reporters discovered that famed profiler John Douglas had offered an incorrect interpretation about something in the Green River Killer case that might have made a difference—perhaps even saved some lives. After Gary Ridgway confessed to forty-eight murders, he said that he'd sent an anonymous letter to the newspaper in 1984, in the midst of his long spree. Douglas had decided the letter was amateurish and had no connection to the murders. While he was correct on several other things in his profile, this mistake made headlines.

A rush to judgment is inevitable when the demand is great and public visibility is high, but that's how mistakes are made. Perhaps it wasn't prudent for the FBI to allow novelists and filmmakers enough access to develop the image of these investigative supersleuths. Or perhaps people (including reporters) who believe that crime solving methods come with a guarantee are just setting themselves up for disappointment. In any event, a method based on behavioral analysis, which has a considerable margin of error in the field, cannot predict every possible human behavior or trait. Yet with additional crime scenes and more behavioral evidence, profiles do evolve. So, also, has the method itself. Still, the mistakes have become fodder for defense attorneys.

TRIAL AND ERROR—

Given the umbrella-nature of criminal investigative analysis, profilers have entered the courtroom in different types of roles. They might testify, consult with attorneys, or participate in sentencing hearings. After they retire, they often become analysts and consultants, although they can now participate on the side of the defense. During the late 1990s, retired agent McCrary was invited into a famous case in which the original prosecutor was now on the defense in a civil suit. The crime had occurred more than forty-five years earlier, but the records from all the proceedings had been preserved. It was the case of Sam Sheppard, on which the television series, *The Fugitive*, had been based.

On the morning of July 4, 1954, someone fatally bludgeoned Sheppard's wife, Marilyn, in the upstairs bedroom of their home in Bay Village, Ohio. The police arrested Sheppard and charged him with murder, but he claimed that a "bushy-haired stranger" had killed Marilyn before attacking him and fleeing. His account had glaring holes, including lies that shielded an extramarital affair, so the jury returned a verdict of second-degree murder and a life sentence.

For his appeal, Sheppard recruited defense attorney F. Lee Bailey, who persuaded the Federal District Court to overturn the conviction. At the second trial in 1966, new culprits were named—the Sheppards' friends and neighbors, the Houks (although Sheppard had called them for help right after the murder, he apparently didn't recognize that Houk was the man with whom he had just grappled). Bailey theorized that Marilyn had been sexually involved with Spencer Houk. After a short deliberation, the jury accepted the reasonable doubt argument and returned a verdict of not guilty. Sheppard was free, but he died young, at the age of forty-six.

Late in the 1990s, Sheppard's son, Sam Reese Sheppard, sued the State of Ohio in civil court for monetary damages for the ten years his father had been wrongfully imprisoned, demanding $2 million. The culprit that he and his attorney, Terry Gilbert, offered was a former window washer named Richard Eberling, who'd allegedly lusted after Marilyn. They theorized that he'd entered through the outside cellar doors, made his way upstairs, raped and murdered Marilyn, and then assaulted Sam.

McCrary assessed the crime records, trial records, and photos, concluding that the crime had been a domestic homicide that was staged (badly) to resemble a home invasion and a stranger murder. The person staging it—presumably Sheppard—had failed to convincingly mimic the behavior of an actual burglar.

For the trial, McCrary qualified as an expert, and his method of analysis was admitted as sound. However, the judge made a qualified ruling: McCrary could testify to "the characteristics of domestic homicide and compare them to the physical evidence at the scene; the characteristics of homicide that are drug-related and compare them to the physical evidence at the scene; the characteristics of homicide that are robbery or burglary-related and compare them to the physical evidence at the scene." In addition, McCrary could describe the characteristics of staging but he could not address the ultimate issue itself—that is, he could not state that the crime scene was staged. That was for the jury to decide.

On the stand, McCrary outlined his assessment, based on the criteria for domestic homicide from the *Crime Classification Manual*, stating how the scene was inconsistent with a sadistic stranger murder. The jury agreed, deciding that the State of Ohio owed Sam Jr. nothing.

MENS REA–

The work the profilers do in any case is performed toward the goal of bringing perpetrators to justice. This means ensuring that they get to trial without technicalities that can derail a conviction. Profilers rarely get into the courtroom to testify as experts, but when they do they must be familiar with issues involving the admissibility of psychological testimony (as must psychologists who consult with law enforcement as profilers).

The legal system relies on the belief that people are generally rational and that they freely make decisions. Thus they are morally and legally responsible for their behavior. Mental health professionals can undermine this notion by introducing psychological factors that mitigate culpability. The law recognizes that responsibility for committing a crime depends on two things: actus reus, which is evidence that the accused engaged in the act, and mens rea, which is evidence that the accused had the requisite mental state to have intended to commit the act or to be able to foresee its consequences. Certain mental states can undermine the mens rea, resulting in defenses for insanity, emotional disturbance, or diminished capacity. Triers of fact—the judge or jury—must consider excusing the behavior of those without mens rea. In brief, to be convicted, the person must have an evil mind and do a bad deed. The absence of either—even the possibility of that absence—constitutes acquittal (sometimes with stipulations or further treatment).

Insanity is a legal concept related to, but not synonymous with, mental illness. Nevertheless, there is no uniform standard across the United States for determining insanity, and a person found sane in one jurisdiction might be considered insane in another. Federal and state courts use a variety of standards, generally grounded in knowledge of right and wrong but sometimes including the ability to conform one's actions to the requirements of the law. Yet it is not sufficient merely to have a mental illness; the illness must be meaningfully related to the crime—that is, the act is the "product" of the illness. A legal defense of "not guilty by reason of insanity" presents the idea that defendants have committed crimes but by reason of "disease or defect" are not responsible for their actions. Thus they should not be held criminally accountable.

An MSO (mental state at the time of the offense) assessment helps determine the type of defense that can be supported. The choices include insanity, automatism, diminished capacity, affirmative defenses, and substance abuse. For example, the Rogers Criminal Responsibility Assessment Scale (R-CRAS) is a structured instrument that quantifies symptoms of organic impairment, major mental illness, evidence of low intellectual function, anxiety, impulsivity, and cognitive control at the time of the offense. Testing for thirty different variables, it considers information about such behaviors as evidence of planning the offense, awareness of its criminality, and reported self-control over one's behavior.

In an attempt to be more precise about mens rea, the ALI's Model Penal Code offers four degrees of culpability: purpose (the defendant's conscious object in the criminal act), knowledge (awareness of criminal circumstances but no intent), recklessness (disregard of the substantial risk of a certain result), and negligence (lack of awareness of a risk that the defendant should have been aware of). Because of these different ways of mentally participating, defendants can give evidence that focuses on mens rea without having to claim insanity. They can say they did not purposely or knowingly commit the crime or that they could not have meaningfully premeditated it. Personality disorders are not considered relevant to an insanity defense, although the issues of dissociative disorders and post-traumatic stress have affected the way some cases are considered. These conditions may be classified as diminished capacity.

Although profilers must be cognizant about MSO issues because their conclusions can contribute to its calculation, a more crucial concern centers on the 1993 *Daubert* decision, the legal standard for federal and many state jurisdictions by which social science testimony is measured. The method of profiling itself comes under this scrutiny.

The judge in this case, *Daubert v. Merrell Dow Pharmaceuticals, Inc*, re-examined the nature of scientific evidence and the issues of legal admissibility. Jason Daubert and Eric Schuller were born with serious birth defects, and their parents alleged in a suit against the pharmaceutical company that the mothers of both children had ingested Bendectin while pregnant to slight nausea. The suit ended up in federal court, where the company attorneys insisted that the drug did not cause birth defects in humans. As their expert, Dr. Steven Lamm offered testimony that upon reviewing more than thirty published studies involving over 130,000 patients, he found no evidence that the drug caused malformations in fetuses.

But the petitioners had hired eight experts who collectively concluded that the drug did cause birth defects, contradicting the defendant's expert. They'd examined test tube and live animal studies as well as chemical studies of drugs that bore a structural similarity to Bendectin. They'd also reinterpreted earlier studies to show that the conclusions were wrong. The court now had to decide between scientific experts and set forth more precise conditions than mere peer review under which scientific evidence should be admissible.

The justices decided that *scientific* means having a grounding in the methods and procedures of science that are sufficiently established as to have general acceptance in the field and any claim of having "knowledge" must be stronger than subjective belief. The petitioners' evidence had fallen short of this mark, because their experts did not sufficiently show causation between the drug and the defects with proven methods. In addition, their approach had not been subjected to peer review and their methodology diverged significantly from that which was generally accepted in the scientific community.

Thereafter, challenges to scientific experts took place in Daubert hearings, wherein judges focus on methodology and on whether the scientific evidence applies to the case facts. In other words, judges now determine whether a theory could be tested in accordance with scientific criteria, the potential error rate was known, peers had reviewed the method, and the method had attracted widespread acceptance within the relevant scientific community. Because a profile is based on behavioral science, which uses probability assessments, whether a profiler can testify is often subject to the judge's discretion.

Even if a profile is not admissible in court, a prosecutor may still seek consultation from a profiler on a range of subjects. As with law enforcement, profilers offer assistance to court personnel in recognizing personality traits and behaviors that are consistent with certain types of crimes. The profiler can also clarify other aspects of forensic evidence, explain technical angles, and help reconstruct the crime. They can offer information on typical behaviors before, during, and after a crime to shed light on how offenders might have been thinking when they made certain decisions. It's important for prosecutors to understand such behavioral manifestations as "undoing," rage, calculation, psychosis, and vengeance. Malice aforethought, or deliberate intention to commit a crime, must be carefully examined and profilers are in a good position to contribute.

Profilers can also help prosecutors with strategy. Relying on behavioral science research, they can devise key questions and maneuvers and predict how a subject will respond. In the Wayne Williams trial in Atlanta, for example, John Douglas instructed the prosecutor to put pressure on Williams because he had the kind of personality that would eventually blow. In fact, Williams did rail against the strategy and the profile in a way that tended to support (but not prove) his guilt.

However, a profiler who relies on behavioral evidence must understand the limitations of probability analysis, a key tool in behavioral research, so as not to overstate what it can prove.

In 1995, Steve Fortin pleaded guilty and received twenty years for a savage attack on a female state trooper in Maine. When she stopped to help him and found him drunk, he reacted by breaking her nose, biting her on the left breast and chin, strangling her into unconsciousness, and raping her. Just then her backup arrived and Fortin was caught. But his story was not over. New Jersey officials investigating an unsolved case from the previous year heard about the case in Maine and noted striking similarities. There in Avenel, Melissa Padilla had been beaten, robbed, bitten on the left breast and chin, raped, and then strangled. Investigators soon discovered that Fortin had lived in the area at the time of Padilla's brutal murder, had been seen abusing his girlfriend at a restaurant near the crime scene, and had committed other violent acts. Fortin was indicted.

During the trial, Special Agent Roy Hazelwood testified

about the MO and signature that linked the two cases. He explained that linkage analysis was not a science, but the deductive reasoning it utilized was based on training, education, research, and experience in working on thousands of violent crimes over an extended period of time. (At this time, he had thirty years of experience.) Hazelwood had been qualified as an expert on the subject of modus operandi and ritualistic behavior in California and South Dakota, and two former FBI colleagues, John Douglas and Larry Ankrom, had qualified in other states.

In the Fortin case, Hazelwood noted the high-risk nature of both incidents (out in the open, in traveled areas), the impulsivity and anger apparent, the similarity in locations, and the nature and location of the trauma inflicted on both victims. The bite marks and injurious penetration, as well as the facial beating and front strangulation method, seemed too similar to him to be coincidence. "In my 35 years of experience with a variety of violent crimes," Hazelwood testified, "I have never observed this combination of behaviors in a single crime of violence . . . it is my opinion that the same person is responsible. . . ." Fortin was tried and convicted for the murder in New Jersey.

Then, on appeal, the court decided that Hazelwood had encroached on the ultimate legal issue, which is reserved for a jury, and that the method he'd used for linkage analysis had questionable scientific credibility. There had been no peer review of this method, or scientific study to support it. Case experience, no matter how extensive, was deemed insufficient. Thus, in 2004, Fortin's conviction was set aside. The case was retried in 2007, this time with better physical evidence, and Fortin was convicted again.

This decision set a precedent that began to erode public confidence in the notion that profiling was a solid methodology. (When the defense attorney on *CM* ridicules Hotchner, the agent starts interpreting the attorney's behavior with uncanny accuracy, as if that proved the method's validity. However, it merely affirms an approach as old as the first tales of Sherlock Holmes: solid skills of observation.)

At any rate, other cases that had included profilers also came up for appeal.

ON APPEAL—

Several cases from the 1990s were reexamined in higher courts. Let's look at one example, which relied in part on the successful appeal in the Fortin case. Cleophus Prince Jr. a convicted serial killer from the Clairemont area of San Diego, appealed his 1993 conviction partly on the grounds that the participation of a profiler was both unnecessary and unfair.

Early in 1990, a man entered the apartments of three different women and murdered them. A fourth victim turned up in her home, and by September "the Clairemont Killer" had sexually attacked a mother and daughter inside their home, slaughtering both. It was not difficult to link these crimes, as the perpetrator had left a distinct signature, known in criminology as piquerism. That is, he liked to stab and gouge with a sharp implement. In particular, he aimed at the heart and left breast, stabbing deeply many times. One victim had been raped.

The Clairemont Killer removed most of his victims' clothing, stabbed them multiple times, and left them on their backs, posed provocatively. He also moved in and out of a victim's home with relative ease, left items strewn about, and often discarded the knife he'd used. Experts believed he was stimulated by violence and the knife was a substitute for penile penetration.

The victims were all white women, and five had been stabbed with a knife found inside the residence. Five were between 18 and 21, and all had been killed early in the day. Jewelry was missing from several. These circumstances were sufficient to justify a behavioral analysis for the possibility that the incidents were all linked to a single offender.

A failed break-in led to the arrest of a black man, Cleophus Prince Jr., twenty-five, and in 1993, Prince went on trial for six murders. Three victims had lived in the same apartment complex as he did, and two others had lived near where Prince's girlfriend resided. The sixth victim had frequented a fitness club where Prince often went and lived in a building next to where he roomed with a friend.

Based on DNA evidence on the rape victim, Prince was convicted of that murder. The other five convictions rested on linking the incidents via the modus operandi, behavioral signature, eyewitness reports, surviving witnesses from failed assaults in the area, and the similarity of circumstances. Prince was also convicted of twenty burglaries and attempted burglaries from the same area and time frame.

Prince's first appeal was considered in 2007. In it, he argued that his trial should have been moved because of prepublicity that had prejudiced the pool of jurors and because of the presence and testimony of FBI Special Agent Larry Ankrom.

In a decision dated April 30, 2007, the California Supreme Court upheld the death sentence for Prince, in a unanimous ruling that dismissed his legal beefs. As for Prince's claim about pretrial publicity, the court found that the majority of the articles published before the trial had been "framed in neutral terms." In addition, the judge had taken pains to keep Prince's picture out of the papers, so there was little basis to the charge of unfair prejudice.

The brunt of the complaint was targeted at the use of a profiler.

After Prince's arrest, several task force members had met with profilers at Quantico to examine the evidence in all six cases. They were clear on the rape case, because of the semen match, but they knew that if the prosecutor could prove the "special circumstance" of six murders, getting the death penalty would be easier. Thus they needed an expert linkage analysis, and the profilers had actually been involved since the third murder.

Former Cuyahoga County prosecutor Tim McGinty had recommended Douglas, then BSU chief, to the San Diego police. Ankrom, also in the unit, had geographical jurisdiction, so they'd entered the case together. They viewed the three murders as high risk for the offender because they'd been perpetrated during the middle of the day when other residents of the apartment complex could have spotted an intruder entering or leaving an apartment. Thus they expected that the unsub was familiar with the complex, known to other residents, and possibly even lived there. He knew how to go about entering apartments and slipping out without being seen, so he might have a record for breaking-and-entering. They believed that other women had been approached or accosted in this same area.

The profilers expected that the first murder, performed in an area familiar to the offender, probably occurred as the result of a stressful incident in the unsub's life. Whatever it was, it would have triggered a desire to punish someone—a woman. His victim would be a stand-in for the person he really wanted to punish. He probably held women accountable for whatever annoyed him, and he'd be abusive with his wife or girlfriend as well. He probably gave the items taken from the victims to his wife or girlfriend, secretly delighting in the fact that he'd taken them from a woman he'd killed. Doing this would inspire an added sense of control. He might also live in a dependent relationship with a woman, which made him resentful and angry, and he'd have a spotty employment history as well as temperamental issues with authority.

Douglas and Ankrom directed the task force to publicize the list of traits, along with the probability that the offender's behavior would have changed somewhat since the first murder, evident in activities such as greater substance abuse or secrecy. Thus people who knew him might recognize his involvement from behavioral clues and his absences during the times of the murders. Someone might step forward to provide helpful information. Because he'd been spotted at this apartment complex, Douglas suggested he'd move on and find victims elsewhere.

What Douglas had anticipated during the first few months of the murder spree proved correct, as three more victims turned up during the next several months at two separate scenes. While it was unfortunate that the unsub had succeeded three more times, it provided a more secure basis for analysis. (At first the profilers had only five crime scenes to examine, but a sixth would turn up as well.)

Ankrom and Douglas noticed that the victims all fit a similar type: white, attractive, and physically fit. Most had been brunette and five had been young women. (The forty-two-year-old mother looked much younger, but she might also have come into a scene already happening and was thus not specifically targeted.) The killer had entered their residence via an unlocked door or window, all of the victims had been stabbed, and five were killed around the same time of day. All were left face-up on the floor of their homes, nude or mostly nude. Three had lived or been visiting in the same apartment complex and three used the same fitness center. Jewelry was stolen from three of the victims, but most telling was the way the deepest stab wounds had always been concentrated in the chest area, revealing a focused and controlled rage.

The profilers used the Violent Criminal Apprehension Program (ViCAP) database, entering information about the race of the victims, their geographic location, the MO of entering their homes, the use of a knife, the time at which the murders generally occurred, and specifically the signature—the tight circle of puncture wounds left on the chest area. The results of the analysis indicated that there were no similar crimes anywhere near this area, and none around the country with this particular type of wound pattern.

"When I start analyzing research into the minds and motivations of serial killers," said Douglas in a newspaper interview, "I would look for the one element or set of elements that made the crime and criminal stand out, that represented what he was."

Considering the differences in the Clairemont-area series, the only victim stabbed only once had been followed and subdued via the same MO as in the other crimes. The assault had been interrupted so it was not clear whether the perpetrator might have continued. In every other way—victim type, time of day, weapon used—it was similar. Only one victim had been sexually assaulted, while only one had been covered after the attack. One victim—a dancer—was higher risk than the others. However, taken all together to determine the links, the similarities outweighed the differences.

"There is simply no way," said Douglas, "of coming up with a numerical value for each piece of information. It can be properly evaluated only by running it though the brain of an experienced profiler." Ankrom and Douglas decided that the motive for all six murders had been controlled sexual rage. They weren't alone in this interpretation since it's highly unusual to have a black serial killer, let alone one who crosses racial lines to murder white women.

Staff writers at the *San Diego Union-Tribune* penned a long article about how Prince did not fit the psychological profile offered by the FBI when they'd examined the crime scenes. Among the details that supported this position were the following: Prince's acquaintances said that he was obsessed with sex and often bragged about his relationships with white women. Yet there was no evidence that he'd had an altercation with a white woman who might have made him angry enough to kill. In fact, there was no indication from anything in his entire life history that he'd become a killer. He'd always been a polite young man, and despite growing up in a rough neighborhood in Alabama as the oldest of eight children, he'd never had a brush with the law. He'd been an average student who enjoyed sports, had completed high school, and had joined the navy in 1987. He'd run into trouble when he stole a postal money order, receiving a sentence of nearly a month in the brig and a fine of $466. Prince was discharged in October 1989. As far as anyone could tell, that had been the extent of his issues with the law.

But that was only because he'd managed to operate surreptitiously. In fact, once he moved to San Diego, he'd been quite busy with thefts and burglaries.

Prince's attorney, Roger Appell, claimed that Prince looked nothing like the composite drawing made from a woman who'd been accosted by a man police believed was also the killer. But the claim that he was the first known serial killer to have crossed racial lines, in the hope of showing the improbability of his guilt, was untrue. There had certainly been black serial killers of white woman in America before this case.

While he was in California, Prince had gotten a job but was soon laid off, so he'd turned to burglary, which he found easy. He enlisted some accomplices, and they donned socks to go in and rob homes without leaving fingerprints. The socks were similar in pattern to the bloody honeycomb marks left on doorknobs where murders took place. Ultimately it was physical evidence in one incident and circumstances coupled with linkage analysis in the others that formed the prosecution's case.

When prosecutor Dan Lamborn requested that both Douglas and Ankrom participate in the trial, the court conducted a lengthy pretrial hearing concerning their qualifications. Douglas was slated to take the stand to provide background about the profiling analysis, while Ankrom would specifically address the series of Clairemont-area crimes. The defense attorneys protested that neither was a psychologist and thus they should not be allowed to make a psychological assessment.

The court concluded that the witnesses' experience and training failed to qualify them to express an opinion about the perpetrator's probable state of mind, so that aspect of their testimony was excluded. However, the court accepted that they had sufficient training and experience in crime scene investigation and linkage analysis to testify about analyzing the Clairemont murder scenes for commonalities. It was also deemed likely that the jury members would need an expert to explain such concepts as signature analysis, so using profilers to address these subjects was acceptable; however, because it bordered on psychological motive and they were not psychologists, they were prohibited from using the word *signature*. Given these limitations, the prosecutor elected to use only Ankrom because he had been more extensively involved in the case.

The trial in the summer of 1993 brought out several interesting items, one of which was a biological quirk that had stalled the investigation. Apparently, Prince was a non-secretor, meaning he failed to secrete in his biological fluids a blood enzyme that was present in 75 percent of the population. Because the tests did not pick it up, the semen analysis from the rape/murder had erroneously indicated that the offender's blood type was O. Prince's was type A. It took a year to discover and rectify this mistake.

Prince's roommate testified about a night when Prince had returned to the apartment they shared with fresh blood on his jeans, offering a tale that he'd gotten into a fight with his girlfriend. However, he'd often bragged about his burglaries and had admitted he'd stabbed some people to death. The roommate even recalled Prince talking about stabbing them in the heart. They'd lived next door to the building where one victim had been murdered, and the roommate had even been involved in some of the burglaries. He testified about how they had worn socks on their hands, and recalled pieces of women's jewelry that Prince had in his possession.

Ankrom testified that all six victims had likely been slain by the same person; his judgment was based on the similarity of the wound patterns from case to case and his experience with crime series. He'd been fully involved in the case, he said, and provided a linkage analysis. Under cross-examination by another of Prince's attorney, Barton Sheela III, Ankrom admitted that during his analysis he did not include information involving knife attacks on area women who'd survived. He also did not include information on murders in other neighborhoods. In fact, the attorney pointed out, there had been an unsolved homicide of a white woman stabbed in her home in the San Diego area, committed *after* Prince was arrested, and Ankrom had not examined it. Sheela believed this raised doubt not only about his client's guilt but also about the profiler's approach, which seemed to have been based on a presumption of guilt. However, Judge Charles Hayes limited this discussion and called for a closed session because he decided that making the details of this crime public could adversely affect that particular investigation.

In closing, the deputy DA made the case that Prince was a sexual pervert who enjoyed watching blood flow from women's breasts, and he emphasized the brutal similarities among the crimes. Prince's attorney countered by pointing out eyewitnesses who were unable to identify Prince as the man they'd seen in the vicinity of the murders. In most of the cases, he said, there was no physical evidence against his client. He described the many differences among the crimes, insisting that they could not be viewed as a pattern. Then both sides rested.

The jurors deliberated nine days before they returned a verdict on July 13, 1993: Prince was guilty for all six counts of murder as well as twenty burglaries and a few other charges. The special circumstance of multiple murder was sufficient grounds for giving him the death penalty. Judge Hayes affirmed the sentence, and Prince joined fourteen other men on California's death row at San Quentin. Thus his appeals began.

In the context of his complaints about FBI profilers, Prince's appeal stated that jury members had not required an expert to help them decide whether the six cases were linked and that inviting an expert into that role had prejudiced them. Chief Justice Ronald George concluded that the testimony had not been improper: Ankrom had described the FBI's method of linkage analysis to indicate how likely it was that the same person had committed all six murders but had not concluded that Prince himself was the guilty party. Ankrom's testimony had been restricted to methodology, which was appropriate; he'd simply provided a context for the jury. Such an analysis, based on his extensive experience, was clearly beyond what a layperson could perform.

The court applied an abuse of discretion standard to examine the use of the expert profiler (*People v. Robinson*) and decided that the trial court had correctly exercised its discretion with an extensive hearing about profiling. It had also stipulated the expert's limitations and the expert had observed them during the trial. It was clear that laypeople could not reach a conclusion as intelligently as the witness had, and Ankrom's testimony had therefore appropriately assisted them. While jurors can examine crime scene photographs and autopsy evidence themselves, the justices decided, they would not have the experience to form a sound decision about wound analysis comparison. Ankrom had testified about the hundreds of cases he'd examined during his career to make his decision, and no juror's decision making could be as accurate.

But there were other issues, raised in previous cases in other jurisdictions. The court noted that a profiler's testimony had been admitted into a case in Delaware.

Three prostitutes had been tortured and murdered in Delaware, each one with wounds worse than the last, and on each battered body were traces of blue carpet fiber. Without leads, the case went nowhere, so an undercover female officer began to watch the area, posing as a prostitute. When she spotted a blue van that seemed to be following her, she strolled over. She noticed that his van had bright blue carpets, so as she talked with the driver, she pulled at the carpeting on the inside of the door. When she stepped back, she had fiber specimens for trace comparison. It was found to be consistent with the fibers on the bodies, so they found the van and arrested the driver, Steve Pennell. With more evidence, he was convicted, and Supervisory Special Agent John Douglas was allowed to testify on the signature analysis he'd done in preparing the affidavit for a search warrant. At trial, Douglas described the similarities of the wound patterns on each victim and the nature of the torture inflicted: "The signature was the pleasure he received out of inflicting pain and hearing his victims' anguished screams."

On appeal, the Delaware Supreme Court had concluded that the testimony's admission in the Pennell case had been proper. That decision strengthened what the California court decided about the Prince appeal. Still, in the Fortin case in New Jersey, an appeals court had ruled just the opposite.

The justices examining Prince's appeal took a hard look at the reasoning in Fortin and decided that the New Jersey decision had been made in error: That court had compared linkage analysis methodology to a much more rigorous DNA analysis, based in biology. Understandably, they thought it fell short. But few methods in the fields of forensic science and investigation have the scientific methodology and error rate percentages that DNA analysis has. "In our opinion," the California justices wrote, "the court applied an incorrect standard in searching the scientific community for peers to test the expert's theories and duplicate his results." Ankrom's testimony, derived from his investigative experience, had not been offered as an approach subject to peer review in the way that biological science is. Thus the decision from the Fortin appeal gave no weight to Prince's complaint.

However, his attorney did raise a key issue, which was not sufficiently addressed in either venue. He noted that there had been another knife murder of a white woman in her home in the same general area, committed while Prince was in custody. On cross-examination, Ankrom admitted he had not examined the details of that crime. While it's possible he was not shown the case because the wound pattern or some other circumstance was considered too different to include in the series, in fact, a profiler is obligated to look at the full range of cases to make his or her own decisions about which belong to a series and which do not. To provide a fair judgment this case should have been included in the analysis.

Whatever issues profiling may invoke in the courtroom, its success has raised its visibility and credibility in other countries. As a result, more investigators have used profiling internationally, and some have even improved on the process.

ELEVEN

−Profiling Abroad−

Who can say how often a casual remark, an observation, a spontaneous
hunch, a bit of advice, or a serious discussion by a BSUer contributed to
the capture of a murderer?

—DON DENEVI AND JOHN H. CAMPBELL,
INTO THE MINDS OF MADMEN

WANDERING PHANTOM−

It's not often that serial killers cross national boundaries, and it's
especially rare that a female serial killer will do so. However, thanks
to DNA evidence left at scenes, it seemed clear to investigators that
a female serial killer was doing just that—and in fifteen years, she
hadn't been identified.

In 1993, the first known victim, Lieselotte Schlenger, was strangled in her apartment in Idar-Oberstein, Germany. The killer left
DNA behind on a fragile china teacup and on the murder weapon—
wire from a bouquet of flowers. The same DNA turned up in nearly
two dozen robberies and break-ins in Germany, France, and Austria as well as at the site of a triple execution—in a car where three
men were shot. Her DNA was also found on a used syringe discarded on a playground, but for a junkie she had been uncharacter-
istically careful. An antiques dealer was murdered in his home in

2001, strangled to death with garden twine that yielded the same DNA. Then in April 2007, two police officers were shot in their car in Heilbronn, Germany, and one of them—a twenty-two-year-old female—died. There were no witnesses or obvious motives. However, the mysterious DNA was in the car's backseat and on the console. A DNA sweep of three thousand homeless women and 800 convicted women turned up no match, and in October 2008, the body of another woman was found in a ditch near her car. DNA implicated the faceless phantom. In fact, the phantom's DNA was found in a car in which three men were executed but the two men arrested for the crime denied that a woman had been with them. Investigators had dedicated considerable resources and posted a sizable reward for her capture. She was fast becoming the most clever, elusive, and perplexing serial killer in all of Europe. The police even asked psychics to ponder the puzzle.

A psychiatrist in Vienna devised a brief profile, calling the "Woman Without a Face" organized and able to maintain her composure, even around law enforcement. She refrains from making mistakes, he said, sticking to the theft of small amounts of cash. She appears to be adept at manipulation, both of victims and accomplices. She has been psychopathic from an early age, suggesting an abusive home life and possibly parents who were addicts.

The case unraveled when the culprit was finally revealed: it was a woman all right, but she was not a killer or even a criminal. She worked in a factory—one that made cotton swabs. The puzzle was solved when someone swabbed a fingerprint from a deceased burn victim in an attempt to provide an identification and the notorious DNA turned up. But the burn victim was male. They realized that the materials were contaminated, which led them to the swab factory. They then learned that the swabs they'd used were not sterile and should not have been sold to law enforcement agencies for forensic investigation. It was a bad day for the police agencies.

Despite the profile offered (from a professional without investigative experience), this case actually confirmed the probability analysis and common sense used in the profiling method: a rare, nomadic female serial killer with several different types of accomplices (who never saw her), and whose behavior was entirely inconsistent with familiar psychological patterns should have raised red flags much sooner. While DNA analysis may be a solid scientific procedure, it's not wise to base an entire investigation on DNA alone. Perhaps a more experienced profiler would have spotted the behavioral contradictions.

Although *CM* is based largely in the United States, they have gone to Mexico and Cuba, and we may yet see more international episodes because the BAU offers expertise to other countries. In addition, other countries have developed psychology-based investigative programs similar to what the BAU has accomplished.

OVER THE BORDER—

It's nearly automatic for investigators to attribute serial murder to male offenders. This miscalculation occurred in an actual case in Mexico, and *CM* featured a similar tale in "Machismo," when the team traveled to Mexico to assist law enforcement there. As with the actual case, elderly women were being murdered, and while the *CM* agents speculated that the perp was a man posing as a woman, in the actual case the suspect in nearly thirty homicides of elderly females turned out to be a female wrestler. (FBI profilers working on this case had wrongly proposed that the "Mataviejitas," or "Little Old Lady Killer" was a transvestite, a man dressing as a woman.)

Juana Barraza, forty-eight and a mother, was caught in 2006 just moments after fleeing from the house of a murder victim. Barraza had strangled the elderly woman with a stethoscope. It turned out that Barraza had an altar in her home dedicated to the scythe-wielding cult figure, Santa Muerte, or Saint Death. As a masked wrestler, she'd been known as the Silent Lady. She confessed to four of the murders but denied involvement in any others, despite fingerprints associating her with nearly a dozen. It was her MO to approach the women and offer to do some work for them; as soon as they let her in, she would kill them with anything she could find, from socks to telephone cords. Ultimately, Barraza was convicted of sixteen murders and sentenced to 759 years in prison. When asked why she had killed these women, she responded, "I got angry." Psychologists thought it was likely that her anger was directed at her alcoholic mother, who'd traded her for beer when she was twelve, abandoning her to sexual abuse and a difficult life.

FBI profilers came to Mexico for another case as well—this one with perhaps one of the highest victim tolls of modern times, and still unsolved. Retired Supervisory Special Agent Robert Ressler went to assess the situation.

In the Mexican border town of Ciudad Juárez, across from El Paso, Texas, many women have gone missing. Since 1993, hundreds of bodies have turned up, hundreds more women have vanished, and dozens of men have been interrogated, but the murders continue. Many victims were young women who'd worked in assembly plants that supply the United States.

In 1998, a women's group from Mexico City had brought international media attention to the fact that nothing was being done about these murders. Mexican authorities contacted Ressler to help narrow down the number of suspects in their investigation and to train their task force in the psychology of serial killers. Ressler went over the documentation for 160 murders from the previous five years and concluded that not all of them were linked by similarities. The case, while shocking, had been overblown. Ressler recalled:

They were talking in excess of 100 women at the time and saying that someone was running amuck and had killed them all.
When we sorted all the cases out, we ended up with 76 homicides of concern. I did a preliminary ViCAP assessment and
determined that a number were connected and a number were
not. Some suspects were clearly family members [of the victims]
and some were gang members. They had one guy in custody,
an Egyptian national who had a record in the United States for
rape and assault. He was charged with half a dozen homicides
[but convicted in only one]. I also believed that some of the murders were done by people—possibly a team—coming over the
border from El Paso. So we also met with the El Paso police to
get their cooperation.

He explained to the officials that the victims whom he believed
were part of the pattern ranged in age from seventeen to twenty-
four and most had been raped and strangled. Ressler set up a surveillance of the buses that let young female workers off at night. "I went
behind the buses with cops and saw that they were dropping these
women in dark locations. Anyone interested in abducting them just
had to follow the buses. Some of the bus drivers knew the routes,
and they could easily come back later when they weren't driving to
get these girls."

Yet a Mexican criminologist and chief of Chihuahua's forensic
department, Oscar Maynez, was certain that the perpetrators were
not from Texas. He'd seen most of the evidence, too, and believed
they were Mexican natives. The ViCAP database was limited to
mostly American serial killers, he observed, and there had never
been a structured study of Mexican killers. Thus Ressler's analysis
was both limited and flawed. In fact, if the police had withheld or
were ignorant of any of the facts, which seemed likely, the profile

would be deficient. He said that the killer or killers were stalkers with knowledge of remote places in the desert and the means to dump victims in these areas.

In November 2001, eight decomposing bodies were discovered in a former cotton field. The following year, five bus drivers were arrested for thirteen of the murders and disappearances on the list, and became suspects in five others. A witness identified a man he'd seen dumping a body, which led to the arrest of bus drivers Javier Garcia Uribe and Gustavo Gonzalez Meza, both of whom confessed to kidnap, rape, and murder. One even said that he'd killed three more, although those bodies were not located. According to their confession, they'd get intoxicated and when they spotted a vulnerable woman, would force her into their van to rape and kill her. Yet both later claimed their confessions had been extracted with torture, and they recanted. Another official claimed that he'd been forced to plant evidence against them.

As of 2006, Amnesty International had reported more than 430 recovered bodies and hundreds of missing women. Among the theories are organized criminals trafficking in sales of human organs, a drug cartel, satanic sacrifices, and copycat killers.

PROFILING IN SOUTH AFRICA—

Ressler assisted to set up criminal investigative analysis in other countries as well, notably South Africa. Between July and October 1994, fifteen bodies of females in their twenties were found near the Pretoria-Johannesburg suburb of Cleveland. All had been raped and strangled, none was hidden, and the killer had removed personal items from the scene. Most were commuters, unemployed, or students. A man was arrested and detained, but when fifteen more bodies turned up the next year in another remote suburb, Atteridgeville, authorities knew that the real killer was still at large.

Seven months later, a cache of bodies was discovered near Boksburg with the same MO but dumped closer together, and these three groups of victims came to be dubbed the ABC killings, after the areas in which they'd been found.

In 1994, the South Africa Police Service had established the Investigative Psychology Unit (IPU), and Dr. Micki Pistorius invited Ressler to supervise her efforts to profile some of their serial criminals. In fact, the rate of serial murder seemed equivalent to that of the United States or Russia. After the practice of apartheid had stopped, the lack of control either inspired more murders or opened the door to journalists for better coverage.

Ressler went to South Africa to see the crime scenes and profile the killer. It was clear to him that he (or they) had returned to the bodies. There was also evidence from one site to the next that the killer was improving as well as escalating. Ressler deduced that he was familiar with the areas, had done prior surveillance before each murder, and had lately grown arrogant. He was probably luring victims with some skill rather than attacking them by surprise. The resulting profile included the fact that the offender was black, owned a vehicle, appeared to be well off, but was young and had a strong sex drive. Ressler believed this man would contact the police or newspapers.

Soon an anonymous caller claimed credit for the murders, saying that he'd once been falsely accused of rape and being in prison had ruined him. When police finally caught him he turned out to be Moses Sithole, a thirty-one-year-old youth counselor. He was convicted of forty rapes and thirty-eight murders, and sentenced in 1997 to 2,410 years. Pistorius trained more investigators in profiling, although the work soon overwhelmed her and she resigned. The IPU formed a partnership with John Jay College of Criminal Justice in Manhattan on the topic of South Africa's serial killers. They have also instituted a series of interviews with convicted killers to develop a scientific database.

THE JOURNALIST AND THE MURDERER—

Among Ressler's international associates is Dr. Thomas Müller, chief of the Criminal Psychology Service within the Austrian Federal Ministry of the Interior. Müller was trained in the Federal Police School in Innsbruck, Austria, and became a member of the SWAT team. He then acquired graduate degrees in psychology. Among the areas in which he now teaches are hostage negotiation, abnormal criminal psychology, criminal profiling, and threat assessment, and he established the Criminal Psychology Service in Austria. He has also worked together with Ressler to train other investigators abroad, notably in Poland, Germany, South Africa, and the UK.

Müller got his taste of the ViCAP system when working with Supervisory Special Agent Gregg McCrary on a serial murder case. He accompanied Chief Detective Geiger to Quantico to learn how the profilers operated. They brought several boxes of documents about eleven murders from three countries, including three from the Los Angeles area. One had been committed in Prague and seven in Austria. The investigators also had a suspect, but McCrary asked them to withhold that information until he'd looked at the crimes and put the information through ViCAP.

Based on the eight European cases, McCrary prepared the criminal profile and compared the facts with crime scene characteristics from the cases in LA. It appeared that they were all connected.

"As I looked through the cases and asked questions," McCrary says, "I took extensive notes to try to distill the significant factors that would help to create a timeline and a means for comparing one case to another. In particular, I was looking for an escalation of certain behaviors."

He realized that they had a similar victimology and manner of disposal. Most of the women had been prostitutes, and in Europe their bodies had been left outside in the woods, with branches or foliage placed over them. Most had restraint bruises on their arms and wrists. McCrary believed the unsub was similar to other prostitute killers: He was insecure about his masculinity, and when he could not perform after being stimulated, he blamed the women and struck out in anger. "The violence itself had become erotic to him."

The ViCAP database contained about twelve thousand solved and unsolved homicide cases, and McCrary entered his signature analysis. "I used a minimum number of variables: age group in the victimology, the fact that they were prostitutes, the ligature strangulation, the outdoor disposal sites, how they had been left mostly or partly nude, and that they had retained their jewelry." He thought they'd get a large number of cases that matched, but in fact they got only twelve. One had been solved, which left eleven—the cases that the Austrians had brought. "It would be highly unusual to have more than one guy engaging in this specific type of behavior during this same time period," says McCrary. "Even more significant, this offender had committed all these murders in less than a year."

Then they compared what they knew against the suspect, Jack Unterweger. The illegitimate son of an Austrian prostitute, Unterweger had first been arrested for assault at age sixteen—an attack on a prostitute. In 1976, he killed his neighbor Margret Schafer, out in the woods, using her bra to strangle her. He was arrested and in court blamed his mother for his anger. He was sentenced to life in prison. This is where it got interesting.

Unterweger entered prison nearly illiterate, but over the years he learned to read and write. He published poems, short stories, plays, and a prison memoir, some of which won prestigious awards. The Viennese literati believed that art had reformed Unterweger, so several politically influential Austrians petitioned for his release.

In May 1990, Unterweger had been granted early parole. As a celebrity already thanks to his prison writings, he made the rounds of talk shows and became a much-sought-after guest at elite gatherings. He also became a journalist, and McCrary saw that he'd written extensively about the failed police investigation for the Austrian prostitute murders. As part of his job, Unterweger had traveled to Los Angeles to write an article about crime and prostitution there. The police, who had no reason to suspect criminal motives, showed him where the prostitutes tended to hang out. It seemed that Unterweger had returned to these areas covertly to select three victims, using a unique knot when he strangled each of the three women with their bras.

Unterweger then went on the run, but he was caught and returned for trial, at which McCrary testified as the first FBI profiler to be used on a criminal case in Austria. Although Unterweger claimed he'd been framed, he was convicted on nine counts of murder and sentenced to life without parole. Within hours, he committed suicide with the drawstring from his sweatpants, using the signature knot that had helped to convict him.

ON PAIN OF DEATH—

Profiling may be useful even after an offender is caught, as illustrated with the infamous Andrei Chikatilo, Russia's most demented and prolific serial killer. From 1978 to 1990, he raped, brutalized, and murdered at least fifty-three women and children. Trying to narrow possibilities for suspects, chief investigator Viktor Burakov read about the FBI's Behavioral Sciences Unit. He wanted to request their assistance, but the Soviet authorities insisted they did not have a serial killer; that phenomenon was exclusive to bourgeois countries like the United States. The next best thing was to ask a local psychiatrist to draw up a profile, but most refused. Burakov despaired, but then in 1987, Dr. Alexandr Bukhanovsky agreed to study the few known details and the crime scene patterns. From this information, he devised an extensive profile. The killer, he said, was a sexual deviate, twenty-five to fifty years old, around five feet, ten inches tall. He thought the man suffered from some form of sexual inadequacy and that he blinded his victims to prevent them from looking at him. He was a compulsive sadist, but not retarded or schizophrenic, as investigators believed. He'd be a loner, ordinary and unassuming, as well as depressed, except during periods when he killed. He brutalized the corpses to enhance his arousal, because otherwise he had difficulty getting sexual relief.

Once Chikatilo was arrested in 1990, state officials could not obtain the confession they desperately needed to prosecute him. Finally, when the probability loomed that the man would be released, they brought in Bukhanovksy. The psychiatrist saw right away that this was the type of person he'd had in mind. He read the profile to Chikatilo, describing his mental illness and the possible reasons for it. As Chikatilo heard his secret life thus portrayed, with apparent compassion, he broke down and said that it was all true. He confessed to fifty-six murders, although there was evidentiary corroboration for only fifty-three: thirty-one females and twenty-two males.

The FBI got wind of this case and notified authorities there that they admired the work that Burakov had done to bring this killer in. Many years later, in 2005, they also invited Bukhanovsky to their international symposium on serial murder.

It's clear that with better resources and a less politicized legal system, Chikatilo would likely have been captured before so many people had died. Burakov had spotted the patterns in 1982, with three corpses found in wooded areas in quick succession, although the authorities had officially treated them as unrelated incidents. The killer had taken some risk and showed evidence of overkill and sexual deviance—a type of offense said by Soviet officials to be exclusive to decadent bourgeois societies. So the investigation had remained both hobbled and secret.

Burakov had noted a signature emerging: The killer had gouged out the eyes of his early victims. On girls and women, this offender stabbed the breasts and destroyed the vagina, uterus, and bladder. On boys, he often mutilated the penis, scrotum, and anus, and once even chewed up a tongue.

Andrei Romanovich Chikatilo, fifty-four, fit the profile. He'd been a lonely child, mocked by others for his clumsiness and sensitivity. Seething but unable to fight for himself, he'd devised fantasy tortures for his tormenters. His first sexual experience as an adolescent involved ejaculating as he struggled with a ten-year-old friend of his sister's. Later in life, the images of this erotic wrestling helped him become aroused. As an adult, when he'd tried to develop a relationship, he could not perform sexually. His mother also endlessly mocked him, so his inner torment grew more intense, fueling his anger against women.

Chikatilo became a schoolteacher and his sister helped him meet a woman suitable for marriage, although his wife, too, belittled him throughout their marriage. Reportedly, he was able to conceive children only by pushing his semen inside her by hand. After his mother died, Chikatilo began to molest young girls. This made him feel powerful, but he made a mistake and lost his teaching position.

He'd become a traveling salesman, riding the trains and picking up vulnerable prey at train stations. Some he'd watched carefully but most had been victims of opportunity who were easily lured. The stabbing, he said, was in place of the sexual intercourse he couldn't perform, and he'd needed violence for arousal. Chikatilo viewed male victims as his captives; in his fantasy world, torturing and mutilating them made him a hero. He also admitted to cannibalism. Sometimes he had removed a uterus and placed his semen inside it, then chewed on it as he walked away from the corpse. Or he bit off a part and swallowed it. "But the whole thing," Chikatilo said,

"—the cries, the blood, the agony—gave me relaxation and a certain pleasure." Found sane, he was convicted of the multiple murders and summarily executed. He'd begged to be studied, but government officials were interested only in being rid of him.

As the Soviet system collapsed, more crimes involving serial killers were revealed, and in 2003, twelve women were murdered in quick succession around Moscow. Each had been walking alone and all were either strangled or had their throats cut. Because the incidents occurred in different parts of the city, the daily paper *Kommersant* suggested that there might be not one but two serial killers at work.

Even as police investigated these crimes, they were aware of crimes in the southwestern part of the city, in Bittsyevskiy Park. Thus far, they'd been stymied in their attempts to catch the person bashing the heads of elderly people.

It was June 2006 before Russian officials stopped the fourteen-year spree of thirty-two-year-old Alexander Pichushkin after he murdered a co-worker from a supermarket, Marina Moskalyova, and left her body in the park. Video surveillance from a train showed Pichushkin walking with her, and she'd left a note for her son that she would be with him.

Under arrest, he initially denied his involvement, but after seeing the surveillance tape, he started talking. He even led police to several undiscovered bodies. To everyone's surprise, he'd sought to break the record set by Chikatilo; he wanted to be the country's worst serial killer. Shockingly, Pichushkin claimed to have killed sixty-two people, and a chessboard drawing found in his room on which he'd placed dates on sixty-two of the sixty-four squares seemed to confirm it. He'd often targeted the elderly, he admitted, inviting them to drink with him in a secluded area of the park—supposedly the grave of his dog—and once they were drunk, he'd bash in their heads with a hammer or pipe, and either leave them on the grounds or dump them into a sewer pit (sometimes alive but too inebriated to save themselves).

In his confession, televised to prove it was not coerced, Pichushkin said that he'd first committed murder in 1992 when he was a teenager (the year Chikatilo was tried and convicted). The victim was a boy he'd pushed out a window. When the police called it a suicide, Pichushkin believed he was invincible. He started up again in 2001, killing people in the park who were unlikely to be reported missing. Nevertheless, the bodies did draw attention, and police were on the lookout for the Bittsa Maniac.

Psychologist Mikhail Vinogradov interpreted the attacks as the result of anger at his grandfather for abandoning him, although they also had a "sexual subtext." Pichushkin had actually described his criminal career as a "perpetual orgasm," and in an interview, he'd stated, "A life without murder is a life without food." It had been his goal, he bragged, to kill sixty-four, to match the number of squares on his chessboard. Three people had survived his attempts to murder them, and one identified him and confirmed his MO.

At the Serbsky Institute, Pichushkin went through psychiatric evaluations and was judged competent to stand trial. He was charged with forty-nine murders and three attempted murders, which irked him, because he wanted credit for more. He claimed he'd been cheated, but investigators had found no evidence to support his calculations. The chessboard killer was summarily convicted, receiving life in prison.

VIOLENT CRIME LINKAGE ANALYSIS SYSTEM—

During the 1980s, complex serial killer investigations in Canada inspired the development of a system similar to the FBI's ViCAP, called the Violent Crime Linkage Analysis System (ViCLAS). Its originators had been trained at Quantico, and the precipitating case reverberated across Canada with its wrenching details.

On Christmas Day in 1980 in Vancouver, British Columbia, the body of a mutilated 12-year-old girl was discovered outside in the cold. She'd been stabbed and strangled. Another victim turned up that spring, and the crime spree continued locally over the next year until numerous children had vanished, with only two more bodies found. They ranged in age from twelve to eighteen. The key suspect was Clifford Olson, an ex-con who lived in the area with his wife and child. He was caught picking up two girls, and inside his van was a notebook that contained the name of one of the murdered children. Olson then offered a deal: He would confess the known murders and provide investigators with locations of six bodies still missing in exchange for $10,000 per victim. Unless they agreed to the deal, he would give no information. The government reluctantly paid $100,000, placing the money into a trust fund for Olson's son. Canadian citizens were outraged. When Olson then tried to make a deal for revealing more graves, no one bargained. He pleaded guilty to eleven murders and received life sentences, although he comes up for parole hearings every two years.

The first attempt at a national automated crime linkage database in Canada was the Major Crimes File (MCF), which could be searched via keyword queries. By 1990, it held details from eight hundred cases but no recorded hits—that is, no one was utilizing it. Around this time, Inspector Ron MacKay from the Royal Canadian Mounted Police headquarters, went to Quantico for ten months. As Canada's first trainee in criminal investigative analysis, he had ideas about what could be done with the MCF. With Sergeant Greg Johnson, he looked at the ViCAP system, as well as linkage systems used in several states. They then incorporated what they deemed were the best features of each approach to develop ViCLAS. They used input from experts in the field of violent crimes, as well as research about specific crimes, to formulate 262 questions for data input that would link offenders to crimes via behavioral and forensic evidence. The booklet took about two hours to complete, but it then guided a comprehensive investigation. Like ViCAP, the crimes in this database included solved and unsolved homicides and sexual assaults; missing persons in which circumstances suggested foul play; and unidentified bodies, for which the manner of death was believed or known to be homicide. They also added parental abductions and attempted abductions.

Once the system was up and running, it proved its usefulness with confirmed linkages. In fact, the first high-profile case in which psychological linkage was employed feature a notorious pair of team killers, nicknamed Ken and Barbie.

Karla Homolka and Paul Bernardo killed three girls, starting at Christmas in 1990 with Karla's younger sister, Tammy. They drugged her to have sex with her, but she vomited while unconscious and died. They quickly covered it up and the pathologist did a cursory autopsy, accepting their story of an accident so they got away with it. Getting married in 1991, they had recently killed and dismembered a second girl, fourteen-year-old Leslie Mahaffy, dumping her remains into a lake. Then another schoolgirl, Kristen French, disappeared. She was seen being forced into a car in the middle of the day while walking home from school. A few weeks later, she was found murdered, her long hair cut off.

Ron MacKay was convinced that the French and Mahaffy murders were related, but ViCLAS was only just being developed. Still, this was a good case for a formal linkage analysis, and a public service television show was produced and aired that offered a profile of the killer. While it featured FBI Special Agent Gregg McCrary, who was consulting on the case, it also introduced Canadian profilers to the public. In fact, the killers were watching this broadcast, and it was Homolka who gave the Green Ribbon Task Force its big break. Abused by Bernardo and afraid that investigators were closing in, she turned him in and orchestrated a deal for herself. For her cooperation and a plea of guilty to two counts of manslaughter, Karla Homolka was sentenced to two concurrent twelve-year terms.

The task force relied on behavioral analysis, supplied by Gregg McCrary, to get a search warrant to find tapes of the sexual torture sessions they believed were in Bernardo's home. Although they failed to find any, they did convince a judge that Bernardo was a dangerous individual. He was convicted of two murders and numerous sexual assaults, getting life in prison. He is still suspected in other assaults and murders. The tapes turned up in the possession of his attorney, showing that he and Karla had acted as a team.

In 2008, Bernardo gave an interview in which he stated that sexual "performance anxiety" had driven him to rape and kill. He said that he cries now over incidents such as 9/11 and Columbine, so he knows he's not the psychopath that psychiatrists claim he is. He'd felt nerdy as a child, so he'd begun by forcing his victims to disparage their boyfriends and tell him how great he was. "It's all power and control," he said, "because you're so insecure in yourself." He believes he's a solid candidate for parole and hopes one day to be free. He continues to insist that while he was present to the murders, Homolka was the perpetrator. He says that the profilers got him all wrong, doing him a disservice.

Little research has been done on the remorseless female who

exploits a man to act out her own violence; this could be a case in which such a dynamic occurred. That Homolka could kill her sister and then marry and continue to participate in more rapes and murders with her sister's co-killer for several years indicates a truly disturbed personality.

Across the country, each ViCLAS unit started with an independent database specific to its province, but they soon became linked via a central server in Ottawa. The ViCLAS booklet is now available online and can be operated in English, French, Dutch, or German. ViCLAS specialists have at least five years of experience in the field of serious crimes as well as experience with computers. Some experts believe that ViCLAS is the best system of its kind in the world, and it's become a model for databases in Australia, Belgium, Holland, Japan, and the UK. In the meantime, the UK had cases that required on-site profiling.

PSYCHOLOGICAL INVESTIGATION–

At the University of Surrey in Liverpool, England, Dr. David Canter developed his own approach for psychological investigation. While the principles are similar to the FBI's approach, somewhat differing philosophies guide Canter's work.

In 1982, the rape of a woman near Hampstead Station in England precipitated a spree of more than two dozen rapes over the next two years. Most victims described two men involved. At the end of December in 1985, nineteen-year-old Alison Day became the next victim, but her attacker also asphyxiated her and dumped her in a canal. Four months later, another murder changed the media moniker from the "Railway Rapist" to the "Railway Killer." The body of the second victim, a fifteen-year-old girl, had been set on fire, apparently to destroy semen. Only a month later, a newly-married woman was murdered shortly after she stepped off a train and got on her bike to go home. There was also an attempt to burn her body.

The police were at their wits' end. They had considered setting up a BSU like the FBI's, so they invited geographical psychologist David Canter to offer a profile. This was a first for British law enforcement; no prior case had used psychology-based offender profiling. Canter was eager to try it. He computerized the data and placed all the incidents on a map to locate where he believed the offender lived and to describe the offender's likely "mental map"— his psychological focus. He then devised a portrait of personality traits and behaviors, offering seventeen observations.

Canter suspected that the offender had once worked for the railroad and had lived in the area since the first rape. He probably had a tempestuous relationship with a wife and was a semi-skilled worker. A good possibility from among over 2,000 suspects was John Duffy. He matched thirteen items on Canter's list, and his former wife supplied a few eye-opening details. The police put him under surveillance.

Duffy was finally arrested for following a woman into a park. Forensic evidence from Duffy's home matched evidence from the murders, so he was charged. While reports had indicated that two men were responsible, Duffy refused to give up an accomplice. In 1988, he was convicted of two of the three murders and four of the rapes.

More than a decade passed before Duffy revealed the name of his accomplice, David Mulcahy, and admitted his part in the murder for which he'd been acquitted. DNA tests proved Mulcahy's involvement, and the married father of four was arrested. Duffy claimed that Mulcahy was the mastermind and the one who'd decided they should start killing. Mulcahy was convicted of the three murders and twenty-four rapes, and he emerged as a suspect in many other sexual assaults.

Canter's approach is a hybrid between a psychologist and detective, although not quite fully either one. Investigative psychologists generally take courses in applied psychology programs such as Canter's, and then learn police investigation techniques. They act as assistants to police, but they don't necessarily have graduate degrees in psychology or a license. Specifically, they gather information and interpret it within a scientific framework that involves background in sociology, geography, and psychology. They might also interview inmates, conduct studies, write reports, and perform document searches.

Also in Scotland, Ian Stephen, a criminal profiler who inspired the television series *Cracker*, has examined the case of convicted sex offender and killer Peter Tobin, who has reportedly claimed to others that he's murdered over forty people. The sixty-two-year-old Tobin has emerged as a suspect in numerous past cases that resemble those for which he's serving a life sentence.

After a double rape in 1993, Tobin hid in a religious retreat under a false name, but thanks to a Crimewatch program, he was recognized and arrested. He served ten years, and when he got out, he turned to murder. While working as a church handyman in Glasgow, he met Angelika Kluk, a twenty-two-year-old student who was staying in the chapel. Her body was found, stabbed and beaten, in an underground chamber beneath the floor of the confessional. She'd been placed there while still alive. Tobin was arrested and convicted in May 2007. That June, one of his former homes was searched in connection with a girl who'd gone missing in 1991. The remains of her body were found buried in the garden, and Tobin's fingerprints were lifted from the bag that she was wrapped in and a dagger left in the house. Tobin was convicted in this murder as well. Then a second body was found on his property, and Tobin was charged.

As psychologists suggested that these murders were not the work of an amateur, the police wondered if he was "Bible John," an infamous killer in an unsolved series of crimes from the late 1960s. Tobin had been a regular at the Glasgow ballroom where the three victims had been picked up, and at the time he'd have been twenty-one. The man called Bible John had shared a cab with his third victim and her sister, who was able to describe the encounter. He'd said his name was John (Tobin often used aliases), and he'd talked about scripture and prayer. All three woman were found the day after they went missing, and they'd been beaten and raped, and their bodies ritually arranged.

Around that time, Tobin had viciously attacked his wife (whom he'd met at a dance hall), raping, stabbing, and strangling her, nearly killing her. Soon thereafter, he'd moved to another town, and several unsolved murders had occurred there. Tobin also fits the description given by the third victim's sister, who'd been dropped off before her sister had disappeared with the Bible-quoting killer. DNA from semen found on this victim's tights does not match Tobin's, but police have not ruled him out. Another man had been with them for a short distance in the cab before getting out, and he might have been waiting at a prearranged site. He was never located, but at the time Tobin worked at a bed and breakfast (B&B) a few blocks from where that man had exited the cab. One interesting clue was that the three Bible John victims had been menstruating, and reportedly the presence of menstrual blood had enraged Tobin.

MIXED BAG–

Serial killers show up in many countries these days, and the international media have given a great deal of visibility to the FBI's profiling unit. Among the countries dealing with recent serial homicide cases are the following.

- *Jamaica:* The Major Investigation Task Force is looking for help from local psychologists to profile what appears to be linked cases of murder, because the island has a "unique brand" of killers: Criminals make bets with one another on how many people they can kill. For example, Damian Thomas, twenty-eight, is suspected in twenty-eight murders, including several committed while he's been in prison. Some were precipitated by dares, others by his need to prove his prowess.

- *India.* A businessman, Moninder Singh Pandher, and his domestic servant, Surinder Koli, have been convicted of murdering a young girl, but it's just the first of nineteen cases. Sewers near the home yielded the bones and organs of numerous women and children, and the servant confessed to having sex with the bodies and eating parts of them. Also, in Mumbai, Ravindra Kantrole, the "Beer Man," was sentenced in January 2009 for three of seven suspected murders, and beer cans were found near most of the bodies. In addition, just as a film about the "Stone Man" murders in Guwahati opened in theaters, two more fatal bludgeonings were committed on sleeping homeless men.

- *Ukraine.* Serhiy Tkach was found guilty in December 2008 of eighty rapes and murders. He was once a criminal investigator himself, and nine other people had been erroneously convicted in some of these crimes.

- *Greece.* Two prostitutes have been killed in Athens, with four stab wounds to the neck. One victim was fifty-seven, the other sixty, and they were killed a week apart.

- *Australia.* Peter Dupas, fifty-four, received a life sentence for the murder of Mersina Halvagis, killed a decade ago near her grandmother's grave. Dupas stabbed her thirty-three times, breaking bones with the force of his thrust and cutting deep into her heart. He'd been spotted at Fawkner Cemetery on that day, and the witness who'd seen him identified him during his three-week trial. A prison cellmate also described how Dupas had pantomimed the killing to him. Dubbed Victoria's worst serial killer, he's already serving life sentences in two other murders and remains the key suspect in three more.

SOUTH KOREA–

In the course of a year, a string of murders in southwestern Seoul inspired journalists to name a potential serial killer the "Rainy Thursday Murderer." Five young women had been murdered, and two were beaten but escaped. Most of the assaults occurred on Thursdays, during bad weather. Also, Yoo Yeong-cheol was arrested in Korea in connection with nineteen murders committed in less than a year, while Chung Nam-kyu was detained for thirteen.

Kang Ho-Sun was charged in January 2009 with the murders of seven women, after he confessed. A good-looking, affable man, he'd used his charm to lure girls into his car. He said he'd developed the urge to kill in 2005 after his fourth wife and her mother had died in a fire. He's charged with murder in that incident as well because he purchased four insurance policies in his wife's name just five days before and he'd already been through three divorces. In addition, DNA from another woman was found in his home and it did not match victims he'd already confessed to killing and burying. Based on the PCL-R, local psychologists have labeled him a psychopath, but a fan base arose immediately, opening a website to collect funds to support his defense. Over half a million people popped in during the first three days, and the killer declared that he'd like to write a book to set himself apart from other serial killers (which makes him even more like them).

In the first research of its kind in Korea, reporters teamed up with the Korean Institute of Criminology to profile fifty-four known serial murders, two of which were female. Researchers conducted interviews with twenty-five of them, finding that most had substantial criminal records and nearly half had been delinquents. More than 50 percent had no prior acquaintance with their victims, the majority of which were either women in their twenties or people in their fifties. Most of the killers had committed their first murder when they were in their thirties, and some had killed more than one person in a given incident. Some worked alone, while others were members of organized gangs.

Many more countries could be added to this list, and will be, as law enforcement around the world gets better tools and more incentive to address serial murder. With the world becoming more globalized, police work has moved toward a community-based philosophy that involves cooperative problem solving and consultation. Information systems are becoming easier to link and share, and technicians are assisting those who need help to get up to speed. The FBI's BSU has changed from the days when a handful of agents went out with little standardized information, and although bureaucracy has its problems, it also offers improvements. More and more countries are setting up psychology-based systems to reveal and study the behavior and motives of serial offenders. The BAU today has evolved into a completely different type of crime-fighting agency from how it began.

TWELVE

−The New Generation−

From childhood's hour, I have not been
As others were.

−EDGAR ALLAN POE, "ALONE"

We can't look into other serial killers' minds as to what they do unless
they allow to give their thoughts and views. You don't find many that
have done this any place.

−CLIFFORD OLSON

On "Bloodlines," a temp is startled by the manner in which the experienced agents offhandedly discuss their cases. She points out that their "objective" terms and phrases buffer them from the horror of what's happened to the victims. Although they counter that it's important to keep some distance, this conversation signals the evolving self-reflection of a new generation of profilers. They don't just do a job, they ponder emotional and ethical implications to gain greater insight about their approach. As profiling becomes part of police procedure, it's important to question how reliable the method of criminal profiling actually is, to subject it to scientific scrutiny, and to make appropriate adjustments for greater professionalism.

MORPHING—

The year 2008 marked a century for the FBI, and some thirty years since the Behavioral Science Unit got solid footing. As threats from gangsters, terrorists, public corruption, cyber attacks, white-collar crimes, and serial killers have grown in the United States, the agency has evolved to identify and defeat them. From postcrime responses to threat prediction and preemptive control, trained agents have focused increasingly more on intelligence-driven approaches. The BAU follows this model.

CM is based on the BAU, not the original BSU. Although one agent, David Rossi, comes from the earliest days of the unit's existence and *CM* addresses his lack of fit with new procedures on "About Face," most have been trained according to the protocol of the new regime. Few viewers even realize that the unit has gone through many changes since its earliest days in the 1970s, because the media tend to repeat what the first generation of profilers wrote in their books (and Rossi, too, is a best-selling author of books about his experiences.)

According to one of the current unit directors, the following changes took place: The Behavioral Science Unit evolved into the Behavioral Science Investigative Support Unit. Then, in 1994, with the creation of the Critical Incident Response Group (CIRG), the FBI integrated crisis management, behavioral analysis, and tactical resources within one entity. By that time the unit had changed its name again to the Investigative Support Unit. Also, the FBI director created the Child Abduction and Serial Killer Unit. Then the whole thing evolved into the Behavioral Analysis Unit, East and West, to focus efforts geographically, until in 1999, based on the Protection of Children from Sexual Predators Act, the FBI received mandates related to crimes against children and serial murder. One of them was the creation of the Child Abduction and Serial Murder Investigative Resource Center (CASMIRC). For a while, CASMIRC was a training and research entity, supporting the BAU East and West, and that was how the situation remained until after September 11, 2001. Change was needed again, urgently.

At this point, the Behavioral Analysis Unit 1 emerged for counterterrorism and threat assessment, while Behavioral Analysis Unit 2 was dedicated to crimes against adults and Behavioral Analysis Unit 3 examined crimes against children. There was also a ViCAP unit, and the NCAVC recently established a Behavioral Research Group (BRG), which employs interns and consultants to provide research resources to personnel in all four areas. There remains a Behavioral Science Unit, but with a different identity from its earlier namesake. The Training Division re-created it for researchers and trainers. The BAU today is interested in more than just the law enforcement angle on serial crimes. Its research advisory board includes outside experts from the academic world with whom agents meet regularly to ensure that academic research supports the NCAVC's operational effort. In every type of crime in which they're involved, there's some type of research project.

Terrorism has become a significant part of the unit's responsibilities, and several *CM* episodes draw the team into investigations of terrorist activities ("Secrets and Lies"). By structuring the approach according to type of crime problem, the FBI has developed a concentration of personnel in each unit who possess specialized training and experience in a specific area of responsibility.

The BAU has hosted a number of international symposia on different topics, such as school violence, domestic violence, workplace violence, and the sexual exploitation of children. They invite multidisciplinary experts to discuss the commonalities, what's currently known in a certain area, and what should still be researched.

In 2005, a five-day symposium was dedicated to serial murder. A total of 135 subject matter experts from ten countries on five continents were invited to initiate discussions and give presentations. This included law enforcement officials who'd successfully investigated and apprehended serial killers, officers of the court who'd prosecuted them, killers' defense attorneys, mental health and academic researchers devoted to the topic, and key members of the media who'd covered such crimes. The agenda included such topics as pervasive myths about serial murder, talking heads on television during ongoing investigations, pathology and causality, prosecution issues and forensics, best practices for task forces, and major case management issues. The goal was to devise better policies and guidelines, and set the record straight on certain facts.

An important issue was to arrive at a consensus on the definition of serial murder. The discussions resulted in a dramatic shift. The professionals at this gathering looked to legislation from 1998 that stated: "The term 'serial killings' means a series of three or more killings, not less than one of which was committed within the United States, having common characteristics such as to suggest the reasonable possibility that the crimes were committed by the same actor or actors."

Symposium attendees decided that this definition, while formalized, was limited in application. Thus they reviewed the definitions offered by a number of prominent criminologists and came to a consensus: to create a simple but broad definition, designed for use primarily by law enforcement. This meant doing away with the concept of a "spree killer," which sometimes overlapped serial murder and sometimes overlapped mass murder. While academics and researchers might continue to rely on the three categories for gathering specialized data, for the designation *serial killer* the BAU adopted the following:

Since the definition was to be utilized by law enforcement, a lower number of victims would allow law enforcement more flexibility in committing resources to a potential serial murder investigation. Motivation was another central element discussed in various definitions; however, attendees felt motivation did not belong in a general definition, as it would make the definition overly complex. . . . The different discussion groups at the symposium agreed on a number of similar factors to be included in a definition. These were:

- one or more offenders

- two or more murdered victims

- incidents should be occurring in separate events, at different times

- the time period between murders separates serial murder from mass murder

Thus, in combining the various ideas put forth at the symposium, the following succinct definition was crafted: Serial Murder: The unlawful killing of two or more victims by the same offender(s), in separate events.

This was distinctly different from the original notion (and the one most viewers of *CM* would know). Even today media sources still promote the idea that a serial killer must kill at least three victims at three locations in three distinctly different events. Although that's clearly problematic, it remains a fixture in the public mind. The BAU composed a publication, offered freely online, to alert principal participants in such investigations as well as the media, but press reports largely neglect to signal this sea change.

The symposium document itself is comprehensive. First, the role of the NCAVC was spelled out, along with changes to the BSU and the current nature of the BAU. Then the authors addressed the most common and oft-repeated myths about serial murder. Most derive from outdated studies, or from fiction and film. While the early studies had their merits, they're not, and never were, representative of serial killers as a whole. The public has been captivated by the psychology of serial killers, but if they look to fiction or television for it, they're getting whatever plays to the ratings but not learning the facts. In addition, among the media commentators are people whose lack of credentials go unchallenged.

The myths about serial killers on which the symposium focused (and hoped to dispel) are as follows:

- They're white males.

- They're dysfunctional loners, without relationships or families.

- They're motivated only by sex.

- They travel.

- They're insane or highly clever.

- They like to play cat-and-mouse with investigators.

- They want to be caught, so they always make a mistake.

The truth is, serial killers are not all alike. There is no single causal factor or set of circumstances that launches such an offender on his or her violent path. They're not all male. Some have been as young as eight and some older than fifty. They're not all driven by sexual compulsion, and most are fueled by multiple motives. They might be profit driven, in search of thrill or self-gratification, or compelled by some other deep-seated desire, fear, or need. Occasionally, serial murder is about revenge or it's inspired by a delusion. They're not all intelligent or clever. A single killer may choose different weapons or methods of operation, and even with rituals, they often experiment and change things. In most cases, the killer does not wish to be stopped or caught. Yet a few do intentionally undermine themselves or stop of their own accord. Some rare killers have even professed remorse or killed themselves.

Jack the Ripper was not the first serial killer. Among the earliest documented killers, as far back as ancient Rome, was a female poisoner, and females have been among those with the highest victim toll (American serial killers don't even come close, with Gary Ridgway holding the documented record here at forty-eight.)

Quite a few killers have had families or been in relationships. Their IQs range from borderline mentally retarded to genius, with most about average. Some have been psychotic, while about 90 percent are psychopaths. About 15 percent work in teams, and teams have ranged from two or three to more than a dozen.

Because so many people are interested in what makes someone into a serial killer, the symposium attendees generated a statement:

> Causality can be defined as a complex process based on biological, social, and environmental factors. In addition to these factors, individuals have the ability to choose to engage in certain behaviors. The collective outcome of all these influences separates individual behaviors from generic human behavior. Since it is not possible to identify all of the factors that influence normal behavior, it similarly is not possible to identify all of the factors that influence an individual to become a serial murderer.

Among the attendees who addressed this idea was Dr. Debra Niehoff, a neuroscientist who had studied the biological basis of violence. Her extensive research indicates that both biological and environmental factors are involved in the creation of a violent person, and each modifies the other such that processing a situation toward the end of a violent resolution is unique to each individual. In other words, a particular type of trigger is not necessarily going to cause violence in every instance because each person's brain keeps track of his or her experiences via combinations of chemical codes. Each new experience brings either new information that could provoke change or information that reinforces what the brain has already stored, creating habits and a sense of status quo. This develops a unique neurochemical profile, influenced by such things as attitudes that have been developed about whether or not the world is safe. It shows up in behaviors and attitudes, and as others react, the individual processes the reaction, updating the profile. Niehoff found that there were different patterns of violent behavior and that certain physiological differences are associated with each pattern.

The symposium's report goes on to describe how all of this begins early in life, as the individual develops coping mechanisms that shape his or her responses to the environment. In some, the failure to develop pro-social skills may result in violence, especially if they grow angry or frustrated and attach themselves to ideas or role models that demonstrate violence as a viable—even satisfying—resolution. While abuse and head injuries do show up among serial killers, they also show up among people who never become violent. Thus there appear to be a "multitude" of factors that contribute to the development of a serial killer, but "the most significant factor is the serial killer's personal decision in choosing to pursue their crimes."

Motives and the role of psychopathy were central to the symposium roundtables, and a number of different typologies were discussed. It was determined that most typologies were too complex and laden with requirements to be useful to law enforcement during an active investigation. However, an understanding of psychopathy seemed to be key to at least understanding the danger of recidivism and escalation.

On a final note, the BAU hoped to alert writers and reporters to realize that "there is no profile of a serial killer." That is, there is no single set of parameters or traits or behaviors that blueprint the clever, white, male, lone wolf, game player who stands out because he's been abused, has a head injury, and is driven to sexually assault and kill white females. They hope that researchers and other qualified personnel will have the good sense to refrain from commenting on active investigations when they don't have all the facts.

FROM COWBOYS TO PROFESSIONALS—

In 1981, not long after the BSU became involved in serial crimes, unit members performed a cost-benefit study of nearly two hundred agencies that had called them in to an investigation. Eighty-eight of the cases were solved (46 percent), and officers said that the profile had helped in about 72 percent of those cases. In 20 percent, it had helped locate a suspect, identifying the right suspect in 17 percent of cases, and assisting in the prosecution in 6 percent. However, the researchers were interested parties as well as the very people who'd assisted, so they did not clarify whether law enforcement responses were skewed by such possible factors as gratitude or being flattered by an invitation to participate in an FBI study.

In 1990, another FBI project pitted profilers, detectives, psychologists, and students with no training against one another. When judging the traits of a perpetrator from a crime scene, profilers were the most accurate in their predictions (29.1 percent), with detectives coming in second (15.8 percent), and students last (6.3 percent). Psychologists were between detectives and students. Some studies have suggested about a 65 percent accuracy rate for experienced profilers. Yet the way success for a profile is defined remains vague. (Another study indicated that for female students, education in psychology enhanced accuracy for profiling physical and cognitive characteristics of offenders.)

In 1999, several law enforcement practitioners and criminologists joined together to found the Academy of Behavioral Profiling (ABP), a professional association devoted to the application of evidence-based criminal profiling techniques. According to the president's statement on the website, "The Academy of Behavioral Profiling is the first independent, non-partisan professional association devoted to the professionalization of evidence based, or 'deductive,' criminal profiling techniques and crime analysis." Divided into three sections—investigative, forensic, and behavioral—the point is to encourage members to develop themselves through education, training, and peer review. "The Academy aims to foster the development of a class of practitioners capable of raising the discipline of evidence-based behavioral profiling to the status of a profession." Toward this end, they set up the *Journal of Behavioral Profiling*. However, not many FBI personnel, current or former, are involved in this organization.

A study published in 2002, conducted at the University of Liverpool, examined the general approach of deriving characteristics from behavior at a crime scene. The researchers called this method—used by most agencies that relied on the FBI's manner of profiling—the "naïve trait perspective." The approach is founded in two assumptions: that behavior will remain consistent across offenses and that there are stable relationships between offense behaviors and personality characteristics. While the first assumption was proven solid, research did not support the second one. Thus the researchers propose that profiling be used with great caution but not used in court until its validity becomes better established.

Yet the studies aren't all critical. Some are even surprising. The news in 2008 was that British scientists were using bees to track down serial killers by refining geographical profiling. Researchers at Queen Mary's School of Biological and Chemical Sciences use computer simulations to replicate the foraging behaviors and geographic patterns of bees that travel from flower to flower to devise a formula for predicting where the hive was located. Similarly, geographical profiling assumes that predatory serial killers tend to kill in familiar territory not far from where they live or work, but there's a buffer zone around the killer's home or workplace wherein there's a low probability of a crime being committed. The researchers assumed that the bees also observed a buffer zone, avoiding flowers near home so as to deflect predators from locating the hive. The results indicated that the distribution of flowers did assist researchers in locating the hives. (However, bees follow their biological instincts and don't read; killers who keep up on law enforcement might learn from this study and find a way to deflect an investigation that relies on its assumptions.)

Another development for geographical profiling involves greater mathematical precision. Relying on information about the layout of a geographical area, notably a city, scientists or profilers with this software can view the relative location of similar crimes. It still relies on the principle that perpetrators will commit more crimes in their zone of familiarity, but it's not solely focused on that series of crimes. To this point, geographical profiling had not recognized the added layer of diversity in city geography surrounding a perpetrator's home base, parts of which could influence what happens where. If the historical records of crimes in the area are analyzed and used, the way one area discourages or encourages crime becomes part of the calculations. Access roads, neighborhood demographics, lighting, and other factors could assist to make the analysis more accurate. Even the age or race of perpetrators might have an effect.

CYBER PROFILING–

A video emerged on YouTube, a popular website, made by a man with a distorted voice like that from the film *Saw* who claimed to have murdered Jennifer Kesse, a woman who disappeared in 2006.

The man stated that he'd killed other people, and he wanted to lead viewers to Kesse's body. However, he then came clean in a call to the media to admit it was a hoax.

Hoax or not, the cyber age has entered the world of profiling in a number of ways.

In Wichita, Kansas, a man calling himself BTK for "Bind, Torture, Kill," slaughtered a family of four in 1974. Six months later, a young woman was murdered in her home, and a local newspaper received a letter with crime scene details of the family massacre, but no killer was identified. In 1977, two more women were murdered, followed by a poem sent to the press. FBI profilers suggested downplaying the murders and dispensing with all the glitzy media, which provoked another letter to a local television station claiming responsibility. This offender wanted the attention he believed he deserved; thus, he revealed his driving motive.

Years passed and in 2004, BTK returned, offering proof that he'd committed an as yet unsolved murder not linked to him. At this time, a computer program generated a profile. A Virginia-based company called EagleForce Associates gathered all the evidence and cross-correlated the data, showing that BTK was likely a white male around 60, with military experience and a connection to the local university. EagleForce saw from a video surveillance tape that he drove a black Jeep Cherokee. While the computer profile did not help to catch him, its designers said it was as accurate as any FBI agent who'd been involved.

Another computerized profiling system involves a linkage analysis developed at DePaul University in Chicago. The Classification System for Serial Criminal Patterns (CSSCP) uses neural network pattern recognition software to connect crimes that show faint traces of commonality across widely disparate jurisdictions. It would work for any type of serial offense—arson, rape, robbery, or murder. Obviously, its success depends on the way the crime details are entered and the entry of all possible cases. Once crimes are linked, suspects—usually already convicted of a specific crime linked in the network—are compared to see if they could have traveled to the different areas, or if there is proof they'd been near a crime scene. While detectives can identify the same patterns with the same information, this system provides a faster, more efficient means for doing so. It operates 24/7 and is sensitive to any type of commonality—even things easily overlooked by human eyes. (In the UK, a similar system is called CrimeLink.)

No one expects that computers will make detective work obsolete, but cyber units will continue to polish and improve systems for aiding the process and accelerating the amount of detailed analysis that must be done in complex cases.

THE BSU LIVES ON—

As the first generation of law enforcement profilers retired—the BSUers—many have become consultants, working alone or forming groups. Robert Ressler drew together investigators from various places as associates for his private consulting firm called Forensic Behavioral Services, and earlier we mentioned Gregg McCrary's work for the Sam Sheppard civil trial in Ohio. His consulting company is Behavioral Criminology International. Former BSU chief Roger Depue founded Academy Group Incorporated (AGI) in 1989, including other retired former FBI and Secret Service supervisory special agents, and among them are the founders of NCAVC. AGI consults with organizations on the motives behind different types of aberrant behavior of employees, customers, and unknown adversaries. They also provide training and expert testimony.

Among the AGI's programs is the Cold Case Analysis Program (CCAP), which offers resources, experience, and knowledge to help determine whether a case can be solved. They assist with crime analysis, the development of an offender profile, and post-offense behavioral issues. They also offer interrogation techniques, prosecutorial strategy, and assistance with search warrants.

On February 3, 1984, inside a Roy Rogers restaurant in Fairless Hills, PA, 25-year-old assistant manager Terry Brooks was found strangled, stabbed, and suffocated. A few feet from her body, the restaurant's safe stood empty. The crime looked like a robbery, similar to others in the area, but for years the case went unsolved.

The AGI assisted with a civil suit in 1990, and the profile indicated that this crime had been staged to resemble a robbery but was more likely the work of someone who knew the victim and was angry at her. The murder was disorganized and unsophisticated, typical of rage, not calculation.

In 1998, as DNA analysis became available to cold case squads, criminalist Diane Marshall re-opened this case and focused on fingernail clippings taken from the victim during the autopsy. She discovered skin cells that produced DNA implicating a male. This was confirmed by a strand of human hair plucked off Terry's clothes.

With this information and the AGI's profile, cold case detectives re-interviewed those who'd been closest to Terry. Included on the list was her fiancé, Scott Keith, and the detectives who'd interrogated him had been of the opinion that he was lying. The new investigators dug deeper into his past, learning that Terry had planned to end their relationship. This could have triggered such rage. But the detectives needed physical proof—samples of his DNA. They retrieved cigarette butts from Keith's curbside trash and matched the DNA profile from his saliva to the skin cells and hair strand. With this evidence, they arrested Keith, and he finally confessed.

Crime scenes always tell a story, and often that story shows up most clearly in behavioral clues. Specialists who can accurately interpret this behavior, such as agents from the FBI's Behavioral Analysis Unit, are increasingly in demand. As the cyber age takes over, some of the linkage analysis will be subsumed by pattern recognition software, but the human behavioral detective will always be among society's heroes. *Criminal Minds* focuses on the procedure, but its strongest appeal comes from the cases—the extreme and even bizarre behaviors that people think up to perpetrate on others. With hundreds of actual cases worldwide to use, there's no end of material for this television show. Serial murder has been a hot topic since the 1970s, and there's no reason to think it will lag any time soon.

GLOSSARY OF
FORENSIC PSYCHOLOGY

ACTUS REUS The physical act or omission required for conviction of a crime; the person must have conscious physical control.

AGGRAVATING CIRCUMSTANCES Conditions that make a crime more serious, such as knowing the risk involved that may lead to injury or death.

ALLEGATION A statement about what the alleging party will address in court.

ALI RULE Ruling of the American Law Institute stating that a defendant is not responsible for criminal conduct when, as a result of mental disease or defect, that person lacks substantial capacity to appreciate the criminality of the conduct or the ability to conform his or her conduct to the requirements of the law.

ANTISOCIAL PERSONALITY DISORDER As defined in the DSM-IV, it emphasizes antisocial behavior over psychopathic personality traits; often confused with psychopathy.

APA American Psychological Association.

BEHAVIORAL ANALYSIS UNIT The investigative part of the National Center for the Analysis of Violent Crime, specific to threat and terrorism, crimes against adults, and crimes against children; formerly the Behavioral Science Unit.

BEHAVIORAL EVIDENCE Forensic evidence suggesting certain behaviors, generally used for criminal profiling.

BEHAVIORAL PROFILING See CRIMINAL PROFILING.

BEHAVIORAL SCIENCE UNIT The first name for the unit of special agents who learned how to read behavioral evidence at crime scenes to assist in extreme crimes such as serial murder; now the research and training division.

BEYOND A REASONABLE DOUBT The degree of proof that will convince a legal trier of fact to a near-certainty that the allegations have been established. This is the highest of the three standards of proof in a courtroom, used in all criminal trial proceedings.

BLITZ ATTACK The delivery of overpowering force to subdue or kill a victim.

BORDERLINE PERSONALITY DISORDER Instability in relationships, job, mood, and self-image, including uncontrolled flashes of anger, impulsive behavior, and self-mutilation; it often shows up among offenders.

BRAIN FINGERPRINTING A technique used to link experiential records in the brain with crimes or alibis.

BURDEN OF PROOF In a courtroom, the necessity of proving a fact in dispute, according to the standard of proof required in a specific proceeding (beyond reasonable doubt, preponderance of evidence, clear and convincing).

CASE LINKAGE See LINKAGE ANALYSIS.

CHARACTER DISORDER A personality disorder that manifests in habitual and persistent maladaptive patterns of behavior; psychopathy, narcissistic personality disorder, and antisocial personality disorder are commonly found among serial killers.

CLEAR AND CONVINCING PROOF The second-highest standard of proof, stronger than preponderance of evidence but less stringent than beyond a reasonable doubt. Generally thought to be about 75 percent certainty, it is applied in matters in which civil liberty interests are at stake.

COMPETENCY Sufficient ability to participate in proceedings, such as to stand trial, to waive rights, to testify, and to die. One must understand the legal proceedings involved and have the ability to consult with an attorney.

COMPLIANT ACCOMPLICE A partner in crime, usually female, who is worn down or heavily manipulated into committing crimes that the person would not otherwise do.

CONDUCT DISORDER A disruptive behavior in childhood and adolescence that involves violating the rights of others, conflict with authorities, truancy, constant disturbance, and petty crimes. There are several categories of conduct disorder, depending on the specific behavior.

CONFESSION Incriminating evidence offered by the defendant in the form of a written or verbal statement. Some confessions are false or pressured, which was a motivating factor in establishing Miranda rights.

CONSULTANT The role a mental health professional might take in offering expertise or research results on a legal issue, policy, or proceeding; some are profilers, and FBI profilers are typically consultants.

COOLING OFF The psychological experience that distinguishes a serial killer from a spree killer, involving the release of tension after a murder and a time of preparation for the next one. The FBI stopped using this concept in 2005.

CORPUS DELICTI Essential facts that indicate that a crime has occurred.

CRIME RECONSTRUCTION Using evidence to determine the sequence and types of actions involved in a crime or series of crimes.

CRIMINAL INVESTIGATIVE ANALYSIS The FBI's structured approach to identifying whether a crime occurred, what type of crime it is, and how it should be profiled and managed.

CRIMINAL PROFILING The use of observation of the crime scene and pattern of crimes to determine investigatively relevant characteristics of the perpetrator; it guides police in narrowing the field of suspects and devising a strategy for questioning.

DANGEROUSNESS See THREAT ASSESSMENT.

DAUBERT RULING The 1993 court decision about the admissibility of scientific evidence. The court decides whether the methodology is scientific and can be applied to the facts at issue.

DECEPTION DETECTION Methods and measurements that determine if someone being interviewed or interrogated is lying.

DEFENDANT The individual formally accused of wrongdoing.

DELUSION A false belief based on an incoherent inference about reality.

DEVIANCE Behavior that deviates from the social norm—for example, a paraphilia or sexual perversion; often occurs in signature crimes.

DIAGNOSTIC AND STATISTICAL MANUAL OF MENTAL DISORDERS (DSM) The official classification manual of the American Psychiatric Association for mental disorders, revised several times and now in its fourth edition, with text revisions; thus, the DSM-IV-TR.

DIMINISHED CAPACITY A psychological defense indicative of an inability to appreciate the nature of the crime or to control one's actions. Not used in all states.

DISORGANIZED OFFENDER Person who commits a crime haphazardly or opportunistically, using weapons at the scene and often leaving clues; usually has a history of mental instability or is criminally inexperienced.

DISSOCIATION Detachment from an idea or location such that it can alter normal organization of thinking; consciousness or identity can be lost.

DISSOCIATIVE IDENTITY DISORDER A disorder, once called multiple personality disorder, that involves several "alter" personalities in a single host body; often malingered by offenders to try to elude responsibility or mitigate a sentence.

ENCODING SPECIFICITY PRINCIPLE In memory research, the idea that memories are more accurate of the retrieval cues match the storage cues.

EVIDENCE Documents, statements, and all items and behaviors that are included in the legal proceedings for the jury's sole consideration on the question of guilt or innocence.

EXPERT WITNESS A person with specialized knowledge about an area or with a special skill that is germane to the proceedings, such as linkage analysis or a mental illness. This person's role is to assist the fact finders (judge or jury) in understanding complicated information.

FELONY A serious crime for which the punishment in federal law is generally severe, including capital punishment.

FORENSIC PSYCHOLOGY A discipline that focuses on psychological issues and situations *in* the law, *by* the law, and *of* the law; most often it involves evaluations for competency or mental state at the time of a crime.

FRYE TEST A test that has governed the admissibility of scientific evidence since 1923, such that evidence entered into a case must be generally accepted by the relevant scientific community.

GEOGRAPHIC PROFILING Using aspects of a geographical relationship among crime scenes to infer offender characteristics.

HABEAS CORPUS An order to bring a party before a judge for evaluation of appropriateness of hospital retention.

HIGH-RISK VICTIM A person continually exposed to danger, such as a prostitute or drug addict.

HOSTAGE NEGOTIATION   The skill involved in trying to resolve a tense situation in which people are held in exchange for something else, and they're usually in danger of being killed.

HYPNOTICALLY INDUCED TESTIMONY   Use of hypnosis to aid in the recall of material relevant to the legal proceeding; has an uneven history in the courts and is only admitted in qualified circumstances; sometimes accompanies a cognitive interview.

INSANITY   A legal term for a mental disease or defect that if present at the time of a crime, absolves the person of responsibility if the person's condition hinders an appreciation of the nature of the behavior and that it's wrong.

INTELLIGENCE TESTS   Psychological assessment techniques to determine cognitive functioning and problem-solving abilities. The most common traditional IQ tests are the Wechsler Adult Intelligence Scale (WAIS) and the Stanford-Binet.

INTENT   Mental state ranging from purpose to awareness of consequences.

INTERROGATION   The act of using questions to pressure someone suspected of a crime to confess.

INVOLUNTARY COMMITMENT   Detaining someone against his or her will in a mental hospital when the person is considered a danger to self or others.

IRRESISTIBLE IMPULSE TEST   A way to determine whether the defendant knows that what he or she did was right or wrong; if that person would have done it even in the presence of a police officer, because he could not help it, then he was acting on an irresistible impulse.

LINKAGE ANALYSIS   Using evidence, particularly behavioral, from a series of crime scenes to indicate that they are associated with a specific offender or set of offenders.

LINKAGE BLINDNESS   Failing to see the commonalities among crime scenes that associate them with a specific offender or set of offenders.

M'NAGHTEN RULE A legal rule first proposed in Britain's common law that states the grounds for a defense of insanity: At the time of committing the act, the accused was laboring under such a defect of reason, from a disease of the mind, as not to know the nature and quality of the act, or if he did know, that he did not know that what he was doing was wrong.

MALINGERING Deliberate simulation of a mental illness to obtain personal gain.

MEMORY HARDENING When hypnotically aided recall results in transforming a belief into a memory that appears to be true and is resistant to attempts to change it.

MENS REA The mental state that accompanies a forbidden act, required for conviction.

MINNESOTA MULTIPHASIC PERSONALITY INVENTORY (MMPI-2) A personality assessment test composed of items organized along ten scales for clinical assessment as indicating exaggeration, defensiveness, and lying.

MIRANDA WARNING The required statement that a police officer gives to a suspect upon arrest, informing that person of the right to remain silent (not to self-incriminate) and to have legal representation before questioning.

MITIGATING CIRCUMSTANCES Factors such as age, motivation, duress, or unstable home life that can diminish the degree of guilt in a criminal offense.

MODUS OPERANDI (MO) An offender's method of carrying out an offense.

MSO Acronym for mental state at the time of the offense.

NARCISSISTIC PERSONALITY DISORDER A personality pattern that manifests as arrogance, entitlement, and the need to be admired by others for one's superiority; often shows up among serial killers.

NATIONAL CENTER FOR THE ANALYSIS OF VIOLENT CRIME (NCAVC) The FBI organizational structure that combines research, operations, training, consulting, and investigation to support local jurisdictions investigating unusual or repetitive crimes. The NCAVC also provides support for national security, nonviolent corruption, and white-collar crime investigations.

NON COMPOS MENTIS Not of sound mind.

ORGANIZED OFFENDER Person committing a crime in a planned, premeditated manner, leaving few or no clues.

PARAPHILIA Deviant forms of sexual behavior in which people get fixated for sexual arousal on items, activities, or events; necophilia, cannibalism, and vampirism are common among serial killers.

PAROLE When a defendant is freed from prison before his or her sentence allows, conditioned on adherence to certain rules, such as seeing a parole officer on a regular basis.

PATTERN RECOGNITION SOFTWARE Computer programs that strive for greater accuracy than humans can achieve in providing linked behavioral patterns for profiles of serial crimes.

PERSONALITY DISORDERS Enduring patterns of thought and behavior that are maladaptive, causing impairment and distress. For criminal proceedings, the most common are antisocial, borderline, narcissistic, paranoid, and schizoid.

PERSONATION The behavioral manifestation at crime scenes of unique individuals; also called a signature.

POLYGRAPH A machine used to determine through changes in physiological functions whether a person is lying.

POSTMORTEM After death.

POWER ASSERTIVE RAPIST   Using aggression to restore an offender's self-confidence, authority, and control.

POWER REASSURANCE RAPIST   Behaviors used to restore self-confidence through low-aggression means, suggestive of a sense of inadequacy.

PREPONDERANCE OF EVIDENCE   The standard used in civil suits; the evidence on one side outweighs the evidence on the other. This is the lowest of the three standards of evidence (beyond a reasonable doubt and clear and convincing proof), generally estimated at 51 percent certainty.

PROBATIVE   Serving to prove.

PROFILER (CRIMINAL)   A mental health professional or law enforcement officer with behavioral science training who helps determine the traits of an unknown offender from aspects of the victim and crime scene.

PROSPECTIVE PROFILING   Devising a series of behaviors of a type of offender before the the crime is committed; used in threat assessment.

PSYCHOLOGICAL AUTOPSY   Methods used to determine the state of mind of a person where the scene of a possible suicide is ambiguous and therefore questionable; also to make a determination about manner of death.

PSYCHOPATHY   Personality disorder defined by long-term unsocialized criminal behavior by a manipulative person who freely exploits others for selfish purposes, feels no guilt or remorse and is not inclined to stop; usually diagnosed with the PCL-R.

PSYCHOPATHY CHECKLIST REVISED (PCL-R)   A tool used to assess psychopathic traits and behaviors and to aid in violence risk assessment.

PSYCHOSIS   A major mental disorder in which a person's ability to think, respond, communicate, recall, and interpret reality is impaired. Psychotic people show inappropriate mood, poor impulse control, and delusions. Often confused with insanity, which is a legal term, and psychopathy, which is a character disorder.

PSYCHOTROPIC Drugs that act on the psyche, such as antidepressants and antipsychotic medication.

RETROSPECTIVE PROFILING Assessing behavior at a crime scene to devise a portrait of the unsub. See CRIMINAL PROFILING.

RISK ASSESSMENT See THREAT ASSESSMENT.

ROGERS CRIMINAL RESPONSIBILITY ASSESSMENT SCALE (R-CRAS) An assessment test for organic impairment or major mental illness specific to the time an offense is committed.

RORSCHACH TEST A projective psychological test that relies on inkblots and free-association to detect patterns of functioning.

SCHIZOPHRENIA A group of disorders manifested in delusions, disturbances in language and thought, mood shifts, and maladaptive behaviors.

SCRIPTING When an offender forces a victim to say or do certain things that fulfill a ritual scenario.

SERIAL CRIMES Any type of crime occurring in a successive pattern that indicates a single offender or criminal team is committing several crimes of a similar nature.

SERIAL KILLER According to the FBI's new definition (since 2005), an offender who kills at least two different people in two separate events.

SERIAL KILLER GROUPIE A person who wants to be emotionally close to a serial killer, such as in a romantic relationship.

SIGNATURE CRIME A crime scene that bears a personality stamp of an offender, characteristic of a need for ritual or theme. These acts are not necessary to complete the offense. Also called personation.

SOCIOPATH According to some theories, a person with behavior similar to a psychopath, but the personality was forged by social forces and environment; however, sociopath has lately been understood as a person with no regard for laws of society at large but who does keep to the moral codes of a select group, such as a family or contained community.

SOUVENIR A personal item taken from a victim and kept by the offender as a memory aid to relive the crime. Also known as a trophy.

SPREE KILLER Although the FBI stopped using this crime category in 2005, they once included it in the crime classification as an offender who commits more than two murders in a tightly related series, with no psychological cooling off period.

STAGED CRIME SCENE A disposal site where an offender has arranged the body and other items to serve a ritual fantasy; also a scene made to look like something other than what it actually is, such as a staged domestic homicide made to look like a suicide.

STALKER A person who fixates on another person, usually following them, sending letters, or making obsessive phone calls and generally harassing them.

SYNDROME A cluster of symptoms that collectively characterize a group of people who share them.

TARASOFF DECISION Court decision deriving from a 1976 murder case in California that stipulates that psychotherapists have a duty to use reasonable care to protect third parties when a patient presents a risk of violence to a foreseeable victim.

TEAM KILLERS Two or more people who commit murder together, usually for thrill or profit; about 15 percent of serial killers.

THREAT ASSESSMENT The procedure for determining how likely it is that a certain person or group might become violent in the future.

ULTIMATE ISSUE The actual legal issue at stake in a proceeding—for example, competence or insanity.

UNDOING BEHAVIOR An attempt to reverse a crime, generally by returning the victim to a natural looking state.

UNSUB The term used in criminal profiling to refer to an unknown suspect.

VERDICT The decision of a judge or jury after hearing and considering the evidence.

VICTIMOLOGY A study of victim information to find clues about the offender's opportunity and selection process.

VIOLENT CRIME LINKAGE ANALYSIS SYSTEM (ViCLAS) The Canadian system of tracking crimes.

VIOLENT CRIMINAL APPREHENSION PROGRAM (ViCAP) The FBI's nationwide data information center, designed for collecting, sorting, and analyzing information about crimes.

VOIR DIRE Process by which a judge and attorneys interview potential members of the jury; they hope to uncover biases that may undermine a fair trial; it's also the process for qualifying experts.

BIBLIOGRAPHY

Berg, Karl. *The Sadist: An Account of the Crimes of Serial Killer Peter Kürten: A Study in Sadism.* London: Heineman, 1945.

Biffl, Elizabeth, "Psychological Autopsies: Do They Belong in the Courtroom?" *American Journal of Criminal Law* 24, no. 1. (Fall 1996), pp. 123-146.

Brussel, James. *Casebook of a Crime Psychiatrist.* New York: Grove Press, 1968.

Campbell, John H., and Don DeNevi. *Profilers: Leading Investigators Take You Inside the Criminal Mind.* Amherst, New York: Prometheus, 2004.

Cannon, Angie. "Crime Stories of the Century" *U.S. News and World Report,* December 6, 1999.

Carlo, Philip. *The Night Stalker: The Life and Crimes of Richard Ramirez.* New York: Kensington, 1996.

Charles Albright v. the State of Texas. 05-92-00005, Fifth District, May 19, 1994.

Clark, Doug. *Dark Paths, Cold Trails.* New York: HarperCollins, 2002.

Cullen, Robert. *The Killer Department: Detective Viktor Burakov's Eight-Year Hunt for the Most Savage Serial Killer in Russian History.* New York: Pantheon Books, 1993.

Daubert v. Merrell Dow Pharmaceutical. 509 U.S. 579 (1993).

DeNevi, Don, and John H. Campbell. *Into the Minds of Madmen: How the FBI Behavioral Science Unit Revolutionized Crime Investigation.* Amherst, NY: Prometheus Books, 2004.

Diagnostic and Statistical Manual of Mental Disorders. 4th ed. Washington, DC: American Psychiatric Association, 1994.

Douglas, John, Ann Burgess, Allen Burgess, and Robert K. Ressler. *Crime Classification Manual.* San Francisco: Jossey-Bass, 1992.

Douglas, John E., and Corinne Munn. "Modus Operandi and the Signature Aspects of Violent Crime." In *Crime Classification Manual.* New York: Lexington Books, 1992, pp 19-30.

Douglas, John, and Mark Olshaker. *Anatomy of Motive*. New York: Scribner, 1999.

———. *The Cases that Haunt Us*. New York: Scriber, 2000.

———. *Mind Hunter: Inside the FBI's Elite Serial Crime Unit*. New York: Scribner, 1995.

———. *Journey into Darkness*. New York: Scriber, 1997.

Ebert. B. "Guide to Conducting a Psychological Autopsy." *Professional Psychology Research and Practice* 18, (1987), pp. 52–56.

Egger, Steven A. *The Killers Among Us*. Upper Saddle River, NJ: Prentice Hall, 1998.

Fox, James, and Jack Levin. *Extreme Killing: Understanding Serial and Mass Murder*. Thousand Oaks, CA, Sage, 2005.

Gerdes, Louise, ed. *Serial Killers*. San Diego, CA: Greenhaven Press, 2000.

Giannangelo, Stephen J. *The Psychopathology of Serial Murder: A Theory of Violence*. Westport, CT: Praeger, 1996.

Godwin, Grover Maurice. *Hunting Serial Predators: A Multivariate Classification Approach to Profiling Violent Behavior*. Boca Raton, FL: CRC Press, 2000.

Gollmar, Robert. *Edward Gein: America's Most Bizarre Murderer*. New York: Pinnacle, 1981.

Grierson, Bruce. "The Hound of Data Points." *Popular Science*, Mar. 21, 2003.

Harris, Thomas. *The Silence of the Lambs*. New York: St. Martin's Press, 1991.

Hare, R. D. "Psychopaths and Their Nature: Implications for the Mental Health and Criminal Justice Systems." In *Psychopathy: Antisocial, Criminal and Violent Behavior*. Ed. T. Millon, E. Simonsen, M. Biket-Smith, and R. D. Davis. New York: Guilford Press, 1998, pp. 188–212.

———. *The Psychopathy Checklist*. 2nd rev. ed.. Toronto: Multi-Health Systems, 2003.

———. *Psychopathy: Theory and Practice*. New York, Wiley & Sons, 1970.

———. *Without Conscience: The Disturbing World of the Psychopaths Among Us*. New York: Guilford Press, 1999.

Hazelwood, Roy, and Stephen G. Michaud. *Dark Dreams: Sexual Violence, Homicide, and the Criminal Mind*. New York: St. Martin's Press, 2001.

Hickey, Eric. *Serial Murderers and Their Victims*. 4th ed., Belmont, CA: Wadsworth, 2007.

Holmes, Ronald M., and Stephen T. Holmes. *Profiling Violent Crimes*. 3rd ed. Thousand Oaks, CA: Sage, 2002.

Holmes, Ronald, and D. Kim Rossmo, "Geography, Profiling, and Predatory Criminals." In *Profiling Violent Crimes.* Ed. R. Holmes and S. Holmes. Thousand Oaks, CA: Sage, 1996.

Innes, Brian. *Profile of a Criminal Mind.* Pleasantville, NY: Readers Digest Press, 2003.

Isenberg, Sheila. *Women Who Love Men Who Kill.* iUniverse.com, 2001.

James, Earl. *Catching Serial Killers.* Lansing, MI: International Forensic Services, 1991.

Jeffers, H. Paul. *Who Killed Precious?* New York: St. Martin's, 1991.

Keppel, Robert D., with William J. Birnes. *The Psychology of Serial Killer Investigations.* San Diego, CA: Academic Press, 2003.

Keppel, Robert D., with William J. Birnes. *Signature Killers: Interpreting the Calling Card of the Serial Murderer.* New York: Pocket, 1997.

Kleinfield, N. R. "Retracing a Trail: The Sniper Suspects." *New York Times,* Oct. 28, 2002.

Krafft-Ebing, Richard von. *Psychopathia Sexualis with Especial Reference to the Antipathic Sexual Instinct: A Medico-Forensic.* Rev. ed. Philadelphia: Physicians and Surgeons, 1928.

Krueger, Anne. "Prince Is Sentenced to Death in Six Killings." *San Diego Union-Tribune,* Nov. 6, 1993.

Lane, Brian, and Wilfred Gregg. *The Encyclopedia of Serial Killers.* New York: Ballantine, 1992.

Leyton, Elliott. *Hunting Humans.* Toronto, Ontario: McLelland & Stewart, 1986.

Lourie, Richard. *Hunting the Devil: The Pursuit, Capture and Confession of the Most Savage Serial Killer in History.* New York: HarperCollins, 1993.

Lunde, Donald T. *Murder and Madness.* San Francisco: San Francisco Book Co., 1976.

Masters, R. E. L., and Eduard Lea. *Perverse Crimes in History.* New York: The Julian Press, 1963.

McCrary, Gregg. "Are Criminal Profiles a Reliable Way to Find Serial Killers?" *Congressional Quarterly,* Oct. 31, 2003.

McCrary, Gregg, with Katherine Ramsland. *The Unknown Darkness: Profiling the Predators Among Us.* New York: Morrow, 2003.

Meloy, J. Reid. *Violent Attachments.* Northvale, NJ: Jason Aronson, 1992.

Michaud, Stephen G., with Roy Hazelwood. *The Evil That Men Do*. New York: St. Martin's Press, 1998.

Newton, Michael. *The Encyclopedia of Serial Killers*. New York: Facts on File, 2001.

People v. Cleophus Prince, Jr. SO36105, Supreme Court of California Apr. 30, 2007.

Pistorius, Micki. *Catch Me a Killer*. Johannesburg, South Africa: Penguin, 2000.

Powell, Ronald. "Suspect in Clairemont Killings Held." *San Diego Union-Tribune*. Mar. 4, 1991.

Poythress, Randy K. Otto, Jack Darkes, and Laura Starr. "APA's Expert Panel in the Congressional Review of the *USS Iowa* Incident." *American Psychologist* 48 (1993): 8–15.

Proenca, Mario. "The Psychological Autopsy," Suicide and Parasuicide, April 7, 2001.

Ramsland, Katherine. *The Human Predator: A Historical Chronicle of Serial Murder and Forensic Investigation*. New York: Berkley, 2005.

Reiser, M. *Handbook of Investigative Hypnosis*. Los Angeles: LEHI, 1980

Reiter, Henry, and Laura B. Parker. "Psychological Autopsy." *The Forensic Examiner* 11 (2002), pp 22-26.

Ressler, Robert. K. *I Have Lived in the Monster*. New York: St. Martin's Press, 1997.

———. *Whoever Fights Monsters*. New York: St. Martin's Press, 1992.

Rossmo, D. K. "Geographic Profiling." In *Offender Profiling: Theory, Practice and Research*. Ed. Janet L. Jackson and Debra Bekerian. New York: Wiley, 1999.

Rumbelow, Donald. *Jack the Ripper: The Complete Casebook*. New York: Contemporary Books, 1988.

Schechter, Harold. *The Serial Killer Files*. New York: Ballantine, 2003.

Schmid, David. *Natural Born Celebrities*. University of Chicago Press, 2005.

Schwartz, Ted. *The Hillside Strangler*. New York: Signet, 1989.

Selkin, J. "Psychological Autopsy: Scientific Psychohistory or Clinical Intuition?" *American Psychologist* 10 (1994), pp. 77-83

Shneidman, Edwin, ed. *Essays in Self-Destruction*. New York: Science House, 1967.

———. "Some Psychological Reflections on the Death of Malcolm Melville." *Suicide and Life-threatening Behavior* 6, no. 4 (1976): 231–242.

———. *Suicide as Psychache: A Clinical Approach to Self-Destructive Behavior.* New Jersey: Jason Aronson, 1993.

Sillitoe, Linda and Allen Roberts. *Salamander: The Story of the Mormon Forgery Murders.* 2nd ed. Salt Lake City: Signature Books, 1989.

Stewart, James B. *Blind Eye: How the Medical Establishment Let a Doctor Get Away with Murder.* New York: Simon & Schuster, 1999.

"Suspect Doesn't Fit Serial Killer Profile." *San Diego Union-Tribune,* Ma. 10, 1991.

Thomas, Charles. *A Glimpse of Hell: The Explosion on the* USS Iowa *and Its Cover-Up.* New York: W. W. Norton, 1999.

Vorpagel, Russell. *Profiles in Murder.* Cambridge, MA: Perseus, 1998.

Wilkins, John. "To Ex-FBI Profiler, Crime Scene Is All in the Mind." *San Diego Union-Tribune,* Aug. 9, 1996.

Wilson, Duff. "Profiler Can't Recall Why He Said Letter Wasn't from Green River Killer." *Seattle Times,* Nov. 26, 2003.

Worrall, Simon. *The Poet and the Murderer.* New York: Dutton. 2002.

Wrightsman, L. S., M. T. Nietzel, and W. H. Fortune, *Psychology and the Legal System.* Belmont, CA: Wadsworth, 1994.

Wrightsman, Lawrence. *Forensic Psychology.* Belmont, CA: Wadsworth, 2001.

The author conducted personal interviews with John Douglas, Robert K. Ressler, Roy Hazelwood, and Gregg McCrary, as well as other FBI personnel not named in the text.

INDEX